Real Estate for Boomers and Beyond

EXPLORING THE **COSTS, CHOICES**
AND **CHANGES** FOR YOUR NEXT MOVE

TOM KELLY

KAPLAN PUBLISHING

President, Kaplan Publishing: Roy Lipner
Vice President and Publisher: Maureen McMahon
Acquisitions Editor: Victoria Smith
Production Editor: Karen Goodfriend
Typesetting: Janet Schroeder
Cover Design: Gail Chandler

Published by Kaplan Publishing,
a division of Kaplan, Inc.

Printed in the United States of America

06 07 08 10 9 8 7 6 5 4

Library of Congress Cataloging-in-Publication Data

Kelly, Tom, 1950 Oct. 8–
   Real estate for boomers and beyond: exploring the costs, choices, and changes for your next move / Tom Kelly.
      p. cm.
   Includes index.
   ISBN 1-4195-2679-0
   1. Real estate business. 2. Real estate investment. 3. Retirees—Finance, Personal. 4. Older people—Finance, Personal   I. Title.
   HD255.K384 2006
   643'.120846—dc222

                                                          2005031868

Contents

PART ONE

IS IT TIME TO MAKE A MOVE?

PART TWO

AGING IN PLACE

PART THREE

FUNDING FUTURE YEARS

Thinking about moving from the family home? How do you deal with 46 years of memories and possessions?

My mother, at least on the surface, chose to take the matter-of-fact road to move out of the family home, a two-story, stucco structure near Hollywood that had become more than an anchor of stability for family and friends: Call the seven kids, have them come and get what they want, give the rest to charity, close the door, and keep moving.

Don't look back.

The decision was very un-Kelly like. Certainly there would be an appropriate prayer of thanks and gratitude, perhaps supplied by the parish priest or the popular Jesuit from the local high school where five Kelly boys left their marks—a few even academic. Clearly there would be another backyard barbecue, a fitting send-off to the home that was headquarters for so many celebrations, tears, reunions, broken bones, and broken hearts. I left blood and sweat on its basketball court, hid cigars in the garage as a teen, and, more than 30 years ago, stood shaking nervously in an upstairs bedroom over the thought of actually losing my bachelorhood as our wedding rehearsal dinner guests arrived at sunset in the festive garden below.

Mom could not, and would not, host another celebration or gathering (always labeled a "session" by Dad) without my father, especially one down this memory lane. That sentimental journey would have to wait— perhaps until even after the final stages of Parkinson's had taken my dad, then her gentle partner of 55 years. He would be with her only in spirit, which might be the only way she could digest moving from this very special place.

Mom had made up her mind that there was simply too much physical work to do to deal with feelings and emotions. This had always been her way, and now she, at age 78, needed again to lean on *her way* despite the expectations. My dad, then 83, never wanted to leave the house.

While several of his buddies headed to the safer beach cities to be closer to their grown kids, there was no doubt Bob Kelly "was staying put." "Really," he always asked, "what could be better than this?"

It was fewer than three blocks to church—and he made an appearance virtually every day. It was about a driver and a nine-iron to the country club where he enjoyed the food ("best chow around") and people ("Bud Rice said to say hello.") more than the golf ("I'm still lousy.").

The subject of moving never surfaced when the kids lived at home. However, it had been nearly 20 years since there had been more than two full-time residents. I followed older brothers Mike and Bill to the Pacific Northwest three decades ago, while Pat, Kate, and Maureen had called the San Francisco Bay area home for nearly as long. The youngest, John, was the only sibling who stayed. Had he known the number of family members that would be seeking sun and relaxation at his Manhattan Beach home, he probably would have relocated elsewhere.

The most less-than-subtle hint at moving my parents out of the family home occurred about 12 years ago. Some of the siblings suggested the folks get an electric gate and floodlights to guard the yard and driveway. The house had been burgled a few times in the later years, including one ugly night when the car was stolen.

But as much as I would have liked to have seen my parents move, it did not surprise me that they stayed. You could see it in my dad's face—the place was crammed with too many memories for him to pack off to an unknown place. And, probably most importantly, it was still the perfect ball yard for the grandkids who arrived for vacations and holidays like we did a generation ago.

When it became clear that my dad would not be coming home from a local nursing home, the size, maintenance, and emptiness of the family house became too overwhelming for my mom. After my sister and I took our families home a few days after a Christmas visit, Mom said it was time to move on.

I remember feeling relieved and pleased she had made the choice. I believe it's far easier to leave the family home when both spouses are still alive. That way, all involved can at least begin to grieve the loss of the home before the overwhelming loss of a partner or parent.

After the last of the heavy furniture had been moved to my mom's new address—a nearby condominium, I pulled the silverware tray from its familiar place in the kitchen drawer and placed it on the floor of the rental car. I had time for one more shuttle trip to the new condo before visiting my dad in the nursing home. Then, it was off to the airport.

I walked out the front door, turned around on the lawn that had served as host to so many football games, and stared up at the house one last time. I thought of the countless number, and variety, of people who said goodbye on that exact spot over the past 46 years.

I also thought of my dad, and how he never really left there. He did not sell and move to the beach. And I knew, very clearly, why he never wanted to say goodbye.

The day I said goodbye to the home in which I was raised was also the last time I saw my father. He died a few weeks later, at age 83, of complications from Parkinson's disease. My mother was already in the nearby condo, nicely appointed by many of the familiar pieces of furniture from the old family home. Her children had been given, or assigned, the beds and desks that took up most of the space in the bedrooms of the old house. She chose to purchase a two-bedroom condo unit so the kids and grandkids could continue to visit. The second bedroom also afforded the possibility of live-in care down the road. She remained in close proximity to her friends, church, golf, physicians, and favorite stores.

However, not all seniors want, or are able, to remain in the same area, especially after the loss of a spouse. While some do choose to stay and "age in place" alone, others head to a community near an adult child or longtime friend. Many seniors want to remain independent and choose a small, single-family home, while others choose to try out an apartment, at least for the short term. Seniors often have specific issues and needs, the same issues and needs Baby Boomers are now just beginning to face.

I am the fourth of seven children, and I am also smack dab in the middle of the Baby Boom generation. Most of our kids are grown and gone. What will we choose to do, and when? What have I learned from my parents' living situation, including the lack of preparation for my dad's in-home care and my mom's move to the condo? I'm not sold on staying in our home forever; but it's a great space, especially for future grandkids. In fact, I would welcome the chance to introduce them to my old, comfy baseball glove and my four-seam fastball in the front yard.

This book is an attempt to help parents, partners, friends—and my family—answer housing questions and explore critical living options that could be just around the corner.

A *c k n o w l e d g m e n t s*

This book is dedicated to my godparents—Tom and Joan Cooney—the pride of San Francisco, California, and McCall, Idaho, who have provided caring, memorable insights in all aspects of living and loving in my 56 years on this planet. They have been the logical sounding board, the different set of eyes that has allowed me to see outside my often too-focused world. They are truly ahead of their time and have been an inspiration for so many adventures, including this book—displaying the same energy and creativity in their 80s as they did four short decades ago.

My genuine thanks to the many individuals from home building, mortgage lending, tax, and accounting who have aided me for years in my newspaper writing and radio work, and who also provided creative insights and useful information for this book. I have called on them often, and their patience, interest, and kindness have been extraordinary. Leading this list are Mary B. Good, Joanne Elizabeth Kelly, Renee Mindas, Jeff Jenkins, Darryl Hicks, Rob Keasal, Laura Shelley, Richard Morse, Jim Hawkins, Christine Hrib-Karpinski, John Tuccillo, and Kevin Hawkins. I also am grateful to the numerous consumers who shared their stories, and to Brad Inman for his vision and cartoons.

UNDERSTANDING THE HABITS OF BOOMERS AND BEYOND

An American turns 50 every seven seconds.

The over-50 population grows by 10,000 people every day, and this trend is expected to continue for the next 20 years. According to the U.S. Census Bureau and the National Center for Health Statistics, the number of Americans aged 45 to 64—who will reach 65 over the next two decades—increased 34 percent from 1990 to 2000. While these numbers bring immense business possibilities and ramifications, the impact on housing is especially significant.

Couple this upwardly mobile, borrow-at-the-drop-of-a-hat group with the older population—persons 65 years of age and older—who numbered 35 million in 2000, and most of whom would like to stay in their homes as long as possible, and you begin to get a broad idea of the two basic demographics that make up Boomers and beyond. The latter age group represents 12.4 percent of the population—about one in every eight Americans.

What do both groups have in common? Neither wants to be considered old, nor do they want to be surrounded by clunky and frumpy furnishings that give off that perception. In fact, "age" to Baby Boomers is only a number—it defines their grandparents and parents. Fifty is the new 30.

Barbara Caplan, a partner at Yankelovich, a consumer research firm, took the idea one step further: "Boomers aren't redefining age," said Caplan, "they're redefining youth."

When the Boomers and beyond hit their prime next residence decision-making time, and that could come earlier in life for some, a couple of moves are predictable. If they don't relocate to a new home with more stylish and functional amenities than they have now, they most likely will reward themselves, at long last, by upgrading their current residence with comfy and cozy appointments they feel they deserve to accommodate their senior years. They also will not like being told what to do and when. They'll make choices on their own time, and adamantly resist even the slightest gesture of manipulation. Their recall of a given service or product, excellent or poor, is extremely vivid. And, for the most part, their pockets are deeper than expected.

According to the Census Bureau, senior citizens in this country, persons 65 and older, have approximately $2 trillion in home equity. This book will target these consumers plus their children—the 77 million Baby Boomers who comprise the healthiest, wealthiest, and largest generation ever seen on the U.S. landscape—who now are asking critical financial and lifestyle questions of their own. At the center of the decision-making process is the choice of a next home. Some homeowners will absolutely stay put, or "age in place," simply because what they have now—house, neighborhood, friends, church, club—is exactly what they'd like to keep. Others who seek the same environment will sell the beloved family home they've occupied for decades yet remain in close proximity to it. This niche does not have a housing issue, it has maintenance and service issues. Still others will buy a completely different lifestyle but enter into it with the same emotional uncertainty and care they brought to their first home. Boomers, in particular, defy a clear and concise description. They demand a different set of options and services than their parents, are often married more than once, are the free spirits of the 1960s, could have small children or grandchildren, and are more than ready to take care of their aging parents. Trying to nail down the Boomer definition? How much time have you got?

Housing's next largest market segment—active adult/early retirement and eldercare—is a complicated, fragmented, and tricky proposition that can change as fast as a Baby Boomer changes cars. So, why are all these seemingly separate and independent housing categories always combined into a gigantic over-55, "active adult" club? For a variety of reasons, not the least of which is that builders and housing developers are having difficulty finding the correct terminology to market communities designed for older adults. In addition, some 80-year-olds want to live like they are 50, while some 50-year-olds seek the privacy and exclusivity once reserved only for older senior citizens. The term "active adult" and others (explored in Chapter 3) have become linked with the large communities where thousands of retirees flee their friends and families to join a resort-like club in a sunny climate. In the future, "active adult" will apply to a much wider profile of homebuyers who will buy locally, as well as in the amenity-laden resort communities.[1]

"Retirement isn't seen as the end game anymore," says Dave Schreiner, vice president of active adult business development for Pulte Homes, the nation's largest home builder. "It's a life transition. These people want to stay active and engaged, mentally, physically

The challenge for home builders, remodelers, suppliers, and real estate professionals is twofold: the number of diverse people entering the senior Boomer group and the speed in which products are introduced, manufactured, and distributed. Toss in the idea that people are living 30 years longer than they did 40 years ago, and the potential housing components, and demand for alteration, become enormous.

Mark Goldstein, cofounder of San Ramon, California–based Impact Presentations Group, is a specialist in the demographic, lifestyle, and psychographic trends of the senior housing market. He continues to remind professionals in the mortgage and housing industry who serve the over-50 markets that the huge Boomer group has revamped every life stage it has entered—and retirement is next.

"Not only will this group reinvent retirement," Goldstein said, "but it also will not stand for hype. The style of marketing must be educational or they won't be buying."

"Most reinventions have begun too late," Goldstein said. "I think the health care industry has found this out. Health care saw the demographic coming but it didn't get what actually drove the people in the demographic. It is the psychographics, or the mental and emotional connections. The strategy for change must come before an industry finds out that things are not going right. It must come when business couldn't be better."

Jack Haynes, executive vice president of the National Builder Division at Countrywide Home Loans in Dallas, said the industry—especially mortgage bankers—is just beginning to realize there's never been a market segment like the senior Boomer group.

"This is absolutely something we've never seen before," Haynes said.

Let's check some of the generational mindsets, numbers, and reasons that will change over time. One trend that clearly must be radically altered is the country's predisposition toward nursing homes. The sheer number of Boomers suggests that many will have to age in place, or move to a more accommodating residence, simply because the country could not fund and build enough nursing facilities to shelter the projected Boomer population. The bitterly ironic piece is many Americans would rather stay at home, but when health care needs arise and associated expenses rise, very few vehicles other than reverse mortgages (discussed in Chapter 12) are enabling them to do so. Medicare and Medicaid funds are curiously more help in an institutional setting than in the primary residence.

Generation Y, or "Millennials"	Born 1979 or later
Generation X, or "Echo Boomers"	Born between 1978 and 1965
Baby Boomers, early members "Nexers"	Born between 1964 and 1946
Silent generation, or "Zoomers"	Born between 1945 and 1924
Greatest generation, or "GI generation"	Born between 1923 and 1901

Ed Note: No universal terminology is used by the industry. "Nexers" can be a younger Silent or an older Boomer. Active adults typically are Silents and older Boomers.

Source: National Association of Home Builders; William Strauss and Neil Howe

In 1990, the traditional stories of white-collar and blue-collar folks retiring at age 65 and looking forward to a life of golf, fishing, and pottery making were still very common and expected. These folks were eager to join the "make do" generation that survived the Depression and World War II in a relatively risk-free retirement where the biggest threat to their well-being usually occurred during the annual Thanksgiving Day flag football game with their suddenly huge grandkids. Now, pushed along by reduced pension plans, higher health care expenses, lost retirement savings due to corporate shenanigans, and the "tech wreck" of once high-flying Internet companies, many U.S. elders are seeking ways of supplementing their incomes merely to meet their monthly bills. Some prolong their working years because they must; others continue in the workforce because they simply enjoy what they do and fear the lull of slowing down. They've seen their buddies become bored, stymied, and often ill as a result of a lack of challenging projects. And, the active grandparent role has become huge. According to the U.S. Census 2000, there were 2,350,477 grandparents in the country who were responsible for raising one or more of their grandchildren.

In the book *Generations: The History of America's Future 1584–2069*, authors William Strauss and Neil Howe describe a generation as a "cohort" or cluster of people born approximately during the same 20-year period. Strauss and Howe contend that because people form values from common historical events, experiences, and influences, we can understand and often anticipate how a specific generation will think and respond. The generational explanations included below will shed some light on how and why certain groups are prime candidates for reverse mortgages. Other researchers have grouped specific segments using different years as guidelines, so there will be overlaps and underlaps in the Strauss and Howe sampling when measured side by side with other data. Here are the capsule descriptions from *Generations* along with brief explanations of how each group thinks and operates. Let's begin with the largest..and most influential:

The *Boomer Generation* grew up as indulged youth during an era of community-spirited progress. These kids were the proud creation of postwar optimism, Dr. Spock rationalism, and *Father Knows Best* family order. Coming of age, however, Boomers loudly proclaimed their antipathy to the secular blueprints of their parents; they demanded inner visions over outer self-perfection, over making things or team playing. The boomer "awakening" climaxed with Vietnam War protests, the 1967 "Summer of Love," inner-city riots, the first Earth Day, and Kent State. In the aftermath, Boomers appointed themselves arbiters of the nation's values and crowded conspicuously into such "culture careers" as teaching, religion, journalism, marketing, and the arts.

During the 1990s, entering midlife, they trumpeted values, touting a "politics of meaning" and waging scorched-earth culture wars. Now on the verge of elderhood, Boomers are rejecting the old notion of "retirement," in part because many have not saved enough to afford it. In old age, they look to be much more influential in the culture than in the economy or politics—much the opposite of the GIs who raised them. Representative members include Steven Spielberg, Meryl Streep, Spike Lee, Bill Gates, Doctor Laura, George W. and Laura Bush, Bill and Hillary Clinton, and Bill Bennett.[2]

Baby Boomers—the largest, healthiest, and wealthiest group ever appearing on the U.S. growth landscape—never met a loan they didn't like. After leveraging appreciation and location in their starter and move-up homes to pay for cars, college tuitions, and trips, their eventual retirement home probably will hold most of the equity in their life. Their last home will not be terribly modest because of this cohort's desire to entertain. Some members will purchase long-term care insurance in their earning years, allowing more cash to be spent on more gadgets. Although some analysts say the Boomers will gain wisdom with age and curb their spending ways down the road, others won't be persuaded. How they will behave continues to confound researchers—but what else is new?

"Baby Boomers are famous for believing one thing and then behaving totally differently from what they think they do," said Eric Snider, who has a doctorate in social psychology and serves as Shea Homes's marketing director for Trilogy, the home-building company's upscale active adult communities. "They have retreated to their homes and away from society. Yet that is not their reality at all."

According to a study Snider conducted for Shea Homes, the Walnut, California-based company that specializes in upscale homes in North Carolina, Arizona, California, Washington, and Colorado, that's one of the reasons why, in the past 50 years, homes have exploded from an average of 953 square feet to 2,200 square feet. At the same time, the size of the family has declined dramatically.

"When you ask Boomers about age-restricted communities, they initially say, 'I'm not going to live in one of those,'" Snider said. "But when you look at the characteristics of the community, it gives them exactly what they are looking for: exclusivity, amenities, and personal experiences. Boomers are all about personal experiences."

In a 2004 economic study prepared by The Urban Institute for the American Association of Retired Persons (AARP), authors Barbara Butrica and Cori Uccello contend that Boomers will amass more wealth in real terms at retirement than will the two previous generations.[3] Median household wealth at age 67 will grow from $448,000 among current retirees to $600,000 among Boomers. Income at retirement is consistent with trends in wealth at retirement the study shows. Projected household income at age 67 will increase from $44,000 among current retirees to $65,000 among Boomers. As with wealth, there will be income disparities among older and younger Boomers. Nonretirement income is expected to decline between older and younger Boomers.

However, other researchers, including Larry Cohen, director of Princeton, New Jersey–based Consumer Financial Decisions, wonder if

Boomers, given their spending history, will ever get to the traditional retirement years with any real assets.

"As the cohort responsible for the explosion of credit in the 1980s and 1990s, Boomers are hardly likely to forgo immediate gratification in their later years," Cohen said. "The trend among seniors will only be exacerbated when the Boomers enter retirement age. The convenience of credit card use with the occasional slip into revolving credit, along with leveraging their assets for around-the-world tours or trips into space, mean that the more responsible Boomers will have credit insurance to cover their inevitable demise. The rest, who are not so wealthy that they simply can afford that type of lifestyle, may wind up bequeathing their debt as their legacy instead of the 'trillions' that they inherited."

Biggest impact on the future: Spend and borrow, spend and borrow . . . Boomers, who will work into their 70s, will continue to do both. Why expect them to change when they've changed the world around them every step of the way? Long-term health insurance policies purchased earlier in their life will leave the idea that more home equity will be available for their consuming habits. They were the main group burned by the high-technology crash, yet they still continued to gamble.

Noteworthy: They will keep the home separate and independent from what they will leave their children—which might be only a bed and a desk unless consuming ways change.

The *Silent Generation* grew up as the suffocated children of war and the Great Depression. They came of age just too late to be war heroes and just too early to be youthful free spirits. Instead, this early-marrying "lonely crowd" became the risk-averse technicians and professionals as well as the sensitive rock 'n rollers and civil rights advocates of a postcrisis era in which conformity seemed to be a sure ticket to success. Midlife was an anxious "passage" for a generation torn between stolid elders and passionate juniors. Their political ascendancy in the mid-1970s coincided with fragmenting families, cultural diversity, institutional complexity, and prolific litigation. They are now redefining elderhood as a time for reconnecting with family, experimenting with new roles, and shedding the stodgy GI "senior citizen" moniker. Their hip style and notoriety for indecision continues to give them a poor reputation for national leadership—and is likely to make them the first generation in U.S. history never to produce a president. Representative members include

Colin Powell, Alan Greenspan, Woody Allen, Martin Luther King, Jr., Sandra Day O'Connor, Gloria Steinem, and Elvis Presley. [4]

William Manchester, the famous biographer, once commented that this group of people was "withdrawn, cautious, unimaginative, indifferent, unadventurous, and silent." The generation's name also picked up steam when it was used in a *Time* cover story in 1951. This risk-adverse group made some wise investments and typically saved more than other cohorts. According to the U.S. Census Bureau, the number of households headed by people age 60 and over with an income of at least $100,000 jumped 27 percent, to 2 million, between 1998 and 2002. They, and others, are taking cash and indulging their youthful fantasies—perhaps for the first time. For example, Harley Davidson reported that customers aged 65 to 74 tripled between 2000 and 2003. The increase in business was credited to focused marketing containing "the fulfillment potential component," such as the company's billboards and television commercials stating, "The Road Starts Here. It Never Ends." The message conveyed endless possibilities, not simply motorcycles.

Other members of this generation now find themselves as grandparents—and as their grandchildren's primary caregivers. A "skipped generation" household is now defined as one where a grandparent and grandchild live with no parent in the home. In 2000, 5.8 million grandparents (60 percent over the age of 60) lived with grandchildren younger than age 18.

"A lot of these people just don't see themselves as retiring," said Donna Butts, executive director of Generations United, a national organization in Washington, D.C., specializing in intergenerational strategies. "They raised their own kids, now they are raising another set. It comes with obvious financial risks and their income will continue to be a challenge."

Biggest impact on the future: This health-conscious group plans to live longer, spending for education, travel, second homes, and long-term care insurance now plus drawing reverse funds later to age in place. They have begun to see the power of home appreciation as the potential backup to their retirement nest egg. Risk-adverse mentality will keep them weighing costs more than Boomers. Silents will keep reverse cash in hand "just in case" something comes up.

Noteworthy: Will splurge for a calculated special occasion—family reunion, coveted toy, "something they've always wanted to do." This cohort has a strong sense of contributing—to children's weddings, grandchildren's education, and people in dire straights.

The *GI Generation* developed a special and "good kid" reputation as the beneficiaries of new playgrounds, scouting clubs, vitamins, and child-labor restrictions. They came of age with the sharpest rise in schooling ever recorded. As young adults, their uniformed corps patiently endured the Depression and heroically conquered foreign enemies. In a midlife subsidized by the GI bill, they built gleaming suburbs, invented miracle vaccines, plugged missile gaps, and launched moon rockets. Their unprecedented grip on the U.S. presidency (1961–1992) began with a New Frontier, a Great Society, and Model Cities but wore down through Vietnam, Watergate, deficits, and problems with "the vision thing." As senior citizens, they safeguarded their own "entitlements" but with little influence over culture and values. Representative members include John Wayne, Ann Landers, Walter Cronkite, John Kennedy, Ronald Reagan, Walt Disney, and Judy Garland.[5]

The GI generation had to "make do" during the Depression and World War II, and that philosophy still influences its conduct today. Members of this group often are reluctant to spend money on themselves to make their lives more comfortable. They definitely subscribe to a pay-it-off philosophy, especially when it comes to the roof over their heads. Very few purchased long-term care insurance and are thus footing the bill for home care assistance. The GI's unwritten goal was to retire without a mortgage, and not achieving this goal was often seen, and felt, as a huge and depressing failure. Many in the GI generation don't see any reason to dive into their financial assets and "would rather leave it for the kids," even though the kids are in a far better financial place than the folks.

Susan Mack, an occupational therapist and president of Homes for Easy Living Universal Design Consultants in Murrieta, California, a company specializing in home modifications for persons with special needs, said she is constantly frustrated by the GI's frugal mindset.

"We'd go to great lengths to explain to these people and to their adult children that when they come out of the hospital it's important to modify their home to make it safer for them, but they wouldn't spend the money," Mack said. "They would go home and compromise their quality of life and put themselves in jeopardy of having another disability because they wouldn't put in a grab bar, or they wouldn't install a walk-in shower. The amazing thing was that they began consoling me, instead of me consoling them. They'd say 'Susan, honey, don't worry. I'll be just fine . . . I'll make do.'"

According to Princeton, New Jersey–based SRI Consulting Business Intelligence, the amount of household debt for people over 65 nearly tripled between 1992 and 2000. Many seniors simply hadn't saved enough for retirement—44 percent of retirees age 60 or older (overlap with the Silents) had saved $75,000 or less. Eleven percent had saved nothing at all. Forty-four percent cited Social Security as their primary source of income.

Biggest impact on the future: This group will continue to be overly aware of the need for basic living necessities, plus property taxes and rising health care costs. They continue to seek ways to supplement dwindling financial portfolios, make home modifications, travel, and assist in the costs of raising grandchildren.

Noteworthy: Even though they are stunned by what appreciation has done to the current value of their home, they still have to be persuaded to "live a little" by adult children. They also have a genuine willingness to help out.

Now that we have considered the primary candidates of housing's next largest market segment, let's explore how they will go about entering that market. Although some Baby Boomers have moved, refinanced, and moved again in the past ten years, many Silents and GIs have been in their current home more than twice that time. The thought of moving is absolutely exciting yet at the same time scary. In Chapter 1, I explore some of the elements to consider . . . especially if you've been out of the home and loan game since the Kennedy, Nixon, or Carter administrations.

IS IT TIME TO MAKE A MOVE?

1

RUSTY...AND REENTERING THE MARKET

Do all you can to
safeguard your ultimate asset

If it's been a while since you've re-searched a new residence, you will probably be surprised at the cost and overwhelmed by the variety. The concept of a home has evolved from basic shelter to the most valuable piece of the average person's invest-ment portfolio. Given the "tech wreck" that rocked Wall Street begin-ning in the spring of 2000, coupled with the overblown quarterly statements of some businesses and the questionable leadership of com-pany executives, consumers are now more protective than ever when the subject becomes the roof over their heads. In many cases, their home has been not only their most reliable investment but also their most emotional.

The best way to choose a community in which to purchase your next piece of real property is to begin with yourself, your spouse, and your immediate family. Putting too much emphasis on "buying where our good friends bought" or on one wonderful amenity, such as a gorgeous golf course, can come back to haunt. Your lifelong basketball buddy may be an entirely different person after he has blown out a knee and has no intention of making the transition to joining you on early morning bicy-cle rides. The golf club that you planned on being the center of your so-cial calendar could suddenly become too expensive, or too crowded, for your tastes. Friends and venues are terrific, yet they should not be at the top of the chart. You need to know what *you* want before you can determine where to look.

TAKE TIME TO PICTURE YOUR PLACE

The best process to begin the selection of your new home and its geographic location—ultimate, last-time residence; cozy apartment; or part-time vacation getaway; and so on—involves creating the most detailed image you can. Picture yourself in your new home and all of its surroundings. If, at the end of the process, you can engage all your senses— touch, sight, smell, taste, and hearing—in envisioning your dream house, it will seem more real to you and will motivate you to proceed with confidence. As you develop the vision, remember that the controlling factor is not whether it exists but rather whether you can fully envision it. Creating that kind of vision involves the following five steps:

1. *Begin by setting a time frame.* When will you want to reach the goal of your next home? Do you want to wait until full retirement to take up residence, or will you want to use it, at least part-time, well in advance of that? Answering these questions will not only help you envision your dream location but also set the timetable for the financing process that will enable you to reach your dream.

2. *Move a little deeper into the process by looking at the things you enjoy now in your leisure time.* These will make up the bulk of your activity in the dream location, so the location ought to accommodate them. If you enjoy reading, cultural plays, and lectures, then a larger community will be best. Access to golf, fishing, sailing, or hiking will dictate a more specific resort community. Don't worry about whether your tastes will change, because you will be revisiting the master picture often. You might want to add and subtract activities to account for new interests and limitations. Going through this step will enable you to define the type of location that will best suit your needs.

3. *Next, focus on the type of house you want.* How much room do you think you will need? If you are planning on sharing the home with family and friends, more bedrooms and more living space are

needed than if you plan to be there with only your immediate household. How much time do you want to spend dealing with the care and maintenance of the property? If you choose a more developed area, would you rather garden or have the time to play golf? Focusing on these decisions will help you choose the type of house as well as the type of ownership that best suits your vision.

4. *Get more detailed.* Think of the configuration of your house and the amenities you want in it. Should it be on a single level, or can you justify climbing stairs to a second-floor home that could double as a grandchild dorm? To what degree will you want it "wired" so you have access to the Internet or even the ability to voice-activate accessories and services? What type of appliances do you want in the kitchen? Do you want the potential for wheelchair accessibility in every room or just in a specific area? In other words, design in your mind the perfect house and then visit it often. The more familiar you become with the house, the more you will want to be in it.

5. *Revisit the vision.* Your tastes might have changed, and your family situation might be pointing you in a different direction, both in the near and long term. Go through the process again with your current status. You're doing this to remake the vision, but you're also doing it to assess your progress along the road to your dream. As you look at your vision again in light of the changes that have happened to you, also look at your financial position and determine whether your current holdings are on the right track. Is the move toward a real estate purchase a better proposition now than it was at your last review? Do you need to be in a different location to take advantage of population shifts and appreciation differences? Answering these questions provides a valuable "midcourse" correction to your progress.

Where do you see yourself ultimately spending the majority of your later years? Right now, what would be your best guess even though you cannot be absolutely certain? Here are a few sample questions to ponder and help guide you through the process:

- *How do you see yourself spending your days?* No last-time home will be enjoyable if its occupants cannot do what they find enjoyable.

Dad's desire to attend downtown plays and pitch softballs in a huge men's city league may not fit Mom's desire for a bit more isolation and rural tranquility. Before you make any exploration of home possibilities, come to a clear understanding of what type of atmosphere, amenities, and facilities both spouses want. Remember that longtime wants are not always absolute needs.

- *Is your decision merely a trip down memory lane?* If you spent many happy hours on vacation with your family in a particular spot, you might want to return there and buy a home in the same location. This is a legitimate wish, but you should consider how important this is to you. Sometimes, you can't go home again. Prices have risen, congestion has increased, and many of the things you fondly remember have disappeared. More important, your memories are not necessarily shared by those around you. If the vacation home is to provide satisfaction, it must meet the needs of the whole household. Even a seemingly familiar place requires investigation before you seek to relive old memories. Don't let nostalgia for the past take precedence over the more important considerations of the present.

- *How long will you own this home?* Do you really think this will be your last home? As mentioned in the Preface, there wasn't even a thought of a move-down or empty-nester residence in my father's plan. The family home, where he lived with my mother for 46 years and raised seven children, was going to be his last address. "You'll be carrying me out of this place feet first" was his favorite line. And he nearly kept his promise. Only a brief stay in a nursing home was spaced between the family home and his final resting place.

If you want to hold your next place for the long term, try to consider how the preferences and needs of you and your spouse will change over time. In-home activities that you once could do easily may soon become difficult. Kids grow up, and their kids will want to visit. Do you have the desire to make your home office into a cozy, comfy dorm for the grandkids? Be sure to consider the following:

- *What is the quality of social services and medical care in the area?* As you age, you will come to rely more and more on the helping professions, and your own mobility will diminish. Whether you are seeking a primary home or vacation getaway, being close to good community hospitals, elder centers, and recreational opportunities suitable to age becomes more important as time goes by.

- *Will the home age with you?* Steps become a barrier as you get older; regular door openings are too narrow and regular countertops are too high for wheelchairs; and regular wall studs are often too weak to hold grab bars. Before you decide on a house, inspect its construction carefully, not just for now but also for 20 or 30 years from now. We live longer these days, and you're likely to spend more time in that house than you think you will.

- *Can your friends and relatives or medical professionals reach you easily?* The visits might be friendly and enjoyable, or they might be necessitated by a crisis, but they will come. Whether you want them to, as a break from the routine of the retirement community, or whether they have to, your friends and relatives will come more frequently if you live near a major airport or train station or bus station. When you select the home, evaluate it for convenience of access.

- *Don't forget the travel toys.* Even though your new address may be the only conventional roof over your head, don't forget about the other travel toys you may now own or wish to acquire. If you have a recreational vehicle, what months of the year do you plan to dart around the continent checking in on former college classmates or the folks you really enjoyed at your former workplace? If you have a boat, will you take the winter months to explore the series of delightful ports that comprise Mexico's Mar de Cortes Project?

If part of your master plan after your primary working years is to travel extensively, does that include home sharing for a year or more in another country? And don't forget that seldom-used time-share. If you were too busy and had to "bank" weeks during your income-producing years but now plan to maximize the time-share time, would the specific weeks you are gone change the reason you purchased a retirement home in a specific location?

The next step is to look at some specific communities and some specific properties. There are three important considerations in this process:

1. *Return to familiar territory.* Think about places you've visited—either on vacation, for family reunions, or for business reasons—that you think fit your future needs. This gives you a valuable head start because you have a working knowledge of the area, have accumulated some information to use in assessing its merits and demerits, and can get a good fix on costs (including travel time and expense to visit children and friends) in having a retirement home there.

2. *Check back once more.* This time, look at the whole community through the eyes of someone who will be part of it and not just a short-term visitor. It's important to visit during all the times you intend to be there. The seasonal mood should match your needs, and you should visit often enough to be able to gauge those moods accurately. The active spring arts scene may turn into a bitter, cold, desolate winter outpost with no ski lifts and awful public transportation.

3. *Recruit some key players.* Although your next home may not be far from your present residence, chances are it will not be just around the corner. Talk to friends who might have expertise in the area you are targeting, or ask associates at work or members of your church. Check with a real estate professional in your own community for a referral. This avoids the shot-in-the-dark approach of simply looking up a real estate professional in the phone book. Alternatively, if you don't have a real estate professional whom you can ask, use the Internet. If you search on the areas of interest, you will find a number of real estate Web sites. You can then e-mail a series of questions that will constitute an interview to screen potential agents. Seek experience, professionalism, and the personality that will work for you. Will this person do an admirable job in representing you professionally and personally? Here's a list of questions you should ask your potential real estate professional:

   - How long have you been in the real estate business?
   - How long have you been doing business in this market? (Obviously, experience is a big plus.)
   - Have you had experience with buyers looking specifically at retirement homes from a distance? (Specific familiarity with your type of need is important.)

- Can you give me the names of some of your past customers I can call? (The agent should be more than willing to share this information with you.)
- What information will you require from me?
- What services do you offer? (If dealing at a distance, an agent who offers all the services that are needed in the transaction will be more useful to you.)
- What is your usual commission?

You can, of course, add to this list, but it does present the basics of what you need to know before proceeding. Going through this process with a number of agents (three to five is usually the most efficient number) will help you find the best fit for your individual needs.

PUT ON A DIFFERENT SET OF GLASSES

Even if you use a terrific real estate professional, and even if you think you know everything about the area, there are some very specific factors that you need to consider in choosing a location. Each of them can be resolved by answering a series of questions. You can score each answer on a scale of 1 to 5 and then compare total scores for each alternative property. Next, consider the factors, presented in order of importance, from the viewpoint of an outsider with no emotional connection to the property or even from the viewpoint of a potential renter.

Access

The most attractive properties will be those that offer the best access to the things that consumers value. For example, renters tend to want to be close to the beach, pool, golf course, recreation center, or the famous amenity that brings the local area its reputation. So in evaluating a location for investment, ask (and answer) the following four questions:

1. How close is it to major recreational sites (beach, mountains, golf, etc.)?
2. Is the property convenient to major transportation corridors? Consider both roads and public transportation.

3. How convenient are shopping, amusements, and recreation? Renters often use public space.
4. Where is this property located in relation to employment and education centers?

Safety

In this environment, safety is a high priority for everyone and is even truer for potential renters than for owners. In part, this is because owners have more direct control over the security of their property. Renters will rate alternative properties in part on the safety of the areas in which these properties are situated. So ask yourself the following three questions to rate the neighborhoods in which you seek to invest:

1. What security precautions have been taken at the property? As a related consideration, think about what you are willing to spend to increase the safety of the property after you acquire it.
2. What is the crime rate in your target location as opposed to the area as a whole?
3. If the property is a condominium, is the community gated or guarded?

Neighborhood Quality

When there is pride in a community, the homes are well kept and inviting. Typically, where the community is strong, house values are high and demand for living in the community is high as well. Most people, renters included, want to live in a vibrant, congenial place. If you are viewing the place more as an investment property, the quality of the development is a very important factor. It will go far in helping you maintain strong cash flow and high appreciation on the property. Here are three issues that might surface:

1. If you are considering a single-family detached house, what percentage of the population owns in that neighborhood? Traditionally, a high percentage of ownership is associated with better neighborhood quality.

2. How strong are the neighborhood organizations? When a community is progressive, the residents will participate.
3. Do the adjacent commercial areas in the community attract a large volume of street traffic? Busy areas are more vibrant, exciting, and attractive; besides, they tend to be safer.

HOME LOAN PUZZLE HAS A LOT MORE PIECES

Does the latest wiggle in interest rates have you nudging your spouse with memories of your first home loan and the question of "What was *our* rate when we signed"? Not only have rates changed, but so have the programs. Even though I explore some creative and underused methods for financing your next purchase in Part Three, let's take a peek at some of the avenues that have been constructed and paved since your last move. Many members of the "Greatest", or GI, generation were "pay-it-off" people, but Baby Boomers love to borrow and are very comfortable in plunking down little cash for a home purchase and taking out the highly controversial, yet seemingly inexpensive, interest-only loans.

If you are out shopping mortgage programs and pricing mortgage money for the first time in decades, you may be confused and frustrated by all the abbreviations and acronyms bouncing around since you last entered the home loan game. Don't know if you should sign a LIBOR loan or ride a LAMA? You're not alone. Some adjustable-rate loan indexes are so new that even veteran loan officers are scurrying to quiz primary underwriters for understandable definitions. Loans now seem to be tied to every conceivable—and available—money average, giving consumers an overwhelming number of programs from which to choose. The National Association of REALTORS® has made available a publication (found at http://www.realtor.com/) as part of a consumer education campaign addressing specialty loans and abusive lending practices. The brochure helps consumers understand conventional loans such as fixed-rate and adjustable-rate mortgages, and more exotic loan programs such as interest-only mortgages, 40-year fixed-rate mortgages, negative amortization mortgages, and option payment adjustable-rate mortgages.

Traditional loan indexes can be traced and charted, providing borrowers background on how a specific index has performed. But lenders are continually seeking that unfilled borrower niche, and the senior boomer segment is a huge, inviting target. By way of explanation, adjustable-rate mortgages, or ARMs, are indexed loans, meaning they adjust periodically according to changes in the index or indexes to which they are tied. For example, the Federal Reserve Bank's District Cost of Funds Index (COFI) is one popular index. All adjustable-rate loans are unpredictable (that's why they come with lower interest rates). If a new variable-rate loan product sounds good but is difficult to understand or perceived to be too risky, consumers typically turn toward the stability of fixed rates.

And speaking of risk, the hottest home loan product of 2004 and 2005 was the interest-only mortgage, which allows the borrower to get a bigger loan and more house with a smaller monthly outlay. Most interest-only payment plans are offered on adjustable-rate mortgages, but they can also be found on fixed-rate loans. However, the "interest-only" portion is only for the monthly obligation because eventually the borrower must repay the loan principal. So if the goal is to pay the loan down while you are still working and then cruise into full-blown retirement with no mortgage, the interest-only loan is not the program for you. You will not be reducing your principal loan amount with your monthly payments, only paying the interest portion. The Joint Center for Housing Studies of Harvard University cited information indicating that one in four home loans in 2004 was financed with an interest-only mortgage. In 2002, these mortgages comprised a few percentage points of the total mortgage market.[1] Although no-interest loans have merit for some sophisticated homebuyers who are not afraid of risk, the loans might bring more anxiety than the average senior wants to digest. Not paying down the principal, and therefore not building any equity through retiring the debt, means that an interest-only borrower is counting on market appreciation (price inflation) to build equity. If prices should fail to increase during the interest-only period, and if the borrower should find a need to sell the home, the borrower could potentially have to make up the difference because of the selling costs involved.

There's no denying the slim interest rate gaps between fixed and adjustable rates. A few short years ago the difference was 3 percentage points and the advantage was clearly toward the adjustable. Now, the gap is in the 1.25 to 1.50 range, making the fixed attractive—even as it continues to rise. Fixed or adjustable? That continues to be the question of the day. If this is going to be your last home, or if you are going to stay in the home for a long, long time, a low fixed-rate loan is what you are after. If you are willing to take on some risk and don't anticipate staying in the home for several years, an adjustable rate mortgage makes sense.

Here is a capsulated explanation of some of the more popular loan indexes. Keep in mind that each one has distinct market characteristics and fluctuates differently:

- *District Cost of Funds Index (COFI).* This is the monthly average cost of funds of member associations of the Federal Home Loan Bank. It reacts more slowly in fluctuating markets. Popular recently because the faster-reacting one-year Treasury index has shot up. The COFI could continue up when others start down.
- *Six-Month Certificate of Deposit (CD).* This is the weekly average of the secondary market interest rates paid on six-month negotiable certificates of deposit. The CD index is generally considered a quick reactor to changes in the market and is sometimes used as a lender's in-house or "portfolio" product.
- *One-year Treasury (One-year T-bill).* This index, sometimes known as a "spot" index, is the weekly average yield on U.S. Treasury securities adjusted to a constant maturity of one year. This index generally reacts more slowly than the CD index but faster than the Treasury Average.
- *Treasury Average Index.* This is a 12-month average of monthly yields on actively traded U.S. Treasury securities, adjusted to a constant maturity of one year. It reacts slower in fluctuating markets.
- *LIBOR.* The London interBank offered rate is an average of the amount international banks charge each other for large-volume loans. The index responds very quickly to market conditions and is calculated for a variety of loan adjustments—one month, three months, six months, one year, and so on.
- *LAMA.* This relatively new and marketed index means LIBOR annual monthly average and is designed to reduce the volatility normally associated with LIBOR-based indexes. Fannie Mae has been publishing a one-month LIBOR rate since 1989, but the composite average index is a relatively new tool. LAMA reacts more slowly to market conditions.

Now that you have taken time to focus and envision your next home—plus received a taste of more lending options than you ever needed—it's time to take a peek at some housing preferences. In Chapter 2, we start to consider home size and shape. Even though you will probably be spending the rest of your life with one other person or by yourself, chances are your next house will not be as small as traditionally perceived. It also will probably cost much more than the prevailing notion of a "downsize" price tag.

2

WHATEVER HAPPENED TO DOWNSIZE AND UPSCALE?

Senior boomers now want amenities AND larger homes

Our home is getting larger. Three of the four kids are out of the nest—another will leave next year. We miss their energy, the chaos of late-night gatherings, and the intense negotiating over who is going to take the car. The entire family dynamic has changed, especially at the dinner table on a Sunday night. If you've ever experienced a child's first birthday away from home, you've got a twinge of the emotional package headed your way.

And as much as we cherish their visits, our kids' return to the family home can only realistically be slotted for short-term holiday seasons and job-cut summers. And so, periodically, we have asked ourselves: Would we ever leave this place? Would it make sense to consider a smaller home closer to town? No more lawn, lower monthly heating costs, walk to the store and the movies?

The first step is choosing the correct time to even raise the question. I've stayed away from pondering the idea during terrific family reunions or lonely, kidless weekends. It's probably best to begin on rather neutral ground, someplace in between those extremes.

Time marches on, and the buying tendencies of specific groups become more apparent than others. In this chapter, we explore what type of home senior boomers are researching and buying—and they are not the smaller, tighter units universally perceived. In subsequent chapters, I discuss the "where" and "how."

Most GI generation homeowners are expected to age in place in their present home or to perhaps make a move to an assisted living community. However, the Silent generation and the Baby Boomers could easily have one more house move in their plan before settling into their eventual retirement home. Some members of these two groups still have children at home and in college, but they are definitely open to discussing one more jump. When they do jump, chances are it will be to a one-story home that is clearly no smaller than the one they will be leaving. The demand by the over-50 buyer for one-story, single-family homes rose from 17 percent in 1970 to 75 percent in 2003. In addition, more than half of those buyers spent the same or more on their next home.[1]

"The move to a one-story home was very clear, but there was absolutely no demand for homes to become smaller," said Gopal Ahluwalia, research specialist in the National Association of Home-Builder's economics department. "In each of our past five surveys, the size of the home requested by these buyers continued to be about the size of their previous home. Depending upon where these buyers were from, we heard they wanted us to continue building homes between 1,600 square feet and 2,400 square feet. There was no 'smaller, smaller, smaller.' We didn't think this was possible."

A surprise that surfaced in the 2003 surveys and studies was the number of senior boomers who indicated "wired" homes ranked as very important on their "want" list. By 2005, a connectivity package was a standard component in many new homes and remodel requests.

"We knew that technology in the home was important to the 45- to 50-year-old buyer, but we did not anticipate how many people over 55 really wanted it enough to pay for it," Ahluwalia said. "Previously, reports indicated some of this group did not want to deal with technology, but now we see a majority of them are as comfortable around a computer as a 15-year-old."

In addition to examining the amenities, features, and services builders are planning and incorporating into communities designed for the over-50 demographic, housing officials continue to track where senior boomers are relocating, how much they are spending on homes, what type of financing they use, and builders' perceptions about buyers' motivations for moving and regional trends.

"Boomers are buying lifestyle," said Chuck Covell, president of Greenbelt, Maryland–based Bozzuto Homes. "Today's 50 and over buyers are more affluent and crave a sense of lifestyle when buying a new home. They are not buying solely based on price or location."

Covell noted that Baby Boomers will continue to work in some capacity, with many trading their primary careers for a part-time job or a job that is more like a hobby. Builders must include high-tech offices and media centers in active adult homes to appeal to these buyers, who see themselves working well past the traditional retirement age. Baby boomers want first-floor living space, including a master suite, as well as high-end kitchens, luxurious master suites and baths, and high-tech media rooms.

Housing analysts say demand is growing for smaller communities with interesting streetscapes and high-end homes designed for individual lifestyles. When the first active adult communities were launched in the 1960s, many were large in size, located in traditional Sun Belt states, and shared similar community format, design, and amenities. However, builders recognize that today's buyers are open to change, demand a variety of choices, and are more likely to consider a community close to home.

"For many buyers, the established concept of the active adult community conjures up images of boring, cookie-cutter neighborhoods with no opportunities for owners to express themselves," said Bill Feinberg of Feinberg & Associates, P.C., a Voorhees, New Jersey–based architect and designer. "Builders understand that the active adult industry is rapidly changing. A single community formula will no longer meet the needs of mature consumers."

Feinberg added that main-street communities, exclusive enclaves, and age-targeted villages within master-planned communities are gaining popularity. In terms of design, these youthful, individualistic buyers want diversity in street patterns and streetscapes, embrace natural features such as wetlands and open space, and favor smaller, more flexible communities. They also may not need a large community clubhouse, preferring more informal spaces that offer different experiences and a range of social and physical activities.

The word *community* has also taken on a new connotation. Whereas most active adult communities have traditionally been built in suburban locations, urban buyers command a greater share of the market, especially for condominiums, town houses, and multifamily apartments. Many buyers are empty nesters who expect a high level of service, spend more on upgrades, and are less likely to consider moving to an age-qualified community.

Buying Preferences, Opinions of the Baby Boom Generation

Real Estate

More than half of Boomers plan on buying a new home for retirement. About half of Boomers expect to move to another state at retirement, with many seeking a better community lifestyle.

- Fifty-nine percent of younger Boomers (ages 41 to 49) and 50 percent of older Boomers (ages 50 to 59) indicate they plan to buy a new home for their retirement.
- Of Boomers willing to move at retirement, 66 percent of older Boomers indicate they would move for a better community lifestyle, and 54 percent would seek a warmer climate.
- Nearly half (47 percent) of all respondents (ages 41 to 69) who will move indicate that staying within three hours of family would be an important consideration when deciding where to relocate for retirement.
- Among those willing to move to a different state, the most preferred states to move to for retirement, by age group, are: ages 41 to 49, North Carolina (14 percent); ages 50 to 59 and 60 to 69, Florida (18 percent and 17 percent, respectively).

Active Adult Community Amenities

Of Boomers (ages 41 to 59) who plan to move and are interested in a new home at an active adult community (for residents age 55 and older), top amenities desired in a new community include full-maintenance lawn care, walking trails, and access to swimming and water fitness programs. Education, social activities, and security features are also important considerations for many.

Ages 41 to 49

- Top preferred amenities and programs include walking (81 percent), full-maintenance lawn care (80 percent), and swimming/water-based fitness (73 percent).
- Hobbies and clubs are important for 75 percent; many want art or photography courses (56 percent) or college courses (55 percent).
- Sixty-five percent would prefer a gated community.

Ages 50 to 59

- Top preferred amenities and programs include walking (79 percent), full-maintenance lawn care (77 percent), and swimming/water-based fitness (68 percent).
- Fifty-nine percent want hobbies and clubs; 41 percent want art or photography courses; and 38 percent want college courses.
- Sixty-one percent would prefer roving security.

Social Security

Boomers most affected by potential changes in Social Security (ages 41 to 54) are more likely to believe they will need another source of income to finance their retirement and are more likely to invest in private accounts.

- Sixty-two percent of Boomers ages 41 to 54 believe the program is in crisis, and 34 percent of this group expressed an interest in investing a portion of Social Security in a private account.
- Although 61 percent of nonretired Boomers ages 41 to 54 say they don't know what their monthly benefit will be at retirement, 75 percent of all respondents ages 41 to 54 say they do not plan to rely solely on Social Security benefits.
- Uncertainty about Social Security has caused 25 percent of nonretired Boomers ages 41 to 54 to admit they won't retire as soon as expected, but 62 percent of nonretired respondents ages 55 and older say they'll retire on schedule.
- 79 percent of respondents ages 60 to 69 believe they are receiving or will receive full benefits.

Finances

Also on the minds of Boomers, according to this year's survey, is the rising cost of health insurance and prescription medicines that they anticipate needing.

- Regardless of age, all respondents said health care–related costs topped their respective lists of financial concerns during retirement, including health insurance (74 percent), prescription medicine (71 percent), and long-term care insurance (58 percent).
- In projecting their longevity (if healthy), 40 percent of all respondents said they hope to live to 80 to 89 years of age, 20 percent said 90 to 99, and 22 percent said 100 or older. But when asked to estimate how long their savings would need to last after retirement, 42 percent of all respondents said they weren't sure.
- Of all respondents, 17 percent estimated they would require savings of between $500,000 and $1 million to live comfortably throughout retirement, 15 percent said between $200,000 to $500,000, and 12 percent estimated needing between $1 million and $2 million.
- A pension from a former employer was the third most important source of retirement income for respondents ages 50 to 59 (48 percent) and 60 to 69 (47 percent).

Retirement Lifestyle

Anticipation of retirement increases with age as Boomers look forward to active pursuits such as traveling, exercising, volunteering, or even continuing working, either full-time or part-time.

- Enthusiasm about pending retirement increases with age among respondents in their 40s and 50s, with 45 percent and 56 percent, respectively, indicating "excitement,".
  Travel (62 percent) tops the list of desired retirement activities across all ages. Other popular interests are spending time with friends/loved ones (42 percent), exercising more (42 percent), volunteering (37 percent), taking up a hobby (33 percent), acquiring new skills (29 percent), and taking classes (25 percent).
- If they could "go back" to another decade of their life, most would choose their 30s (31 percent) and 20s (28 percent).

Work Habits

Although some Boomers plan to continue working because they enjoy it, 64 percent of all respondents still working outside the home said they will fully retire from their current line of work at some point. But among those planning to continue working, the reasons differ by age.

- Of those who will continue to work, 49 percent of younger Boomers, ages 41 to 49, and 37 percent of older Boomers, ages 50 to 59, plan to continue because they need the money.
- Of those who will continue to work, 33 percent of pre-Boomers, ages 60 to 69, say they will continue because they enjoy it, and 22 percent of this group will continue because "it keeps me active."
- Forty-five percent of all respondents working outside the home say they typically work 31 to 40 hours per week.

Source: 2005, Harris Interactive, Del Webb Baby Boomer Survey

SENIOR BOOMERS' DEMAND FOR SERVICE

The upscale condominiums atop some of the world's most exclusive hotels are not the only homes driven by exceptional service. The nation's top homebuilders, including Pulte, the huge developer that guides Del Webb, have sought counsel from service-oriented leaders, such as Ritz Carlton hotels (operated by Four Seasons), in an attempt to corral loyalty and its incredibly powerful result—marketable referrals—to subdivisions and planned developments throughout the country.

"We are constantly looking for a 'wow' effect," said Rob George, corporate director of The Ritz Carlton Hotel Company's training and development division. "We also know that today's wow will be tomorrow's norm. Remember, we are all in the service business—whether it's selling homes or laying carpet. Why not look at the companies that are best at what they do and take from them what they do best?"

The Ritz Carlton's motto—"Ladies and Gentlemen serving Ladies and Gentlemen"—carries a message of "who we are and how we should behave." It also is part of the panache of The Ritz and a constant attempt to retain guests and nurture loyalty. The company's guests are the last bastions of the group willing to proclaim, "I want somebody to do it for me." Why not find out what they want, provide it for them, and hope they come back with their family and friends?

According to George, changing to a resort attitude doesn't cost very much.

Sheryl Palmer, who led Del Webb's Arizona division before moving over to head the Nevada division, said her company approached The Ritz Carlton when the homebuilder wanted to adopt a resort atmosphere for a 1,850-home community near Chandler, Arizona. The typical owner at Corte Bella has a net worth of $1 million, annual income of $100,000, and an average age of 62.

"We wanted to know more about specific expectations right from the start," Palmer said. "This was going to be a resort-oriented community, so why not find how to execute from those that have been successful in the resort atmosphere?"

Service experts like George say providing homeowners with something extra, a gesture or amenity they did not expect, will not only lead to loyalty but also to priceless promotion. According to The Ritz Carlton's research, a 5-percentage point increase in customer loyalty could produce profit increases of 25 percent to 80 percent because of the potential for peripheral services. In addition, the cost of attracting a new customer is 5 to 20 times greater than maintaining current customers.

"We've found through our research that 67 percent of customers leave because of an attitude of indifference on the part of a company employee," George said. "That is something you can modify and do something about. So, we empowered every one of our employees."

All Ritz Carlton employees are allowed to spend up to $2,000, without supervisor approval, to correct an error or satisfy a specific customer need. All employees are encouraged to create a "wow" experience geared to making a stay memorable.

For example, a guest asked a beach attendant to leave a chair on the sand late in the evening. He planned on asking his girlfriend to marry him under the bright stars and soaring moon. The attendant not only made arrangements for a special chair but also then purchased flowers and candles for the big night. He also folded a huge towel near the chair so the man would not get sand on his trousers when he popped the big question. When the couple eventually arrived, the attendant, in a rented tuxedo, stood quietly in the background with champagne cooling in a silver ice bucket.

Why not give in-house designers a $2,000 pool of funds to spend on an amenity the buyer could not afford, a special planting, a custom door mat, or a stocked freezer?

"You do everything you can to know what your customer wants," George told the homebuilders. "We have a database of one million of our customers that includes specific requests and preferences we've experienced during their stays. Our guests, like yours, are buying a lifestyle, a feeling, and an experience. If you give them what they want, they will come back and bring their friends."

ONE EFFORT TO PINPOINT FUTURE HOME SIZE

Downsizing may have worked for the GI generation, but keep in mind the homes of the 1950s and 1960s were small by today's standards. The Silents clearly feel they deserve their upgraded amenities, yet the Boomers, again, stunned planners with their attitudes and demand for space. In an effort to pinpoint factors for the potential size and shape of homes, Shea Homes recently completed a survey asking Baby Boomers if they were politically active, if

"EMPTY NESTER"

they were involved with their children's educational experience, and how often they had guests over for dinner. According to the findings, the assumption that Boomers are politically active is incorrect. The huge group that once protested, waved banners, and flashed the peace sign has not remained politically involved.

"The results were surprising because of the perception we still retain of the1960s," said Eric Snider, Shea Homes's marketing director for Trilogy, the company's upscale active adult communities. "People immediately shift their minds to that decade when Boomers even begin to be mentioned. After the war, Boomers put their signs down, went home, and essentially turned on their televisions."

That's one reason why today's homes are so large, researchers say. During the past 50 years, homes have gone from an average of 953 square feet to 2,200 square feet. At the same time, the size of the family has declined dramatically. An interesting section of the poll asked Boomers if they were involved in their child's educational experience. Even though most replied yes, very few were members of the PTA or part of policy decision making at the school or larger-based school systems.

"What they mean is that they engage with their child about school or a specific teacher," Snider said. "They're not talking to the principal nor are they key players of the PTA."

The most surprising revelation in the Shea data was that Boomers are no longer social beings or so inclusive.

"They have retreated to their homes and away from society," Shea said. "Yet that is not their reality at all."

The over-65 group will not be pressured into buying before they have "kicked a lot of tires" and found a lot of bang for the buck, according to Ron Bonvie, whose DJG Construction is based on Cape Cod. "I will not permit any of my salespeople to take a check from a customer on the first visit," Bonvie said. "There are several reasons, not the least of which is that you don't want to push this group into anything. Another reason is that we don't want to come off as hard sellers looking to swoop down on folks as soon as they come in the door. A lot of builders talk about providing a great lifestyle, but people still want to make sure that they are getting a great shelter value. The best thing you can do is show them that you are getting this amount of product for this amount of dollars. Show them a list and check off all the features they are getting."

William E. Becker, longtime builder from Teaneck, New Jersey, said the two biggest deal killers for older buyers are homeowner fees and taxes. "We are no longer in the housing business—we are in the retail business," Becker said. "You have to show customers a value point for everything. If the homeowners' fees are $250 a month, show them that they were paying that much at the gym, ceramics class, and pool already. If you don't take the time to relate all costs to something present now in their lives, you stand a good chance of losing them."

Builders, analysts, and consultants say it is critical for every new home community to have a large, flexible center that stresses not only physical fitness but also arts and crafts. "We now calculate about 15 square feet of the rec center for each home in the community," said David Smith of Cambridge Homes based near Chicago. "This building has to be front loaded (ready for viewing) before your first home is sold. You have to have something to show people what you are talking about, and the rec center has become the center of these people's lives. It is an absolute necessity and an invaluable sales tool."

WOMEN ARE CLEARLY THE DECISION MAKERS

The initial view of retirement in the United States was focused on Dad and his golf clubs. What was this man who had spent years in the working world going to do with all of his spare time? Builders and developers are now well aware that women make a majority of the decisions in the homebuying process and are no longer merely housewives of a nuclear family. Since the 1960s, the percentage of men entering the workforce has diminished. During this same period, the percentage of working women has increased substantially. Today, women are independent, empowered, educated, and employed—and often single. A profile of homebuyers and homesellers from the National Association of REALTORS® (NAR) showed nearly 30 percent of all U.S. homebuyers were single. Single women accounted for the second-largest segment of homebuyers, accounting for 21 percent of transactions, after married couples, who bought 59 percent of homes. NAR also estimates that 47 percent of condominium owners are single women. Women are choosing to live in communities that emphasize social interaction and convenience, enabling them to simultaneously nurture and multitask. The experience of community is a key driver for women as well as the proximity to jobs and public transportation.

As for home amenities, women are very much focused on security. They are attracted to high-tech home security systems as well as automated home-lighting systems. Women are just as busy as men and they appreciate anything that saves time. Convenience, in terms of location and saving time and effort, is a big plus with female homebuyers. They also look to have amenities that play into the needs of children. Shared areas are critical to community life, as are well as nearby stores, parks, and recreational areas. Communities centered on a single amenity (e.g., golf clubhouse) are perceived as less welcoming for women and children.

According to Doris Perlman, founder and president of Denver-based Possibilities for Design, women control 80 percent of consumer purchases, direct 91 percent of housing decisions, and guide 94 percent of home-furnishing choices. Perlman's research has delineated many of the specific home features that are likely to particularly attract older women, but in their shopping habits she suggested that these customers are apt to be "circular, exploring, and tactile" and "do not make linear decisions."

"Her needs for personal connection and security are key," Perlman added. "Women don't just buy a product; they join it."

Among Perlman's observations on what will sway Boomer women homebuyers:

- Women are very attuned to colors. In 2005–2006, the color trends include brown becoming the new black; grayed-out greens; reds coming up orange; classic colors with such new names as Wasabi, AeroBlue, and Vanilla; and textural effects suggesting copper, pewter, and stone.
- Illumination—both task lighting and natural light—is of major importance to compensate for declining vision and to add drama.
- Feminine buyers are looking for strong character in home design, such as cottages with a crisp and clean look, urban enclaves with rich colors and textures, and calming and contemporary Asian influences.
- Women who are 55 or older are cyber savvy and use their computers for ordering and correspondence.
- Women this age now have more time to relax, engage in social activities, and explore hobbies, making "special interest" rooms an essential feature in new-home marketing. Perlman also says that "women shop with peripheral vision: they notice everything," and they "harness the power of grandparenting." It's okay to include a grandkid's room. They also want walking trails and a hotel/resort fitness feel.

Sara Lamia, founder and president of Fort Collins, Colorado-based Home Building Coach, Inc., said that builders who hope to succeed in selling to the older woman need to learn how to build their trust first. Lamia cautioned that women over 50 "are especially perceptive and will know if you appreciate them or not."

"We need to be respected and heard and expect nothing but the best including luxury and superb customer service," Lamia said. "We want to be able to die in our new homes and don't want to ever have to move to an institution."

The aging Baby Boomer female buyers are not only active, but they are also proud and extremely good listeners, according to Joanne Chappell-Theunissen, president of Mt. Pleasant, Michigan-based Howling Hammer Builders. Unlike younger women, the over-50 female buyer is also likely to be relatively unaccustomed to business dealings, but the average 70-year-old thinks of herself as middle-aged.

Builders and remodelers wanting to focus on this category will be working with a woman "who likes to have the rules set for her," so it is important to set them at the start, explaining her responsibilities and what can, and cannot, reasonably be expected as the construction process moves forward.

"What isn't she saying to you, and why? She's not comfortable talking to you about her frailties. Turn it into a third-party conversation and take the onus off her," Theunissen said. "Don't say, 'Don't worry about that, we'll fix it.' Instead, tell her how it's going to be fixed, who's going to fix it, and when it will be fixed."

NEW DESIGN IDEAS WILL SURFACE

The aging Baby Boomers will continue to redefine new-home design. The new-home industry built its large homes on small lots in the 1980s and its gate-guarded castles in the 1990s. In this decade and the next, builders and developers will build the homes and communities that allow retirees to reconnect with their friends and family. Current and future retirees do not want a house built for old people. They want an easy living home that an Olympic athlete would also enjoy, and their preferences will vary greatly based on their socioeconomic status and their values.[2] Here are the prime generalities about the future of new-home design for retirees:

- Inexpensive, commonsense universal design concepts (see Part Two) that are designed to make life more enjoyable will grow in popularity.
- Retirement home segmentation will occur, allowing developers to maximize absorption by building multiple types of homes and neighborhoods that appeal to different psychographic categories of retirees.
- Home designs will vary dramatically based on the socioeconomic conditions of local retirees and their psychographics.

FEW AFFLUENT BOOMERS SEEK A SMALLER HOME

Affluent Baby Boomers have shown a propensity for selling sooner and buying larger. According to an online random sampling of 363 sales associates who market homes priced at greater than $500,000, more than half (52 percent) who purchased a luxury home through them within the past two years told their sales associate they plan to spend fewer than five years in their current home. [3]

In addition, 65 percent made their most recent home purchase because they wanted a bigger residence. A mere 17 percent were looking to scale down, whereas another 15 percent were buying a second or vacation home. Eighty-six percent of these homebuyers said they have purchased three or more homes throughout their lifetime. Almost half said they have lived at their most recent residence for a period of only one to five years.

The typical size of a luxury home purchased, according to the survey, was 4,500 square feet or less with four bedrooms, three bathrooms, and a backyard. The overwhelming majority (88 percent) of these luxury homes cost approximately $1 million, whereas only 12 percent of the sales associates reported recent sales of homes costing more than $2 million. Approximately 60 percent of these buyers purchased existing single-family homes, whereas 21 percent opted for new construction, and 16 percent purchased condos/town houses.

Affluent Boomers were most interested in the following home amenities:

Luxury Home Amenity	Percentage Interest
Main-floor master suite	47%
Three-car garage	44
One-floor home	40
Home gym	28
Home theatre	15
Guest house	12

According to the sales associates surveyed, Boomers expect to make changes to their new home:

Type of Renovation	Percentage Interest
Any renovation	87%
Kitchen	79
Bathrooms	70
Backyard deck	28
Complete renovation	27
Bedrooms	16

In the opinion of the sales associates surveyed, Boomers want to live in the suburbs:

Where Boomers Purchased Homes	Percentage
Suburbs	67%
City	21
Country/rural	10
Senior community	1
College town	1

Coldwell Banker sales associates said Baby Boomer clients told them they wanted their home to be located where they can continue to pursue favorite pastimes:

Favorite Activities	Percentage Interest
Shopping	71%
Golf	69

Favorite Activities	Percentage Interest
Enjoy beach/waterfront	47
Biking	24
Hiking	22
Fishing	12
Athletic leagues	6

Source: Zoomerang Research, January 2005, for Coldwell Banker Previews International

COMMUNITY SERVICE, SOCIAL ACTIVISM WILL DRIVE HOME SALES

Although the nation's home-builders say they are selling a new lifestyle—not homes—to the over-55 market, researchers believe that they need to hone their marketing efforts to a deeper philosophical level to stay ahead of the competition. Think about it: If most builders produce terrific interior spaces, countertops, cabinets, and tile work, and provide attentive service in a wonderful location, what element would make the difference to an experienced, discriminating buyer?

NO PROBLEM. WHAT ARE NEIGHBORS FOR?

David B. Wolfe, author and one of the nation's leading experts on the "second-half" housing markets, contends home marketers should be aware of the "older-wiser" customer and focus on reality and authenticity to enable this huge population segment "to be all they can be."

"At this stage of life, it's about being, not about having," said Wolfe, author of *Serving the Ageless Market* and *Ageless Marketing*. "The companies that are going to be successful in the future will be those that help people through a self-actualization process."

Everybody knows that a majority of Baby Boomers have wanted all the toys—much more so than their thrifty, make-do parents—as they have moved through every phase of the life cycle. But companies can no longer merely sell products to gain market share. As Wolfe and other analysts contend, the fulfillment potential component must be present. This concept is exemplified in Harley Davidson's message ("The Road Starts Here. It Never Ends."), which conveys endless possibilities and not simply motorcycles. Richard Steckel, president of Addventure Network, an international marketing firm, said the physical items in a house are important, yet they can be imitated. He suggested there was "more to life than just 'more,'" and that builders strive to leave a corporate legacy to society, something that can be identified as a specific "cool factor" that consumers would support.

"If you do things as a company that connects philosophically with your customer base, it's more difficult to imitate," Steckel said. "What will you do that would cause a consumer to choose you over another company?"

Steckel pointed to a Target campaign that earmarks a portion of its revenues for schools, thereby showing the community it values an individual's economic power in making a difference. He also told of a New Zealand phone company that paid four consumers to take a year off and do "something they always wanted to do for the greater good." The phone company invited people to write, in 400 words or less, what they would do with a year away from the job. Because we are all so busy and often wish we had more time to delve into a special project, the phone company decided to take action. It paid not only the four winners' salaries but also the salaries of the replacement workers.

"The result was the phone company was overwhelmed with business," Steckel said. "People wanted to spend their money with a company that had these ideas and goals. It also got a significant number of job applicants from people who wanted to be a part of this kind of organization."

One suggestion of a "soft social activism" program that builders could promote and finance was to offer "civic certificates" toward a local scholarship or community fund to households that learned three life-saving techniques—basic first aid, the Heimlich maneuver, and CPR. In addition, the community would garner the reputation of being caring, safe, and involved.

"People will always rise to the occasion to buy in a community or from a company that hits an important and emotional note," Steckel said. "It becomes part of the area's folklore, part of its cool factor."

Laura Wilson, director of the Center on Aging at the University of Maryland, has focused her research the past 18 years on the aging of Baby Boomers with specific focus on civic engagement, employment, and lifelong learning.

"These people are looking for purposeful social networks," Wilson said. "These are learners who may have left the conventional business workplace and no longer have a typical business card. They will be seeking new business incubators where they can share experiences and ideas. They will be moving toward a new kind of work that will give them personal fulfillment. They're aging, but they are a long way from being done."

What no longer works in communities aimed at folks over 50?

"If I had to do it all over again, I'd take out all of the shuffleboard," said Ron Bonvie, whose DJG Construction is based on Cape Cod. "Most of these people wouldn't be caught dead on a shuffleboard court. They think that game's only for old people, and none of these customers consider themselves as close to old."

Now that we have gauged a number of preferences and examined some of the attitudes of today's older homebuyers about the shape and size of their next home, we check in on the draw to a specific environment. What's the difference between an age-restricted, or qualified, community and an age-integrated, or targeted, community? How did they get that way? In Chapter 3, we take a look at the history and evolution of "age-targeted" communities and some of the other terms aimed at Boomers and beyond.

3

AGE RESTRICTED, TARGETED, QUALIFIED, OR INTEGRATED?

Exploring and defining what has propelled "mature" housing choices

I've known Stan Johnson for more than 25 years. He is 60, divorced, and the father of two children, the youngest a girl who will graduate from high school next spring. He's had the same job since he was 21 and will retire soon on a comfortable government pension with the maximum of 40 years of benefits. He has been known to have more than one cocktail between quitting time and supper, and spouts streetwise wisdom most of the day.

"Will you tell me something?" Stan asked one Saturday afternoon while tossing his posthole digger into his pickup truck. "Is everybody over 50 an active, health-frickin' adult? What do you call guys like me who simply want to come home, relax, pour something special into a glass with ice, and eat popcorn on the couch?"

Stan Johnson, as usual, had a point. Why are potential homebuyers in this country age 50 and older typically corralled into an active adult group even though some of them could be worlds away from being "active"? In this chapter, we explore what Boomers and seniors like to hear, and why they are so conveniently bundled together when the groups should be separate and independent. This bunch includes some of the different buyer types you've heard about—move down, empty nester, last time, or any other moniker you would like to place on a homebuyer older than 50.

The bottom line is numbers, money, and need. The developers, builders, remodelers, and suppliers that see this enormous customer base are racing to get their product to market to capitalize on need-based opportunity. Those who do the research and truly understand their specific local niche market are successful, whereas others in the industry are tossing it all together and hoping one size will fit all. Stan Johnson is just beyond the upper age limit of 77.5 million Baby Boomers who were born between 1946 and 1964. Because so many of these people will soon be over 50, they are grouped into the largest definable category—active adult. Harris Interactive conducted an online survey on behalf of Pulte Homes from April 14 to April 20, 2005, that included 1,802 adults aged 41 to 69 who live in ten different regions of the United States. Of the group in the 60 to 69 age bracket, 46 percent said they would consider moving to an active adult community. The numbers were about the same for the 50 to 59 group—47 percent said they would consider the active adult community, and 41 percent of respondents aged 41 to 49 would consider the move.

POWER BEHIND THE NUMBERS

Housing analysts, designers, builders, and planners have spent millions of dollars in research trying to ascertain what most people around Johnson's age would like in a home *IF* they were to move. Understanding a retirement lifestyle for a typical buyer in a specific area is extremely difficult, yet let's look at a conservative estimate of what Boomers "say" they are going to do. (Remember, this has been the group that's been nearly impossible to predict.) If 40 percent of 77 million people contend they would consider an active adult community at some point in their life, that's 28 million potential customers (not including Silents and the GI generation) with typically more money than any previous generation. Where do you guess marketing dollars will be aimed? These are typically couples and singles who, with the kids gone and work finally slowing, have shifted their activities and energies onto themselves and become more aware of their diet, physical fitness, and eagerness to learn new skills and hobbies. They now are seeking a home that can better accommodate those changes and allow them to age in an area with more security and comfort with people their same age. More than 60 percent, like Johnson, may move to a smaller home in the same community, or simply age in place, surrounded by people of all ages. Although aging in place is not as glitzy as moving to a new place, it probably will be the reality for a majority of the population, despite what you read from homebuilders, apartment managers, and any community in the Sun Belt with an active chamber of commerce. The challenge is that an overwhelming number of Boomers live in the suburbs, and many suburbs, unless reconditioned and retooled, will be lousy communities in which to age in place. As discussed in Part Two. "new urbanism," the concept that promotes community and aging in place through planning and encourages the interaction of neighbors with housing, workplaces, shops, civic events, entertainment, schools, and parks all within easy walking distance of each other, is difficult to accomplish in many suburban areas because of zoning restrictions. In fact, it helped to launch "urban rejuvenation," a movement that sparked more interest and energy in living, shopping, and entertaining downtown. Pushed along by working couples, single professionals, and aging executives who could not find a similar experience in suburbia, it is alive and well in many metropolitan areas.

As mentioned in the introduction, the term *active adult* soon will apply to a much wider profile of homebuyers who will buy locally as well as in the amenity-laden resort communities.

Like so many things in life, a move often does not turn out the way it's planned, and the Boomers have compounded that notion. An empty nester grandpa is suddenly asked to raise a granddaughter, the move-down buyer ends up paying more instead of less for the next home, and last-time buyers eventually come to see that they will actually move two more times. Many, like Stan Johnson, probably will never move again. His pickup will be parked in the same driveway, and he will relax on the couch with popcorn and something wonderful in a glass. If the time comes when he will be unable to march up and down the steps to his front door, he will simply get somebody to build him a ramp.

According to William E. Becker, a veteran homebuilder, and architect Bill Feinberg, both based in Teaneck, New Jersey, Johnson is not the only person voicing annoyance about the active adult label. Even though 67 percent of homeowners aged 65 or older who currently live in age-restricted communities say they would not have purchased their home if it were not in that category, Becker and Feinberg discovered younger buyers (ages 43 to 54) are absolutely turned off by any mention of restriction. The team conducted focus groups divided by income level: either $150,000 to $200,000 a year (called "Professionals") or $50,000 to $80,000 a year (called "Middle Americans). Terms such as *active adult* irritated almost everyone in the groups, as did catchphrases such as *age restricted* and *age limited*. According to Becker, age-restricted communities offer little to this generation. "They don't like restrictions saying you can't put a pool in or put a fence up. What they're asking is, 'What is this place giving me that I don't already have in my current lifestyle?'"

Becker and Feinberg found that the upcoming Boomer generation is looking for a "slower-paced life" free of congested highways, with a small-town feeling that reminds them of where they grew up. Yet they also want all of the perks of a luxury subdivision, such as pools, clubhouses, and proximity to entertainment and restaurants, in a diverse community without age restrictions. The groups also have high expectations about living space; although they may no longer need a larger house, most participants wanted 2,500 square feet of floor space. They also had strong aversions to "cookie-cutter" houses. Other preferences included low maintenance, nearby convenience stores, close proximity to offspring rather than far-away resort areas, and proximity to higher-education institutions. In addition, the Silents, or Nexers, may be empty nesters, yet they do not plan on retiring any time soon.

Becker's peers say Baby Boomers are not at the age where they see age-restricted products as appropriate. There is approximately a seven-year difference in the ages of those buying age-targeted housing and age-restricted housing. Concierge services, valet services, dog walkers, elegant finishes, and upscale amenities can help create the lifestyle that will draw reluctant Boomers.

What are the terms that housing industry experts expect to run with? Have they found the words that are absolutely taboo when marketing to senior Boomers and aging Baby Boomers? It would help if everyone spoke the same language. A Nexer to a builder could be a member of Generation X to a real estate professional. A Silent to a developer could be a member of the silent majority to a marketer. Even though "universal design," "visitability," and "aging in place" (all discussed in Part Two) have become important to builders and designers of all marketing niches, Boomers and senior Boomers have keen ears and sharp eyes for specific terms and identifiers, and they all should be accurate and consistent.

"The word that tests best with young senior Boomers in our research is vitality," said Sharon Brooks, partner in Brooks Adams Research, a Richmond, Virginia–based firm specializing in research for residential real estate companies and economic development agencies. "Other strong choices are **comfortable, choices,** and **individuality.**" Brooks said words her company was trying to eradicate from the industry vernacular included *facility, unit, ambulate, socialization, activities, residents,* and *dementia. Mature adults* was considered the best descriptor, whereas *seniors* was not seen as a bad word nor was retirement, according to the Brooks Adams surveys.

And it's important not to loop all seniors into one category—especially regarding electronic communication. Brooks said that although older seniors (75 and over) rate the words *computers* and *Internet* negatively, younger seniors (60 to 75) rate them very positively, in fact significantly more positively than Boomers rated the two words. As expected, not all analysts agree on the terms that should be highlighted or discarded. John Rude, president and CEO of Eugene, Oregon-based John Rude and Associates, a consulting firm that explores gerontology (the study of aging), marketing, and communications to specific age groups, told attendees at a National Association of Home Builders gathering to avoid seniors, elderly, and *golden agers* because they are labels that carry negative stigmas. "Our propensity is to relate to this market as special and then build products especially for it," Rude said. "The outcome is that the product becomes stereotyped. It's best to make a product as mainstream as possible by focusing on function as opposed to age."

Tracy Lux, president of Trace Marketing, a Sarasota, Florida-based company specializing in the "mature" market, said she is encouraging her marketing and builder clients to use the term *age qualified* instead of *age restricted* in regard to communities targeting persons aged 55 and over. "We think 'age qualified' is much more positive," Lux said. "We also like to have fun with our prospects by saying, 'Just think, you are chronologically advantaged enough to *live here.*'" *Lux said her research confirms that lifestyle community and resort-style living* have been effective marketing terms. She also said the new generation of seniors—the in-betweeners that some industry analysts refer to as "Zoomers"—are more sophisticated than the World War II generation.

"These are people who were born between 1928 and about 1946," Lux said. "I call them the 'crown-molding crowd.' They don't want a large space but they do want high-level finishes such as Corian and granite counters, special interest or hobby rooms, fine outdoor living accoutrements, and cute rooms for the grandkids."

Some of these Zoomers, or Silents, plan to continue working for the foreseeable future and find downtown living to be an attractive alternative to mature adult communities. This movement, developers say, has spawned its own terms that already have been recognized by the housing industry. Reportedly, persons in childless households seek an in-city environment conducive to *hiving*, or frequent social interaction, rather than *cocooning*, in which they feel isolated from friends, neighbors, and community activities. The terms were first used earlier this year by the Yankelovich market research firm. Greg Currens, CEO of Style Interior Design in Irvine, California, cited results from the Yankelovich survey in which 64 percent of the participants identified themselves as *hivers*, compared to 33 percent who identified themselves as *cocooners*. The majority of the respondents said an ideal characteristic for their home is for it to serve as a hub of activity for friends and family. The majority also said they preferred maintenance-free living.

BIT OF HISTORY: WHY THE BENEFITS FOR OVER-55 HOUSING?

Why are developments and buildings for age 55 and older persons exempt from restrictions, and why do they seem so privileged? A brief review of this country's housing laws and the reasons for their enactment would be a logical place to begin that explanation. The Fair Housing Act of 1968 was crafted from the Civil Rights Act of 1964 and prohibits a broad range of practices that discriminate against individuals on the basis of race, color, religion, sex, national origin, familial status, and disability. The Fair Housing Act applies to municipalities and other local government entities and prohibits them from making zoning or land use decisions or implementing land use policies that exclude or otherwise discriminate against protected persons. However, in some cases, the Fair Housing Act does not preempt local zoning laws. According to the U.S. Department of Housing and Urban Development (HUD), the enactment of the Fair Housing Act on April 11, 1968, came only after a long and difficult journey. From 1966 to 1967, Congress regularly considered the fair housing bill but failed to garner a strong enough majority for its passage. However, when the Rev. Dr. Martin Luther King, Jr. was assassinated on April 4, 1968, President Lyndon Johnson utilized the national tragedy to urge the bill's congressional approval. Since the 1966 Open Housing Marches in Chicago, Dr. King's name had been closely associated with the fair housing legislation. President Johnson viewed the act as a fitting memorial to the man's life work and wished to have the Fair Housing Act passed prior to Dr. King's funeral in Atlanta. Another significant issue during this period was the growing casualty list from Vietnam. The deaths in Vietnam fell heaviest upon young, poor African American and Hispanic infantrymen. However, on the home front these men's families could not purchase or rent homes in certain residential developments on account of their race or national origin. The Fair Housing Act was a move to resolve that growing concern.

In 1988, the Federal Housing Act was amended to prohibit discrimination based on disability or family status. The focus quickly targeted children under the age of 18 and pregnant women. The formation of families as a protected category suddenly collided with the operation of retirement or adult communities, so the 1988 amendments included exemptions for housing developments that qualified as housing for persons over the age of 55. Congress countered with the Housing for Older Persons Act of 1995 (HOPA) in an effort to resolve the conflict between protected family status and the exemption for older persons. HOPA was crafted and reconditioned the exemptions for elders, and the law has become the guideline for developers and owners of senior housing.

HOPA maintained the requirement that at least 80 percent of exempt housing must have one occupant who is 55 years of age or older. It also still required that the exempt housing publish and follow policies and procedures that demonstrate an intent to be housing for persons 55 and older. The new law also abolished the requirement that housing for those 55 and older had to maintain "significant facilities and services" designed for the elderly. Communities that are occupied solely by persons who are 62 or older are also exempt from the prohibition against family discrimination under a different section of the law. At first glance, the 80 percent requirement appears to give a developer, owner, or builder a cushion against 100 percent compliance. HOPA allows a 55 and older community to be "exempt" from the preference for families if (after September 13, 1988) 80 percent of the units are occupied by at least one person aged 55 or older. Apartments or owner units occupied by persons who are disabled and require reasonable accommodation also do not count against the 80 percent rule. In addition, units occupied by employees of the housing facility or community who are under age 55 do not count against the 80 percent as long as the employees perform actual duties related to the management or maintenance of the community.

The 80 percent requirement does not mean that the developer or owner can utilize the remaining 20 percent of units to be occupied by any age person he or she chooses. There is an additional "intent" provision that is scrutinized. The 80 percent occupancy requirement is coupled with a condition that the building or community adheres to policies and procedures that demonstrate the intent to be a 55 or older place. A developer cannot merely choose to sell to qualified nonseniors or families just because the facility is greater than 80 percent senior occupied. That's HOPA's most often debated and discussed provision. The law provides that each housing community may determine the age guidelines for units that are not occupied by at least one person 55 years of age or older. Although the stipulation appears to allow a community to set any age requirement it deems fit for the 20 percent of spaces that are not required to be occupied by a person 55 years of age or older (including requiring the occupants of the remaining 20 percent of spaces to be adults), in realty it appears to be contrary to the general intent of the Fair Housing Act, which is to prohibit discrimination on the basis of "family status." So rather than set specific age rules, what some communities have done is allow 20 percent of the units to be occupied by persons who do not otherwise satisfy the community's minimum age requirements.

A challenge then could surface when an older tenant dies or moves out and the building already has used up its 20 percent quota and subsequently finds itself below the 80 percent requirement. When called into question about dropping below stated age guidelines, builders, developers, and housing officials have relied on the all-encompassing "intent" provision, which has come to the rescue in more than a few communities. They also have pointed to the fact that no party deliberately allowed more underage occupants into the community than the threshold permits. Conversely, would an owner or manager violate the Fair Housing Act if the community excluded families with children after the 80 percent threshold is met? HUD says the answer is no, because the property is under the over-55 exemption umbrella. Many states require owners and managers to diligently enforce all age rules consistently so that the 20 percent guideline for persons under 55 is rarely even a factor. And in addition to age occupancy ratios, HOPA requires that the community "publish and adhere to policies and procedures that demonstrate its intent" to qualify for the 55 or older exemption.

DEL WEBB REINVENTS THE ADULT WHEEL WITH SUN CITY

On January 1, 1960, the Del Webb Corporation created the now legendary senior niche when it opened the Sun City community near Phoenix to a reported 100,000 visitors on its first weekend. The company vision was to offer a desirable "lifestyle," which featured relatively small, simple modestly priced homes, to an age-qualified audience. The retirement lifestyle was also fairly simple and the time was filled with recreational activities such as shuffleboard, lawn bowling, crafts, and golf on shorter courses. Cleary, "sun" was at the center of the message and began to connote where retirement should be enjoyed, not merely spent. By the time it was built out, Sun City would become home to 46,000 residents in 26,000 homes.

Over four decades, the Sun City concept lured dozens of builders and developers who were intrigued by the idea and demographic. As more consumers entered the over-55 category, preferences changed. In the 1980s, large, luxurious recreation centers began to surface and included the latest in exercise equipment, indoor walking tracks, and swimming pools. For many years, Del Webb and others in the business focused on providing a retirement lifestyle in warmer climates, often requiring residents to relocate from other states. Ironically, as the wealthier retirees became more and more mobile, the company that attracted thousands of retirees to Sun Belt states discovered through its research that many people preferred to retire within driving distance of their longtime family home. That discovery drove builders to introduce smaller, more intimate lifestyle communities in regions once regarded as taboo for retirement living—the Midwest and Northeast. K. Hovnanian Homes's Four Seasons communities, which offer resort-style living and activities year-round, are among the popular 50-plus projects in nontraditional senior states.

SUGGESTING AN AGE RESTRICTION . . . BUT NOT THE AMENITIES

But do you really want to live in a neighborhood without younger people? Many people over the age of 60 absolutely do, and they extensively research the community type before making their final choice; and they offer both age restrictions and amenities as the primary reasons they bought in an age-restricted community. They seek a complex where they find neighbors of similar age and interests, and where friendships might be easier to make. The sense of security, especially among those who want to lock and leave a home for several months, is also a huge consideration. Living in an area with no teenagers eases the security factor for many elders. Home purchase price is important, but their relatively fixed-income status makes them more concerned about high monthly dues. Age-qualified buyers require a more expensive community because they need to be close to health care facilities, shopping, and highways yet not too far from family and friends. Their community is now the core of their social scene and a total living experience within it is the ultimate goal. It features a comfortable mix of a residence and recreational facilities, such as a pool, a health club, educational auditoriums, and social events. A community van for short errands is a plus, especially to church, travel seminars, and crafts fairs. They don't mind having neighbors close by and want to develop new relationships with different friends. They don't mind smaller kitchens because they like to dine out often in the immediate area.

However, some potential homebuyers were skittish about an age restriction or the perception of living in "an older community." After decades of building age-restricted communities, builders and developers have recognized that the traditional elements of planned community living, such as security, on-site amenities, and low-maintenance housing, appeal to homebuyers of all ages. The construction of multigenerational communities represents a recent trend in planned community home building. The underlying idea is to attract a diverse population of families, including retirees and young professionals of varying income levels and backgrounds, to establish an active and vibrant community. Many developers say older buyers congregate in certain streets and neighborhoods of age-targeted or family communities, thereby setting up their own area of people with the same age and interests.

The major difference between age-qualified and age-targeted communities does not really surface in the type of home or its furnishings but in integration and socialization. Age-targeted buyers, unlike age-qualified occupants, are more likely to be still employed, whether full-time or part-time, plus having their primary contact with friends and family outside the community. They continue to participate in the same clubs and teams and don't necessarily need the integration brought by socialization and recreation that comes with an age-qualified community. Age-targeted buyers prefer individual design features within the home, such as larger, gourmet kitchens for entertaining, instead of a long list of community amenities. Depending on the region, they typically are a larger market segment because they don't need on-site facilities like hospitals and classrooms.

Both groups prefer two or more bedrooms, garage access or underground or covered/secure parking, and huge storage space and more than adequate closets. In fact, they are both willing to sacrifice bedroom size and bathroom size for larger closet and storage space. The variations in floor plan were subtle with age-qualified folks readily accepting smaller single-family homes or condominiums on one level. Age-targeted purchasers require more space than a condo or town house provides yet also prefer a single-level space. They seek more of a traditional family home with more privacy and less density than an age-qualified community.

Now that we have defined various community types, let's drill down another notch and consider geographical location. In the next chapter, we will discuss where the mature adult tends to buy his or her next home. Do these savvy consumers head to the sunshine in search of daily vitamin D, head back to a college town and the last true learning environment of their life, or settle closer to the child who never felt very close to them when growing up?

4

WHERE DO OVER-50 BUYERS CHOOSE TO GO?

Demographics have changed with the present wave

If you jump, where will you land? Where are other people your age deciding to spend their later years? Nearly two decades ago, Lee Fisher, a Northwest researcher and mortgage specialist, began to write a compelling evaluation of where retirees preferred to relocate. Historically, at the center of most decisions was the presence of an adult child and the need for an excellent community hospital. The need for the hospital remains, but adult children no longer "stay put" as they did in previous generations. Fisher's group went on to develop a program to attract urban retirees of moderate means to areas that welcome their presence, providing a more stable base to the community's economy.[1]

That's not a bad sales pitch: Rejuvenate your town by luring interested, wise, talented, and creative individuals and the significant financial assets that come with them. The idea would make sense to seniors as well: Why gamble by moving across the country to be with your grandkids when your children could relocate at any time? The fallout of the "tech wreck" of 2000 was a great indicator of growing unpredictability and the variety and number of careers today's parents experience. Families now move more unexpectedly to a new job or different career, and that can happen shortly after Mom and Dad have moved into the adjacent neighborhood. If the grandparents really want to spend quality time with the grandkids, it's often better to block out extended vacation periods, especially if the long-term job picture is cloudy.

In this chapter, I analyze the demographics of the retirement home market, not only for Boomers but also for those preceding and following the boom who have leveraged the prosperity of the 1990s into a ton of home equity in their traditional family home. We'll glance at the scope of the market, historical trends in relocation decisions, and the demand for retirement homes by prospective buyers and the reasons for those choices. The objective is to indicate the potential size of this market for the benefit of both those seeking retirement homes for their own use and those who cater to them.

Baby Boomers, and the generations before and after them, are looking at the possibility of a retirement home in increasing numbers, creating a very competitive market for builders, developers, and buyers. Regions that were once pristine and quiet are now hosting huge planned unit developments. Areas that once were run-down and unacceptable have been reborn as trendy retirement-compatible places to settle. In other words, the aging of the Baby Boomer has transformed the real estate market as it has influenced every other aspect of the American economy.

POPULATION MAKEUP AND HOUSING FORMATION

The housing market has set records for sales activity in every year between 1996 and 2004. That means approximately 48 million American households (about 42 percent of the total number of households) either bought or sold a house (or did both) during an eight-year period. That frenetic activity marks the maturation of the Baby Boom generation. The boom peaked in 1957. In 2003 there were more 46-year-olds than any other single age category. It is traditional behavior to move into the best house one will ever inhabit during the 40- to 50-year-old decade. Thus, this surge of housing demand reflects the Boomers doing what comes naturally. But now, because they are living longer and their equity is greater, they will lengthen the best-home purchase time frame into their 60s.[2] This ought to come as no surprise. As mentioned previously, the American economy and American society have reflected the impact of the Boomers during all their ages. Now their major impact comes in the housing market.

Masked in these housing statistics is the growth in sales of retirement, investment, and vacation homes. During this great housing boom, the number of those homes sold increased from 296,000 in 1995 to 415,000 in 2000. Between 1980 (when the leading edge of the Boomers was 34) and 2000, the number of those homes in the United States increased from 1.7 million to 3.6 million, rising from 1.87 percent of the housing stock to 3.09 percent.[3] This suggests that the Boomers used the good economy of the 1990s as a boost to buy a bigger and better principal residence and then indulge their desire for a comparable valued retirement home. As we explore in the next section, the number of older Americans will grow, and with that growth will come the demand for retirement homes and home modifications to age in place.

AGING TURNS A CORNER IN AMERICA

The United States is getting older, due mainly to the great population surge we experienced after World War II. Although there has been a second surge since 1979, the dominant demographic fact in this country is that the Baby Boomer is aging. Figure 4.1, showing the projections used by the U.S. Census Bureau based on the 2000 census, indicates the speed at which Americans are aging. By 2020, there will be as many Americans over 65 as there are now over 55 and nearly twice as many Americans over the age of 85.

FIGURE 4.1 *U.S. Population by Age, 2000–2020 (Population in thousands)*

Age Year	2000	2005	2010	2015	2020
Total Population	275,306	287,716	299,862	312,268	324,927
55 and over	58,836	66,060	75,145	85,878	95,841
65 and over	34,835	36,370	39,715	45,959	53,733
85 and over	4,312	4,968	5,786	6,396	6,763

Source: U.S. Bureau of the Census, Middle Series Projections

Even in 2000, the number of Americans over 55—the preBoomers—constituted more than a quarter of the population. By 2020, when the Baby Boomers reach 65, that percentage reaches nearly one-third. By 2050, it's over 40 percent. This is a major and growing market for retirement homes and major remodels, not only in the future, but also now. Like all projections, these depend on a lot of "ifs." Although the Census numbers appear to be reasonable and reliable, the market projection will be affected not only by demographics but also by interest rates, prices, and alternative big-ticket purchases, such as cars, boats, travel, and recreational vehicles. The reliability of any projection over time will be subject to prevailing conditions. That said, the underlying base of demand for retirement homes and remodels established by the structure of the population is very strong by sheer numbers.

WHY THE SURGE IN NEXT HOME INTEREST?

Although the current population numbers are beneficial to the senior home market, there are other reasons why the numbers have been up so dramatically. Clearly, the prosperity of the 1990s gave reality to the desires of younger Boomers to own a larger, nicer home than they originally anticipated. With unemployment low and productivity up, discretionary income was sufficient to carry the cost of a bigger, better-placed home. In addition, interest rates have been low by historical norms and therefore the cost of owning, as expressed in the monthly payment, is low. But there are some more significant forces at work in the marketplace. These forces have pushed demand for more expensive retirement homes and will continue to do so as the Baby Boomers age. What are they and what will they mean for the future?

Years of Double Incomes

One of the legacies of the 1970s has been the growth of two-income households. The women's movement eliminated to a degree the economic discrimination facing half the population and made success in the marketplace possible for all adults. The Great Inflation that sprung up in the 1970s made participation in the workforce by all a necessity. For these reasons, Boomers and their older brothers and sisters now typically (53 percent) live in households with two or more adult earners. This has increased the disposable income available to the typical household and thus enabled households to expand their consumption. It has also contracted the time they have available, making time the scarcest and most valuable commodity in the modern economy. In a two-earner household, there are often three full-time jobs; such stress is often the most intolerable. Thus, the lure of leisure time is extremely valuable.

The two-earner household and the stress related to a shortage of time have produced a new kind of retirement buyer. These buyers want a home as pleasant and comfortable, or even more so, than was their previous home. It is a place they can absolutely enjoy, share, and celebrate with others. Today's last-home buyer is also driving demand in nontraditional areas, usually those within a one-hour or two-hour drive from a business core. The pressure on households to generate income to maintain lifestyle into retirement or semiretirement will continue, because the typical Boomer has not prepared financially to slow down. Savings rates are at historic lows, Social Security is under threat, and the shift from defined benefit pensions to defined contribution retirement plans shifts risk from the employer to the employee. As the Boomers age, this will enhance demand for retirement homes and aging-in-place remodels close to metro areas.

The Lure of Appreciation

The run-up in home values over the past 15 years has Americans thirsting for more. Although some more conservative households may fear the bursting of a housing bubble or merely choose to surrender the responsibilities of home ownership (discussed in Chapter 6), a majority plan to again reap a significant return on their retirement housing dollar. Also, Uncle Sam continues to provide its citizens with a tax benefit. Although many senior buyers pay cash or make a significant down payment on their retirement home, the tax deduction for mortgage interest payments still remains one of the major tools available to the American public for sheltering income. The 1997 change in the tax treatment of capital gains from home ownership ($250,000 tax free of gain for single persons; $500,000 for married couples every two years) basically halted any tax on the sale of most primary residences. The impact of both of these is the same: The cost of owning many homes is reduced and the return on investment in home ownership is enhanced. In a normal financial environment, this might not be enough to foster investment in real estate, particularly the purchase of a retirement home. Traditionally, equities carried with them a greater return on investment than did real estate. But the first years of the 21st century have hardly been normal financial times. The bursting of the tech bubble has reduced the value of most investment portfolios and severely damaged confidence that these values will be restored. This has pushed many investors out of the stock and bond markets with more of their money going into a more reliable place, like the roof over their head. This shift has been made more convenient by a reduction in underwriting requirements for mortgages. Lenders, now viewing the significant equity position of the majority of older buyers, have bent over backward to make first and second mortgages in every region of the country.

Technology in the Home

One of the major changes that has occurred in the American economy over the past quarter century has been the shift in the way work is done. Adult buyers, whether strapped or not, will also redefine "work" (basic office communication, consult, create, evaluate) at home. The change in the conventional workplace is most obvious in the time aspect of work. The cut-and-dried, nine-to-five routine is increasingly less dominant as the rule for work time. The first aspect of this change was the introduction of flexible time, which recognized the needs of working women seeking to balance family life with a career. Now "nine" came to mean "ten" or "eleven" and "five" became "six" or "seven." The eight-hour day, five-day week morphed into the ten- hour day, four-day week, and then evolved into other variations on that same theme.

The second stage of this transformation occurred as an outgrowth of the information revolution. We are no longer primarily a manufacturing economy. Rather, we are increasingly a knowledge-based economy. That means that wealth is created from ideas rather than from transforming things into other things. White-collar workers are less and less paper pushers and more and more wealth creators. With the changes engendered by the technology revolution, the notion of work time has also become less than clear-cut. The concept of a nine-to-five job in a technologically based economy is still dominant but not nearly so much as in the past. Traditional companies now see the clock in a whole new light. More important for our purposes, they see attendance in a different light as well. The improvements in communications technology have created the opportunity for large-scale telecommuting, allowing workers to operate away from the office as effectively as if they were there. And although the growth of telecommuting has been consistently overestimated, it now clearly appears on the radar of the American economy.

All this has added to the appeal of purchasing the next, best home sooner. Employees can roll into semiretirement in the comfort of their own living room. The ease of telecommuting has added another dimension to the demand for retirement homes. As mentioned, it has increased the demand for retirement homes located within easy commuting distance of employment centers and increased the demand for "wired" homes. Today's high-tech consumer is not only going to demand broadband communications capacity in his or her new home, but this capacity will also be a requirement for aging in place. If Boomers choose to remain in their present home, home modification will include high-tech applications for the first time.

SENIOR BOOMER BUYING AFTER SEPTEMBER 11, 2001

The strong domestic magnet that has pulled Americans closer to hearth and home since September 11, 2001, began to lose its strength about three years later when a greater percentage of homebuyers over age 50 considering a move admittedly were "seeking distance" rather than buying a home within three hours of their present residence. Even though the "grandparent" factor was still an enormous incentive for senior Boomers to keep at least some geographic tie to the traditional family home, the results of a national survey demonstrated that U.S. citizens had begun to shed some of their safety concerns.

"I was absolutely stunned by it. It caught us all by surprise," said Sheryl Palmer, Nevada resident and one of the key officials in Pulte's Active Adult Communities for Pulte Homes and Del Webb. "People are looking at the next step in their lives as 'a time for me.' They are planning to slow down and do what they want where they want. There's more volunteering . . . a move to things they've always seen themselves doing but were too busy to do. I think the distance piece is probably a part of that."

Retirees, or those seeking to retire in the near future, are also looking for a quieter environment where the hassles of congested areas are absent. In more popular areas, like Florida and Arizona, gated communities are growing. These afford the advantages of community while screening out the dangers that are always present in city life.

EXPLORING MOBILITY

Having looked at why people are motivated to buy retirement homes or make a significant remodel to stay where they are, the next question is: Where are they moving? In this section we'll look first at the general patterns of mobility of the over-55 group, as revealed in the 2000 census, and then look at some more specifics of the types of places people seek. While all statistics are rather dry and difficult to make exciting, the numbers can help us point to the future.

The habits of older Americans are an understudy for the behavior of the Baby Boom and ensuing generations. The basic results are not surprising. There has been a general population movement from the Northeast to the South, both among older Americans and among the general population. And Americans, with the exception of the years 1998 to 1999 and 1999 to 2000, have been moving out of metropolitan areas and into nonmetropolitan areas.

Figure 4.2 shows the mobility patterns of older consumers in the last year of the 1990s, which was the most recent census data available.

The numbers here are not surprising. Even though they depict only a single year, they seem to conform to conventional wisdom, as follows:

- In percentage terms, the lowest mobility rate for older Americans is in the South.[4] This is consistent with the perception that the South is where one finds a second home. Recall that Florida leads the nation in retirees. Conversely, the highest mobility rates are in the Northeast. Again, conventional wisdom says that "snowbirds" migrate south in the winter. When they are ready to retire, they stay closer to home.

FIGURE 4.2 *U.S. Population Migration, 55 and Over, 1999–2000*
     (Population in thousands)

Census Region	Northeast	Midwest	South	West
Total Population	51,364	62,618	94,646	61, 592
55 and over	11,541	12,454	21,591	11,420
Percent of Total	22.5%	19.9%	22.1%	18.7%
Movers	2,534	2,560	2,190	776
Within Same County	246	234	401	328

Source: U.S. Bureau of the Census, 2005

- A large number of movers move within the same county. Interregional migration is considerable (see Figure 4.3) but the number staying near home is also significant.
- The West shows a relatively low rate of mobility. Part of this is a function of high house prices in many parts of the region. Part of it also deals with the regional climate.

To determine where people are moving, we need to look at the migration patterns among regions. These are best summarized by looking at the difference between the total number of people moving into a region and the number of those moving out. To avoid the impact of immigration—considerable during the 1990s—we only look at internal migration. Unlike the previous section, Figure 4.3 looks at total internal migration, not just older Americans.

The analysis of internal migration patterns also squares with expectations, as noted:

- The Northeast has shown a consistent loss of population to other areas. In no year during the decade was there positive net migration from the rest of the United States.
- The main beneficiary of migratory patterns during the decade was the South, reflecting retirement demand.
- The Midwest and the West were minor players in this people movement, with the Midwest losing a bit and the West gaining.

FIGURE 4.3 *Net Internal Migration by Region, 1990 to 2000*
            (Population in thousands)

Year	Northeast	Midwest	South	West
1999–2000	-252	82	227	-57
1998–1999	-163	-171	271	63
1997–1998	-203	120	230	-146
1996–1997	-119	-154	391	-118
1995–1996	-234	68	150	16
1993–1994	-328	-31	376	-17
1992–1993	-334	233	101	-1
1991–1992	-292	-62	224	129
1990–1991	-585	-15	433	167
Source: U.S. Bureau of the Census, 2005				

Yet another demographic phenomenon of the past decade has been the movement between city and suburb and metropolitan area and nonmetropolitan area. For the most part, metropolitan areas have seen a decline in population over the decade. While the numbers in Figure 4.4 show this, they actually understate the shift. There has been a decided shift from central cities to suburbs. Because both are included in the metropolitan figure, they mask a much greater shift out of urban areas and into (presumably) less populated areas.

Some of this is a function of the availability of space and housing at affordable prices. But part of it represents the desire for the safety and lower levels of stress offered in less urbanized areas. The statistics described above were created by the generation that preceded the Baby Boomers. Is it likely that they will continue as the Boomers age and move heavily into the retirement market? In a word, yes. As the Boomers age, these trends are more and more likely to continue.

The movement to the sun from the northern side of the country will continue, but it will exist side by side with the choice of a retirement home closer to the original primary residence for reasons of family and convenience. If Boomers do not age in place, the most common choice of a retirement home will be either in an obvious retirement community or in a neighborhood close to home. In addition, the movement from the city to the country could be intensified by the actions of a segment

Figure 4.4 *Net Migration in Metropolitan Areas, 1990–2000*
(Population in thousands)

Year	Net Migration
1999–2000	137
1998–1999	71
1997–1998	−182
1996–1997	−216
1995–1996	−275
1993–1994	−86
1992–1993	−317
1991–1992	73
1990–1991	117
1989–1990	128

Source: U.S. Bureau of the Census

of Baby Boomers who will be seeking places where recreational facilities are inexpensive and accessible, and where their active lifestyles can be best accommodated. Others will stay tethered to the job center to produce needed income.

But there is a second dimension suggested by these statistics. Right now, a large portion of these numbers represent primary home moves, younger households seeking to acquire housing that is affordable and reasonably close to their jobs. As the economy has changed and as the technology boom has erupted, burst, and started to flower again, jobs increasingly are located in the southern and southwestern parts of the country where costs are lower and unions weaker. These areas also have abundant land and thus low housing costs. Dallas, Las Vegas, and Phoenix have told this story in the past.

As the Boomers continue to hit the historical retirement years, the concept of job location will fade. Either the Boomers will be employed and able to work part-time from home or they will be retired and not even entertaining the notion of a job. Potential relocation areas will be looked at for their facilities and environment. The luxury of never again having to shovel, rake, or mow will still be measured with the presence of jobs and the cost of housing. In a capsule, today's numbers tell a story about relocation for economic reasons while the same numbers in the future will tell a story about lifestyles.

What are some common mistakes people make when researching retirement destinations?

The basic problem is not considering all the factors necessary for making an optimal choice.[5] Most important, perhaps, people often neglect to investigate medical care in their preferred community before relocating. Here are some examples of erroneous moves:

- To a vacation home (the weather is different in winter/summer)
- To their children's town (the children tend to move, as discussed earlier)
- To a favorite resort area (it grows and changes)
- To a climate rather than to a place (many bad choices in a good climate)

The statistics generated in the decennial census and compiled by the government tell many stories, but some, important for our purposes, can only be told anecdotally. Right now, stories are appearing about retirees settling on retirement in traditional areas like Florida and Arizona and then leaving. Either they will sell the house in the Sun Belt and move a bit farther north (say to the middle South or Colorado) or buy a condo back near home to avoid the discomforts of weather that afflict traditional retirement areas.

The issue, however, is more than weather. In many cases, retirees are seeking active lifestyles for both their body and their mind. You can't play golf or lounge in the sun all day and never at night. The presence of a full range of recreational and cultural activities is already important to the current generation of retirees and will be even more important to the Boomers when they retire. This means that smaller university communities are an attractive location. This means the obvious, like the research triangle area of North Carolina but also less obvious places like Hattiesburg, Mississippi, and Boone, North Carolina. They are situated north of the very torrid weather in much of Florida and Arizona yet south of where home was and family and friends probably still are. These places scattered through the middle South combine a mild climate, abundant recreation opportunities, and cultural activities. They provide a unique mix of ideals for the retiree. This option will be even more attractive to the Baby Boomers, who will have spent their life for the most part in urban environments. They will have become used to the easy availability of restaurants, movies, and theaters. Wherever they retire will have to afford similar amenities.

In this chapter, I've shown that people would be willing to move to what they perceive to be a better home for a variety of reasons. The numbers indicate that this trend will accelerate as the Baby Boomers leave the workplace in droves after 2010. In the next chapter, we will explore if that move—maybe to a second home—should be made before that crunch begins. Given the number of potential, emotional buyers down the road, perhaps securing a retirement spot now for part-time or full-time leisure makes sense.

5

CONSIDERING
A SECOND HOME

*Is it time to invest in another place . . . and
audition for retirement?*

It's usually easier to justify a real estate purchase, especially if it's an expensive, dreamy retreat clearly beyond your affordability comfort zone, by going into the deal thinking it will eventually become a primary residence. You know the drill: "Jane, I know we will be stretching to make the payments on this place, but think about how great it will be when the kids are gone, we no longer need renters, and we are living here full-time."

Well, most of the time, it just doesn't happen. According to the National Association of REALTORS (NAR), approximately one-fifth of all second homeowners see their second home as a potential retirement residence, but even fewer actually make that move.

In this chapter, I spend additional time exploring the astonishing rise in second home sales by U.S. consumers. The key reason for the activity is no longer to spend quiet hours by the lake but for financial diversification. It now appears that the purchase of investment property and vacation homes accounts for more than one-third of residential transactions.

A comprehensive NAR study, based on two surveys, shows that 23 percent of all homes purchased in 2004 were for investment, while another 13 percent were vacation homes. There was a record of 2.82 million second-home purchases in 2004, up from 2.42 million in 2003. The investment home component rose to 1.8 million sales in 2004 from 1.57 million in 2003, while vacation home sales rose to 1.02 million in 2004 from 850,000 in 2003.

"The study shows the majority of the real gain in single-family home sales can be attributed to the vacation and investment property markets," said John Tuccillo, real estate analyst, author, and former NAR chief economist. "Not only are Baby Boomers looking for weekend getaways but we are also beginning to see young retirees auditioning for their retirement location. As the Boomer group ages and the demographics change, a larger and larger number of consumers will be targeting that potential retirement home."

According to the NAR analysis, 86 percent of vacation home buyers do not rent their property compared with only 21 percent of investment buyers. It appears that the majority of investment homes are actually a renter's primary residence, and only 10 percent of investment buyers intend to use their second property for recreational purposes.

Data from a 2003 study revealed the typical vacation home buyer is 55 years old and earns $71,000, while the investment property buyer has a median age of 47 and earns $85,700. For properties purchased between mid-2003 and mid-2004, the median price of a vacation home was $190,000 compared with $148,000 for investment homes. In contrast with the last available full-year price data in 2001, vacation homes have appreciated 12.8 percent from $168,500, and investment homes have risen 25.4 percent from $118,000.

FIND ANY VACATION HOUSES WE CAN AFFORD?

Among the reasons given for why they bought second homes, 30 percent of buyers wanted to diversify investments, 28 percent sought rental income, 14 percent wanted a personal or family retreat, 6 percent planned to use the property for vacations, and 5 percent had extra money to spend.

YOUR NEXT PROPERTY PURCHASE . . . PRIMARILY AS A SECOND RESIDENCE

If you are considering buying a second home that could easily turn into a retirement option, the following are some significant considerations that are often overlooked in an emotional decision that you should put on your list as you evaluate your options:

- *Picking your place.* The three most used words in real estate—location, location, location—are repeated for good reason. If the property will be solely a personal residence, will its style and layout hold its appreciation over the long term? Then think resale: If you had to sell it five years down the road, what would lure the next buyer? Finally, if you had to rent it out, is this the type of property that could definitely catch your eye and possible rental dollars? What appeals to just you may not appeal to the rental pool you will depend on for consistent income.

- *Picking your community.* Even if the house is perfect, is the neighborhood one that beckons late afternoon walks and friendly shopping? Do you think most of the people you know would like it too? Remember, you can always add a bedroom or convert patio space, but the area is set. Again, play the dual role of renter and retiree. If the parcel will eventually serve as your retirement residence, you need to choose a place where you will be comfortable later in life.

- *Finding the cash.* If you don't want to take cash from your old home and roll it into your new home, you definitely will have other choices. One of the biggest changes that have occurred in U.S. mortgage markets over the past ten years has been the introduction of a myriad of creative loan programs. If you have not purchased or refinanced a home recently, you could easily be overwhelmed with the attractive and useful loan options available today. (I also discuss different types of funding in Part Three.)

- *Tax is a benefit, but . . .* While mortgage interest is deductible on your primary residence and second home, it's usually not wise to buy a home solely for tax reasons. Most accountants will not tell you to move into a big, expensive palace just because your old mortgage has been satisfied. If your property eventually becomes your primary residence, you can sell it after two years and pocket $500,000 of gain (married couple) or $250,000 (single person). Sale of an investment property would not qualify for such generous tax treatment.

- *Who's minding the store?* Before you invest in real estate, you must decide how you will handle management. Having tenants, short- or long-term, will require that the property be managed effectively. It's a business unless you will be the only occupants. This means maintenance and improvement, as well as simple rent collection. You will either do it yourself, or you will hire others to do it for you. Management is a cost and will diminish your cash flow. Choosing the more cost-effective approach will affect the return on your investment.

- *How much can you handle?* Real estate that will ultimately prove a good investment because of price appreciation might be a challenge every month because of negative cash flow. You are responsible to pay for and maintain your property regardless of whether the property is generating revenue. Before you invest, you need to create and hold a cash reserve to cover those weeks when the house is not rented, when the rent is late, or when the toilet needs repair.

Any investment needs to be evaluated for its total rate of return over its holding period relative to alternative investments. The holding period is completely under your control. You might decide to buy a second home as a prelude to retirement—vacation in it now, live in it later. Or your second home could be the stepping-stone investment that appreciates and provides the down payment for a third or fourth vacation rental. The alternatives against which you compare a real estate investment are also subjective. Consider how you would use the money if you didn't buy that second home.

The total return on your investment in real estate is not subjective. Rather, it has several very specific components. If you are evaluating the potential return from a second home, some of these must be estimated.

It's usually wiser to be conservative in making these assumptions. The components of total return that affect your profitability are:

- *Cash flow.* Rents provide a stream of income to sustain the expenses of the house and provide profit. In evaluating the investment, you need to adjust your projected rents in two directions. Each year, the rent should be adjusted upward for any increases because of inflation and improvement of market conditions. The weekly rental income might need to be lowered during slow periods. Talking with other owners or property managers in your market will enable you to get a good feel for what rent levels are and what vacancy rates you can expect.

- *Potential appreciation.* Over your ownership period, the house will change in value—hopefully for the better! With the way U.S. properties have been appreciating, there's a good chance the value will increase over time. You have control over when you will sell the property, and thus you can time the market to ensure the best chance of a capital gain. It is rare that an investment property *must* be sold, so you can continue to rent it out during slow sales periods and wait for a better time to sell.

- *Managing, maintaining, and renovating.* There are expenses attached to owning investment or personal real estate. On the investment side, these need to be offset against cash flow and appreciation in calculating your return on investment. Any expenditure on a rental property to maintain or improve it is an expense that will diminish your near-term return. Also, any outside management expenses reduce cash flow to you. That doesn't mean you should let the property run down or quit your day job to manage it. Two things need to be emphasized here. First, major changes (repair or remodeling) in the property can be depreciated over an extended period. Thus, the amount deducted each year is only a portion of the total expense. Second, your estimate of repair and renovation expenses is sensitive to your chosen holding period. A roof replacement might be of concern if you are planning to own the home for 30 years but not if your time horizon is 5 years.

- *Mortgage interest deduction.* If a home is your primary or secondary residence, the interest you pay to finance the purchase of the house is tax deductible. Because you benefit from this, it represents part of the positive return from your investment. Conversely, rental income is taxable to you and is thus reduced by whatever your marginal tax rate is. Finally, tax schedules govern the allowable depreciation deductions for major home repairs and renovations. IRS schedules provide most of the information you need to factor in the tax considerations of real estate investments.

- *Compare and contrast.* You need to adjust your return for the time value of money. In other words, if your rental house yields a return of $10,000 in three years, you need to determine that amount back to today's dollars used elsewhere to see how much it's really worth. Using the return on an alternative investment— perhaps a bank account or certificate of deposit—is usually a good assumption.

All of these considerations can be plugged into a formula that will enable you to get a good estimate of what return you can reasonably expect on your real estate investment. That formula looks rather complicated but merely does what I described above. In fact, most advanced hand calculators have the formula already plugged in. All you need to do is put in your assumptions, and you can get an answer that will guide your decision. Check out some of the real estate calculators on the Internet to help you along your way. Some terrific calculators and real estate formulas are offered by Dr. Jack (The Mortgage Professor) Guttentag at http://www.mtg.professor.com.

Turning the possibilities and creative ideas you have for your next home into reality is a straightforward process that requires both thought and work. It should be done jointly by everyone who will participate in the dream house. If you want to include children, close friends, and other family members, that's fine. But remember, this home will be mostly just for you, so don't be saddled with somebody else's idea of a dream.

IS IT TIME TO SERIOUSLY CONSIDER RENTERS?

Many people might not be able to simply become second homeowners and drive over the hill to their fabulous retreat at the drop of a hat. For the first few years of ownership, it might be imperative to have renters help you with mortgage payments and maintenance fees. The best way to ensure your sanity, and your home's safety, is to first consider renting only to family, friends, and neighbors. In a capsule, you *usually* get the renter you know, and hopefully trust, who will give you less hassle and is most likely to leave your getaway in the condition it was found. And renters quickly become your best—and least expensive—marketing source.

Think about it: How many weeks do you realistically have available? Wouldn't you want to fill your available weeks with somebody that you know? Why rent to a stranger who has contacted you off the Internet when the Porters from the parish church, known for their altar-boy kids, would die to have the two weeks before Labor Day? Owners of second homes often underestimate the large pool of potential renters created by the number of neighbors and friends near their primary residence and second home. These two separate and independent areas can often produce more than enough people to fill your rental calendar. And it's a huge advantage to have personally witnessed how potential renters keep their own home. You'll rest easier knowing they probably will keep your place in much the same condition that they keep their own home. Conversely, your visit to their home may be the primary reason *not* to rent to them!

FRIENDS TYPICALLY EXPECT TO PAY

Remember, friends know the going rate and usually *expect* to pay—so charge them. If your place clearly is on a resort's 50-yard line and has the best beach, kitchen area, and beds, your friends and neighbors will be prepared to pay top dollar for your top spot. (Family sometimes can be a totally different matter, but . . .) If the getaway is in the middle of nowhere with no obvious amenities (besides serenity) and you have never rented it out, at least consider charging a price low enough to cover your utility and cleaning costs. If you are renting to people you already know, one of the most important things to do is set or review some ground rules before they move in. Discuss any issues (inconsistent drinking water, best place to park the boat trailer, no lifeguard at the pool) that you think could arise while they occupy your place. Preparation always helps prevent some awkward situations down the road.

MARKETING IN YOUR OWN BACKYARD

You can reach plenty of potential renters by using local marketing techniques. The power of these is that they can be focused to have the greatest chance of reaching those you wish to attract. When you do advertise locally, be sure to list a phone number or e-mail address that you can use as a message drop, particularly if the rental market is tight. You might be deluged with unnecessary communications if you use your main numbers or addresses.

Consider the following local marketing techniques:

- *Bulletin boards.* These are everywhere, and they are very effective. To use them, create an attractive ad for your property. The ad should emphasize the advantages of location as well as the amenities of the property, and it should contain a color picture. All of this is quite inexpensive. Your cost consists of the time it takes you to compose the ad, the paper it is printed on, and the time you need to post it. It helps if you have access to a digital camera, but given the power of the word-processing software that is standard on most personal computers, this is a relatively easy process (and you probably know a ten-year-old who can do it for you in minutes). Common locations to post your ad include the following:
- *Supermarkets.* Everyone shops for groceries, so the audience here is composed of locals. This is a good place for ads about your vacation home because family traffic here is strong. Given the volume of ads on supermarket bulletin boards, you might want to take care that your flyer stands out.
- *Coffee shops.* These are today's town squares, and they serve the same gathering function. The crowd that loiters here tends to be younger, somewhere between college graduation and first-time

homebuyer, so the demographics are good for someone offering a place to rent.

- *Local government offices.* You might want to investigate the possibility of using the bulletin board in your local housing office to advertise your rental property.
- *Merchandising circulars.* The *Penny Saver*-type merchandising newspaper is everywhere. It reaches a geographically targeted audience and generally is read by people who are motivated to find something they need—a car, a boat, or a beach rental. Unlike bulletin board ads, merchandising paper ads will cost you something, with the cost varying with the size of the ad and the length of time the paper carries the ad. Yet given the readership—interested in buying and local––this might be a very cost-efficient strategy.
- *Real Estate Books.* Find out if the specialty real estate books that feature homes for sale and rent are open to advertising by individual property owners. These books are used primarily by large property owners and real estate professionals, so it might not happen, but it's worth a try.
- *Local newspapers.* While readership is interested in nearby areas, ads for warm weather properties are very popular—especially in colder environs where residents constantly seek sunshine in winter.
- *Church bulletins.* This is an old standby, and one glance will tell you about the concentration of real estate advertising in church bulletins. Marketing your property in the church bulletin gives you an automatic bona fide status with the readers. If you are advertising there, you must be like them—you must be honest and you must be good-hearted. Who wouldn't want you for a landlord? The bottom line here is that local advertising offers the opportunity of reaching high-probability prospects for very little cost. It's well worth thinking about.
- *The Internet.* The Internet is particularly useful for vacation properties where the owner and customer are usually widely separated. It also gives your unit exposure all over the globe. Property owners like Christine Karpinski, author, teacher, and vacation homeowner who wrote the bestselling book *How to Rent Vacation Properties by Owner,* swear by the Internet and say they would not be handling properties by themselves without it. "People new to Internet marketing are always concerned with problem renters,"

Karpinski says. "In my experience, I've learned that most people spending money for a nice place usually are not going to trash it. There are a lot more good people out there than bad, and you can take steps to eliminate the bad ones before they rent."

Internet advertising should be as painless as possible. You can easily create a Web site for your property. If you have the computer training (or know someone who does), it is a fairly simple proposition to craft the property page and then place it with any number of popular vacation sites. The "Big Four" vacation rental sites are VRBO (http://www.vrbo.com), Great Rentals (http://www.greatrentals.com), A1Vacations (http://www.a1vaactions.com), and CyberRentals (http://www.cyberrentals.com). Each has its own major plusses. For example, CyberRentals will be happy to share all comments about a specific home.

SNOWBIRDS ARE OLDER, WISER, USEFUL TENANTS

Karpinski has been a consultant to owners of vacation rental properties for the past five years. Her helpful Web site (http://www.HowtoRentbyOwner.com) offers tips for renters as well. Some of her favorite clients are older homeowners who head south for the winter ("snowbirds"). Karpinski said a few of her clients are on set incomes and have established monthly payment plans. They simply pay a little each month toward their next rental. That way, they can earmark an exact amount each month and don't have to pay one lump sum every year. Typically, the owner would require a reservation deposit, then the balance to be paid in one or two payments. (Most owners require full rent plus a deposit paid prior to the rental period. Payment methods vary, but most will take personal checks.)

"I love my snowbirds because many of them are so willing to help when little things go wrong," Karpinski said. "If they see something that needs attention, like a leaky faucet, they just fix it. Unlike a family that's renting for a week at prime time, snowbirds are more flexible on their days of arriving and departing."

SATISFIED RENTERS WILL CALL BACK AND WILL TELL THEIR FRIENDS

No news here: The key to a successful, moneymaking second home is satisfied renters who want to return because of the special experience they enjoyed at your place. And if they were impressed with their time and accommodation, they are going to tell their friends and acquaintances. Although you often can't be there to place a rose in every room every time a new visitor arrives, make sure you or your representative takes the time between cleanings to scoot back to your property and make certain your people are getting the kind of dwelling you want them to enjoy.

The goal is to provide a relaxing environment. Help ensure that goal is reached by investing in great bedding—especially in the largest, typically the parents', bedroom. Kids are resilient and can curl up in a sleeping bag in the most curious of places. But go out of your way to pamper, and even indirectly coddle, the people most likely to write the check. A great night's sleep brings people back. If they don't receive it, it's often downhill from there. They'll find fault with the inefficient corkscrew, comment on the poor water pressure, or complain about getting a splinter while walking on the deck.

At least once or twice a year, put yourself in the renters' shoes. What would you expect to have in a vacation home at the rental price you are charging? When compared to your competition, are your rates fair and in line with the rest of the pack? When it pours rain for three straight days, is there enough to do to keep your renters from harming themselves? While cable television is the scourge of many vacation-bound parents, some owners have found cable has really made a difference for some of their customers. What could be done right away--perhaps deeper cleaning than you are getting from your service--that would make the stay more enjoyable? During the high season, what could you accomplish with $20, one helper (your loving husband?), and four hours dedicated to intense elbow grease? Be sensitive to smell, aware of color.

A couple of times a year, substitute the throw rugs in the kitchen with inexpensive, colorful new ones. Not only do they help give the home a clean and fresh look, but such moves show renters that you care about the condition of your home--and that you expect the same from them.

Top Ten Tips to Keep Renters

Here is a quick honey-do list you can complete with that 20 bucks, one helper, and four hours. Never underestimate the renter's first upclose look. Remember, these people are on vacation! Do the following to make it memorable from the start:

- Buy a welcome mat if you don't have one. This will save you time and effort cleaning interior rugs and also gives a good impression.
- Clean the front door and make sure the doorknob and lock work and look sharp. It's a pain to wrestle with a difficult lock in the dark.
- If the street numbers are dirty, paint or clean them. If you have a screen door, repair any holes in the screen and wipe the metal frame. Clean all cobwebs from the light fixtures and fingerprints from the entry.
- Do not make any sideyard or backyard area the dumping ground just because most people probably will come and go from the front of the house.
- Make sure your shrubs don't look like grubs.
- Make sure your deck surface is not slippery, sending a visitor for a surprise slide ride.
- Clean all kitchen appliances, and don't let the refrigerator resemble a bulletin board. Save the kid's photos for home. Replace Teflon pans when they get scractched. Make sure drinking glasses shine.
- There should be no mold—anywhere—especially in the bathrooms. If necessary, replace the toilet seat.
- Find an easy, safe place to put keys while out of the house.
- Never apologize for the condition of your home. Offer a clean, comfortable home for rent and hope for the best.

BE CLEAR ON THE TERMS OF THE RENTAL

At the time of occupancy, tell the tenant in writing what your responsibilities and theirs are. You will be grateful later on if the tenant does something you forbade or doesn't do something you specified and a disagreement ensues. Unless you are clear at the outset who will do what, you open yourself up for a lot of headaches. Some responsibilities you want to make clear at the outset include the following:

- *Use a printed lease*, even if you're leasing your waterfront condo to a cousin. This might sound like a burden for you, but it will minimize the hassle of disputes that can turn into a "he said, she said" type of argument. Spell out all the terms that are important to you, such as:
  - *How much of a deposit is expected on the property?* Usually, the landlord requires the first and last months' rents as well as some amount for damage.
  - *When and under what conditions will that deposit be returned or kept?* Increasingly, the law requires landlords to hold the deposit in escrow and to return it with some form of interest accrual attached.
  - *When, where, and how will the rent be paid?* The last day or the first day of the month is traditional, but you need to specify whether that day is for postmark or for receipt. You might specify a grace period, but be specific as to how long and any penalties that will be incurred if the grace period is exceeded.
  - *Who will be responsible for utility hookups and payment?* This can be either you or the tenant. Putting the account in your name ensures continuity of service when a tenant leaves. Because utilities are requiring large payments to reestablish service, continuity is a considerable benefit. Even though you will put some estimate of utility costs in the rent, having the account in your name puts you on the hook for more outlays, whether your tenant pays the rent or not.
  - *Can the tenant sublet the property?* Subletting can reduce the gaps you might experience in tenancy, but it will also decrease your control over who is in the property.
  - *Will the property be furnished or unfurnished?* This also includes the appliances that might be part of the lease and should specify the condition of the furnishings as agreed to by both owner and tenant.

- *What restrictions will you impose on the use of the property?* This will cover things like the number of adults who can live in the house, any pets that are allowed or banned, or any age restrictions on occupancy. It also can cover whether the premises can be used for other than residential purposes.

There are three potential sources for a lease document. First, you can simply draw one up yourself or get a generic form on the Internet or at a stationary store. For most property owners who have a single investment property or whose needs are simple, this is the most cost-effective and efficient way of creating a lease document. If you have a number of rental properties or if there are some complications attached, you might want to consult an attorney who can draw up the lease for you. In general, it is a good idea to talk with a real estate attorney before you launch into the investment just in case there are local ordinances that will affect your ability to rent your property or your flexibility in its use. For example, Florida imposes a tax on any rental of fewer than six months in duration, treating such rentals as the state treats hotel rooms. Using annual (or semiannual) leases will avoid that extra cost.

The third source of lease documents is the management company if you own an investment or vacation unit. In many cases, condos are built with the expectation that owners are investors and will seek to lease their property. Generally, the management company will use standard documents that cover all local death knell requirements.

MANAGING THE PROPERTY YOURSELF

If you have your mind made up to take on all management responsibilities, here are some items to consider before making that commitment:

- *Are you a people person?* Do you have the time and patience to field inquiries and calls from potential applicants? Check the costs of hiring a local rental manager who often arrives with solid, reliable leads. Good managers can be worth an entire season's commission by quickly handling an emergency.

- *Don't sell in public.* More people know about you and your home than you realize. Save conversations about your—and your renters'—comings and goings for the friendly confines of your home.
- *Friends come first.* They're usually good renters. Rent to friends (or friends of friends) you know. They'll usually treat your place with care—and often leave it in better condition than will strangers.
- *Off-limits space.* Don't forget to keep a locked closet or storage area for your supplies and favorite possessions—like a prized water ski you want no one else using. It's also a good idea to load up on cozy comforts such as a large-screen television with DVD player and VCR, a top-of-the-line gas grill, and all kitchen essentials. You want renters to return, and nothing's a bigger turnoff than having only three plates and two forks.
- *Bulk is best.* Rent by the month or season. It will lessen cleaning and maintenance—and extend the life of your favorite throw rugs.
- *Know the territory.* Your group of luxury homes or condos may limit—or prohibit—renters. Research any association restrictions before you rent.

Owning real estate is different from other investments in one very large way—it usually requires interaction with people. When you own a share of stock and its price falls, you don't need to confront your broker. You just dump the stock. With investment real estate, it's a different ball game. We get to know the tenants, albeit sometimes only electronically. It's harder to simply cut and run because it requires that we confront a real human being. Hard decisions and difficult conversations are often necessary in the rental business, and property managers do this for a living. Remember, though, this service comes at a cost and you will need to factor that into the rent you charge.

PROPERTY MANAGERS: DEFINITELY AN OPTION

Perhaps you don't want to be in the marketing business. You bought your investment property as a source of income and capital appreciation, and you'd rather do the things you really enjoy. On your scale of pleasure, dealing with renters is not even on the radar. It is possible to hire someone to manage your property, market it, collect rents, and arrange for necessary repairs.

Property managers are pretty easy to find. If you've purchased a home in a development, the management of that property will probably come along with the purchase. Either the developer will have an on-site manager, whose job it is to represent the owners in all these matters, or a local real estate firm will have the franchise on marketing and rental management for the development. In many cases, except for specific rentals that you would like to carve out (say for friends or relatives) and the time you will be using the property, you will be required to use the on-site property management.

For your individual full-time rental unit, you might want to hire your own manager. Real estate professionals will be a good source for developing a list, or they may even handle the chores themselves. Be clear on the services that the property manager offers and the cost to you for these services. You should expect that the property manager will send the rents to your specified location (lock box, bank account, etc.) within a certain number of days of the rent due date and ensure the enforcement of any late penalties for unpaid rent. The manager should be available to tenants and responsive to their requests within a (short) specified period. The manager should also maintain a reference file of reliable tradespeople who can be used to fix anything that goes wrong with the house. Check references, not only to assure yourself that this property manager is a reliable and effective one, but also that the property manager has the experience in managing your type of property—be it single-family house, high-rise or garden apartment, condo, high-rent, low-rent, and so on.

This might not seem like marketing, but it actually is. Using a property manager can ensure that you have as few gaps as possible in the rental period for your house. For this peace of mind, you can expect to pay about 10 percent of the rent for the property management service, yet some larger firms demand a 50-50 split of all rental income.

THE BOTTOM LINE IS A
DELICATE FINANCIAL BALANCE

Matching what you want with what you can afford can be a delicate, sticky balance. It's human nature for our wants to exceed our capabilities, so you will probably never get all you desire. The key to integrating needs and wants is to organize your goal in two different time frames. The first time frame is your best future prediction. Will the place you want to buy now be the same place 20 years from now? Will you seek a different beach or neighborhood? What does your getaway look like down the road? This involves envisioning in great detail the retreat where you will spend your leisure time when you retire from the conventional nine-to-five world. (Is there anybody who *really* still works nine to five?) The more detail you can gather about this place, the greater the chance that you will attain your dream or something in the neighborhood.

The second time frame is the present. For many consumers, the next home they purchase will be the one they keep down the road. No stepping-stone moves to see if the grass is greener or the pool larger. Ask yourself, which area—at least at this time—do you believe would be best for you? Will the place hold mostly renters in the first five years? What assets would you use to get you there? What can you do now to begin to move toward that goal? If you are currently an investor, the solution may be to ask yourself, How can I leverage/sell property to move closer to my vision of the future? The answer will be in terms of a particular property, including a plan for the property and a strategy to acquire and hold it. You should keep asking yourself this question on a regular basis to keep you on the path toward your goal.

These are the steps in the visioning process. Creating a vision enables you to have a specific orientation, and having that orientation forms your decision making when it comes time to choose.

In fact, unless you bring a good business sense and a sharp pencil to your second-home investment, you'll spend many sleepless hours wondering why you ever did this and feeling worse because your getaway may not be exactly around the corner! Before you make your leap into a property other than your primary residence, you need to be honest with yourself. It's time to roll the dice and discover whether this potential financial move will end up benefiting your wealth or whether you would be better off holding the cash in a certificate of deposit or in another no-risk financial vehicle. If you can't afford to be in the deal for personal use only, follow these steps:

1. *Calculate the total cost of the investment.* This cost consists of the down payment on the property, the settlement costs of the transaction, and the interest forgone because you chose to buy this property rather than to invest in something else. The two most common omissions here are to forget the settlement costs and to ignore the opportunities that might have been seized if you had not chosen to invest in real estate. Settlement costs can be more than expected, so get a real figure early in the negotiations. The proper measure of the opportunity cost is the rate of return on some low-risk security such as a Treasury bond.

2. *Figure an estimate of the monthly cost of owning and maintaining the property.* This includes the monthly mortgage payment—including the payment on your home equity line of credit if this is how you are financing the down payment and monthly maintenance, such as utilities and repairs. If you make any major alterations or repairs on the property, you can spread the cost over a number of years, but you should include some monthly charge to your costs of ownership.

3. *Determine the rent that you can reasonably expect to charge in your market.* This can be determined by analyzing what other similar properties are being rented for in the area. The help of a real estate professional will be valuable here. As mentioned, the rent you charge should at least cover the cost of owning and maintaining the house. But you're not going to get this rent every single month. There will be gaps between tenants, and some tenants will miss a month or pay late. Because the house will go through periods of vacancy, you need to adjust your rental income estimates to reflect these gaps. Doing so allows you to more accurately project your cash flow. After all, you are not buying the house to lose money.

4. *Estimate the price at which you will sell the property.* This is tricky because real estate markets boom and slump. You have no way of knowing what the condition of the market will be when you plan to sell. The key here is flexibility—you usually can wait and con-

tinue renting the place out until the market rebounds before selling.

It's also important to factor in the tax consequences of your investment, discussed in Chapter 14. The tax laws favor investment in real estate. Interest paid to finance the purchase of real estate is deductible against income, and major repairs or renovations that enhance the attractiveness of the property to potential renters can be amortized over a number of years and deducted from income as an expense.

All of these positives and negatives will net out to the expected return on your investment. Remember, your numbers need to be adjusted for the time value of money—a dollar given away today is worth less than a dollar returned tomorrow. Inflation reduces the buying power of money because you forgo the use of that money. If you don't adjust for the time value of money, your estimates of the return from your investment will be biased upward. Check with an accounting professional to find the right way to factor in the time value of money.

Remember, making a profit anywhere—stocks, bonds, commodities, real estate, and sales—requires basic understanding and research. Regardless of what you read in the newspaper or see on television, there is no blueprint that will absolutely guarantee big-time revenue and success. Your return, however, will be gauged differently if you decide it is only for personal use and not necessarily for investment income. How can you put a price on experiences and memories?

HOW TO DETERMINE WHAT YOU REALLY CAN AFFORD

There are two ways for determining how much cash you can afford to put toward a second residence solely for your personal use or part-time rental. The first is the *asset method*. Start by taking stock of your present wealth. Create a balance sheet of your assets and liabilities. Don't forget to include the equity in your primary residence, even though you may be dead set against borrowing against the roof over your head. Homes are no longer cumbersome and difficult-to-liquefy assets, thanks to the integration of home equity lending with other financial opportunities.

If you have refinanced your home recently or have children needing loans for college, you are familiar with filling out forms provided by mortgage lenders and universities. You know the drill—list all of your debts, including credit cards, cars, boats, mortgages, and anything else you view as a "minus" on your financial chart. Balance these against all of your assets, including your savings, individual retirement accounts, home value, stocks and bonds, and other assets. The net of these two numbers will give you your net worth and be an indication of the amount you have available to transfer into your investment.

Although it sounds simple and gives you a good ballpark number, the actual net number is more complicated. Some of your assets might be unavailable for reinvestment. For example, if your retirement program does not have a loan program attached, those assets are tied up until you reach age 59½. Withdrawing retirement savings prematurely subjects the taxpayer to a 10 percent penalty, and the withdrawal amount is included in ordinary income for tax purposes. It would take a rather large rate of return to make the alternative investment worth the withdrawal. So to determine exactly what you have available for investment purposes, subtract those restricted retirement savings. What's left is your capacity for acquiring investment real estate.

The resulting numbers here don't have to be great for you to get into the investment real estate game. With as little as $8,000 to $10,000, you can control a modest yet potentially lucrative investment or vacation property. It may not be your absolute dream home, but it can get you in the door somewhere. Once you acquire the property, the actual cash flow cost to you should be relatively low. Rental income will help offset the monthly costs, including your mortgage payment.

The second method to determine your capacity to buy property is the *income method.* This uses cash flow rather than net worth as the deciding variable. Once again, it requires offsetting positives and negatives. Calculate all your monthly obligations—mortgage and other loan payments, credit card debt, tuition payments, and so on—and subtract them from your monthly income. We'll call this discretionary net income, and it is the amount that is available to handle the cost of carrying the property. As mentioned, rental income will cover a good part (hopefully all) of the negative cash flow. The ability of your discretionary net income to support an investment property is substantial because of the initial unknowns about the amount of time the property will be rented.

To prove this to yourself, try a little exercise. Look on the Internet or contact a real estate professional and research prices in your targeted area. Now calculate the gross cost of owning that property. This will include the mortgage (pick your own down payment), perhaps a property management fee (10 to 15 percent of the monthly rent), and some amount for replacing house components, such as plumbing, electricity, roofing, siding, and other depreciable items.

When you've calculated this figure, ask a real estate professional and the present owners what you could expect to receive in monthly rent—especially if you are going to rely on rental income to make your plan work. If it's strictly for investment, it's critical to determine how often and for how long you intend to rent it. Decrease this number by 10 percent to account for likely vacancies. Compare the estimated rental income with the gross cost of owning, and the balance will either be the net cash flow to you or the amount you need to supply to carry the property. Remember that this is a cash flow number and ignores the tax benefits of owning investment real estate.

If you are thinking of eventually living in the house full-time, consider both your preferences and the renters' preferences. What do renters really want? In a capsule, they typically value convenience to water, transportation, and entertainment more than space and landscaping. Choose a property that will appeal to the renter, not to you, if the rental use will absolutely come first in your master plan. Decorate the property to accommodate common tastes, not necessarily yours. Furniture will rub against walls, so use heavy paint that really covers. Appliances will get more than usual wear, so buy those that are reliable.

If you choose a location, you also probably have envisioned your target renter. The next question is what type of property you will look for or build. This is a decision similar to location but focuses more on the configuration of the actual dwelling rather than on the neighborhood in which it is located. The number and types of bedrooms, the size of the lot, and other amenities will all factor into your decision as to the specific property to buy.

Besides looking at the location of the property relative to water, shopping, and entertainment, your target renter will be more attracted to a home that suits his or her needs. If you seek families, then a quieter, more spacious property convenient to the pool or beach will be best.

Where you are renting to groups of unrelated adults, think about family reunions—multiple bathrooms and larger bedrooms are a must.

With this background, you will be able to choose a property that will be in high demand by potential tenants.

Two suggestions:

1. Ask other investors and real estate professionals about the demographics of the rental market. Who will make up the next great wave?
2. Talk to resort and vacation community managers about the types of renters who enjoy that community.

A TOOL TO HELP COMPARE PROPERTIES

There are two keys to finding an investment property that will at least track the market. First, after you choose an investment area, find a property for sale whose price is lower than the average price for the entire neighborhood. Such a property has the greatest potential for appreciation. In most housing markets, all the units in a given area will eventually move toward the average, so the lower-priced comparable units will be the ones most likely to appreciate the most. Granted, these houses might be underpriced because they need some work, but ultimately they will pay off. Problem developments and condominium buildings/associations can also skew the norm.

Professor Edward Leamer at UCLA developed a creative gauge that can help you evaluate different properties for their appreciation potential. It is a variation on how stocks are evaluated. When analysts look at stocks, they often focus on the price-earnings ratio (PE) as a measure of whether the stock is overvalued or undervalued. The higher the number (especially relative to either the market as a whole or to historical averages), the more likely the stock is to decline in price over time. For example, when technology stocks were the place to be in the 1990s, most of them not only had high PEs relative to more traditional stocks but they also were trading at extraordinarily high PEs. Consequently, the "tech wreck" really came as no surprise.

What Leamer proposed was to view real estate in a similar light. In this case, though, the ratio is the price of the investment property to the annual rent it will earn. This calculation will give you a standard by which you can judge the relative potential for appreciation of different properties in different neighborhoods, and even in different cities. In other words, it helps to make sound investment decisions by giving you a tool to measure alternative investments against each other. Here's how it works:

- *Plan A.* Suppose you're looking at a $255,000 property that will rent for $1,500 per month, or $18,000 per year. (We can assume there is no vacancy period, but you can figure in whatever you deem to be reasonable.) You are also looking at a $120,000 property that will rent for $850 per month, or $10,200 per year. The PE for the first property is approximately 14 (255 divided by 18), and for the second it is approximately 12 (120 divided by 10.2). The second property appears to be a better candidate for appreciation because it has the lower PE.
- *Plan B.* For a truly effective comparison of the two properties, you need to make a second calculation. You need to look at the PE average for both properties relative to those properties in the same neighborhood. If the ratio for the neighborhood of the first house is 20, while the ratio for the second house is 10, then the first property might be the better buy. It is underpriced relative to its surroundings, whereas the second property is overpriced.

Although all this might appear complex, it's really quite simple. After all, you already know the prices being asked for the properties you are evaluating, and you should know what rent you can charge once you own them. All that's needed is to find out the averages for prices and rents in the immediate neighborhood, and you're done. Any local real estate professional or property manager should be able to help you out with these two numbers. This is a helpful process to go through if you want to choose a property that will propel you to financial success.

The second strategy for finding the most promising investment property is to look for the next hot vacation spot. Some savvy investors simply have followed in the path of large, proven developers who have been extremely successful in other areas. How do you find them? There are several ways to determine the next booming area:

- *Ask the professionals.* As we've stated many times, the people who best understand the housing market are those who are in it every day and who depend on it for their livelihood. If you are interested in where prices will rise the most or where the best rental property buys are in your area, seek out real estate professionals, developers, builders, and city planners. They have a feel for the market and will be able to point you in the direction of the bargains. Try this: Interview a number of the top people in each of these fields and ask them about the future of the community. Try to understand who is now living in the community and who they think will be living there in the near future. Find out which neighborhoods they think are the best values and which neighborhoods will be boosted by the development going on in the community. From their answers, you should be able to form a clear picture of where the opportunities for investment are in your area.
- *Read the local brochures.* Promotional material, news circulars, and community associations have newsletters and bulletins that contain real estate information and potential projects that could affect the value of housing.
- *Visit the building department.* Ask what major employment, transportation, or development projects are on the drawing board. Is the municipality using federal money to place new facilities? When will these come on line and begin to change the location of jobs and residences?

In this chapter, we have explored what it takes to acquire and keep a second home. Renters often can be the answer when monthly costs begin to deflate the pocketbook and you simply don't have time to get away to your getaway. In the next chapter, we move on to what has been the last move for many Americans—assisted living and nursing facilities. While today's seniors and aging Boomers will take more steps earlier in their life to age in place, there are a dizzying number of choices if you choose to leave your last personal residence.

6

THE MOVE BEYOND YOUR OWN HOME

A look at retirement residences, assisted living, nursing homes, and the like

As we carried the last boxes—silverware, dishes, favorite kitchen seasonings—up the stairs to my mom's newly rented condominium, my brother stared me down with a sweat-stained grin.

"Am I nuts, or will we be doing this again in a couple of years?" Bill asked. "Mom's not going to be carrying groceries up these stairs forever."

That was seven short years ago. The steps were few—a half dozen reaching from the basement garage to her first-floor unit—but far too many for a woman, now 86, to take on more than once a day. Three years later, the siblings moved Mom into another condominium across the street—complete with a large, spacious elevator. The unit was even a bit larger than the previous one so that the kids—and grandkids—could continue to visit. The second bedroom also afforded the possibility of live-in care down the road.

Well, we are now down the road, and it's decision time once again on Move Number Three since mom left the family home. In this chapter, we summarize the number of possibilities available when residents leave their last "personal" residence. The capsules later in the section focus on the public sector, yet units and services in private facilities are readily available with immense cost differences depending on region, amenities, and service. Private companies, hospitals, and universities often underwrite and sponsor retirement residences for individuals who were once affiliated.

Preferences and opinions can change (especially for octogenarians) faster than baseball teams change pitchers during the hot weeks of August. Mom doesn't care to have live-in help ("I don't need anybody *that* often"), and we should have seen this coming. She was opposed to the idea of having "a stranger" live in our family home to care for my ailing dad, so why would she be open to a similar arrangement for herself? She now maintains she might consider an assisted-living apartment near my sisters' homes in the San Francisco Bay area, and she even put a deposit on the place, perhaps more to pacify her children than to show her genuine interest. I continue to remind her that we need to move her "while she can still dance," because this complex will only admit her initially while she is still able to walk and feed herself. We fear she simply will wait too long and that an accident, perhaps a fall, instead will spark the next move.

While my mom's experience is a terrific example of why consumers should consider buying adaptable homes where they can bypass a series of moves and age in place (which we explore in Part Two), it also proved to be a learning time for her children. We got a taste of nursing homes and coverage (which I explain in Part Three) during my dad's final days, yet his physical status curtailed him from having the options now afforded Mom.

YOUR "RETIREMENT HOME" CAN HAVE A VARIETY OF MEANINGS

A "retirement home" can mean different things to different people. It can be a place on the beach in Mexico, a golf-course residence in Arizona, or one of the many assisted-living communities, congregate care facilities, boarding homes, and apartments available around the country. Unlike your private dream home that you envision as your retirement residence, eligibility for assisted-living programs and nursing homes varies greatly depending on location and situation. Typically, many communities around the country offer federally funded conventional housing for persons 62 years of age and older, those who are disabled or handicapped, or families who meet financial requirements. These communities usually receive primary funding from the U.S. Department of Housing and Urban Development (HUD). While federal preferences are no longer required by law, some properties still continue to honor them. (See http://www.hud.gov./local). Some properties can provide medication services and limited nursing services. In general, residents must be able to function semi-independently.

First priority is given to applicants who are involuntarily displaced through no fault of their own and those who are homeless. Second priority is given to those applicants who are occupying substandard housing that is unsafe, inadequate, or overcrowded, or to those who are paying more than 50 percent of their gross monthly income for rent and utilities.

The priorities mentioned above usually are applicable to all federally funded housing programs and are known as Federal Priority Guidelines. The required rent under a Federal Priority Guideline program is typically 30 percent of the adjusted annual income. Adjusted income is calculated by subtracting allowable deductions from gross income. HUD's rental subsidy programs for apartments (Section 8, Section 202, and Section 236, for example) differ considerably. Each program has a variety of income limits, eligibility requirements, and methods for calculating rents. All income, assets, allowances, and eligibility information must be verified from third-party sources.

INDEPENDENT LIVING COMMUNITIES

Independent living, often referred to as retirement communities, congregate living, or senior apartments, are designed specifically for independent senior adults who want to enjoy a lifestyle filled with recreational, educational, and social activities with other seniors. These communities are designed for seniors who are able to live on their own but desire the security and conveniences of community living. Some communities offer an enriched lifestyle with organized social and recreational programs as a part of everyday activities (congregate living or retirement communities), while others provide housing with only a minimal amount of amenities or services (senior apartments).

Services. Some independent living communities offer abundant recreational activities, which may include a swimming pool and spa, exercise facilities, a clubhouse or lounge, and a library or reading lounges. Communities also may provide laundry facilities, linen service, meals or access to meals, local transportation, and planned social activities. Communities can be either "age inclusive" or "age exclusive." Age-inclusive communities attract retirees but do not have age requirements, whereas age-exclusive communities do have senior age requirements (usually age 55 and older).

Cost. Prices are generally dependent on the local market. Most communities that provide services are market rate, but some subsidized senior apartments cater to seniors with limited incomes. Plans can include housekeeping, laundry, or van or scheduled transportation. Most communities with these services also provide at least one group activity per day.

Regulation. Because these communities are not licensed by local, state, or federal agencies, there is no formal regulation. In those communities that provide services and activities, the rules are set and governed by the management company providing the services. In other communities, an on-site or off-site manager will help address any problems.

Payment options. Private funds are most often used, although some senior apartments are subsidized and accept Section 8 vouchers. Medicare and Medicaid do not cover payment because no health care is provided.

Care. Health care is not provided with your normal fees, but many communities will allow you to pay for a home health aide or nurse to come into your apartment to assist you with medicines and personal care.

ASSISTED LIVING

For people who need assistance with self-care but prefer to remain independent, assisted-living facilities may provide the additional help that makes that possible. Assisted-living residents occupy private apartment-style units with care provided as it is needed. Not all residences offering assisted living are capable of serving, or are willing to serve, all clients. Individuals dependent on a walker or wheelchair, those who need multilevels of care (bathing, dressing, ambulation, toileting, behavior, and medication management), and residents who are incontinent may have difficulty finding an appropriate assisted-living residence.

Assisted-living facilities differ in their design and usually fall into one of five categories:

"...AND TO THINK THEY USED TO CALL THIS A REST HOME!"

1. A personal wing in a retirement complex for those needing to have such care.
2. A separate facility located within a retirement residence. Contracted health services are provided when the resident needs to move to an increased care facility.
3. An independent facility with the potential of 24-hour health care provided in-house, often referred to as an assisted-living center.
4. A campus or "pod" design with several freestanding residences built adjacent to an existing health care facility. Residents have bedroom units with shared kitchen, dining room, and living area.
5. A special wing or facility with the capability of working with dementia- or Alzheimer's-diagnosed residents, who move to the wing as the disease progresses.

Facilities also differ in how costs are established. Typically, the basic rent charge includes only room and board. Other personal care needs are usually additional cost items. Charges for these services may be handled as a fixed fee for each service or as a group of services delivered for a flat monthly rate. Several states also subsidize adult family homes where individuals typically are given their own bedroom in a private, single-family home. However, there are many issues to keep in mind when considering an out-of-home option for an individual who can no longer manage living independently. Concerns about cost, quality of care, and safety will be large factors in your decision making.

Assisted living provides a special combination of residential housing, personalized supportive services, and health care. These residential settings maximize independence but do not provide skilled nursing care. Assisted living may offer the same features as independent living communities, with the added assistance of personal care. It is designed to meet the individual needs of those requiring help with activities of daily living but do not need the skilled medical care provided in a nursing home.

Services. Assisted-living communities can be free standing; part of a continuing care community that provides independent, assisted, and nursing care; affiliated with a nursing home; or specialized services brought into independent retirement communities. There are a variety of names used to describe assisted-living facilities, many of which are specific to certain regions of the country, including the following: board and care, residential care facility, community-based retirement facility, personal care, adult living facility, adult foster care, and the like. The generic term throughout the country, however, is *assisted living*.

Care. These residential settings maximize independence, but they do not provide skilled nursing care. Assisted living offers the same features as retirement communities with the added assistance of personal care. It is designed to meet the individual needs of those requiring help with activities of daily living but do not need the skilled medical care provided in a nursing home. Although the variety of services and level of care will vary, most communities provide assistance with dressing, grooming, bathing, and other daily activities. Assistance with medications differs according to state regulations; this is reflected on each community-listing page under supervision, administration, or monitoring.

Cost. The cost of assisted living depends on the number of services and accommodations a facility offers, and the charges will reflect the number of services that you will have access to. Most plans include meals and laundry, but some may limit the number of meals per month.

Payment options. Most assisted-living communities accept private pay only; however, in some states, there is assistance with payment. Some long-term care insurance policies may cover assisted living. This type of information is best determined on an individual basis.

Regulation. Assisted-living facilities are regulated and licensed at the state level. Each state does so according to its own laws—there are no federal regulations covering assisted living.

NURSING HOMES

Nursing homes, or skilled nursing facilities, are designed for seniors who are in need of 24-hour nursing care. Nursing facilities provide many of the same residential components of other senior care options, including room and board, personal care, and protection supervision, and may offer other types of therapy. Their on-site medical staff sets them apart from other types of senior housing. Nursing care is provided by registered nurses (RNs), licensed practical nurses (LPNs), and nurses aides at all hours of the day.

Standard services. Standard services for nursing homes include the following:

- Clean, furnished room
- Housekeeping and linen service
- Medically planned meals and snacks
- Trained medical staff
- Professional service staff-activity director, social worker, etc.

The following also are available for an extra charge:

- On-call physician and physician services
- Physical, respiratory, and speech therapists
- Medications
- Personal care items
- Laundry service

Care.
- *Basic care.* These are services required to maintain a resident's activities of daily living. Basic care includes personal care, supervision, and safety. A nurse's aide, practical nurse, or a family member can provide this care.
- *Skilled care.* This is the level of care that requires the regular services of a registered nurse for treatments and procedures. Skilled care also includes services provided by specially trained professionals, such as physical and respiratory therapists.
- *Subacute care.* This is comprehensive inpatient care designed for someone who has had an acute illness, injury, or chronic illness. Subacute care is generally more intensive than traditional nursing facility care and less intensive than acute care, requiring frequent (daily to weekly) recurrent patient assessment and review.

Regulation. Nursing homes are licensed and regulated by state departments of public health, and are individually certified by the state for Medicare and Medicaid. They offer a staff of licensed and/or registered nurses, nurse's aides, and administrators as required by licensing standards. The health care is supervised and authorized by a physician. They must also meet federal requirements.

Payment options. Nursing homes charge a basic daily or monthly fee. Often families purchase long-term care insurance in anticipation of the cost, while others must depend on other forms of financing. Facilities accept a variety of Medicare, Medicaid, private insurance carriers, and private funds. The nursing home will ask you for financial information in order to determine the appropriate payment source.

CONTINUING CARE
RETIREMENT COMMUNITIES

Continuing care retirement communities (CCRCs) are residential campuses that provide a continuum of care—from private units to assisted living and then skilled nursing care—all in one location. CCRCs are designed to offer active seniors an independent lifestyle from the privacy of their own home but also include the availability of services in an assisted-living environment and on-site intermediate or skilled nursing care if necessary.

Services. CCRCs offer a variety of residential services, including the following:

- A maintained apartment, town house, or other unit
- Cleaning and laundry services
- Meals in common dining areas (number per day varies)
- Grounds maintenance
- Security
- Social, recreational, and cultural programs

Health care services include:

- Care covered for contracted services
- Personal care and help with daily activities
- Nursing care
- Rehabilitative care
- Respite and hospice care
- Alzheimer's and special care

Payment. With continuing care there are many different types of contracts and fees to consider. An extensive contract offers unlimited long-term nursing care for little or no increase in monthly fees. A modified contract includes a specified amount of health care beyond which additional fees are incurred. Some communities may require residents to purchase long-term care insurance as criteria for acceptance. There are also communities that provide services and access to medical care on a month-to-month basis.

Cost. The monthly fees generally cover the following:

- Meals (number may vary)
- Scheduled transportation
- Housekeeping services
- Unit maintenance
- Laundry

- Health monitoring services
- Some utilities
- Organized social activities
- Emergency call monitoring
- Security

Regulation. CCRCs are highly regulated in some states but not in others. There is no federal agency that oversees them. The Continuing Care Accreditation Commission (CCAC), a private, nonprofit organization, accredits these communities. This voluntary process involves a review of finances, governance, and administration; resident health and wellness; and resident life. Although many assisted-living communities and nursing homes cater to individuals with Alzheimer's disease and other related memory disorders or dementia, there is a growing trend toward facilities that provide specialized care and housing tailored to the special needs of individuals with Alzheimer's disease and other memory disorders. These facilities offer care that fosters residents' individual skills and interests in an environment that helps to diminish confusion and agitation. Specialty services are provided in a secure environment, such as activity programs designed to include reality orientation classes and specially trained professional staff skilled in handling the behavior associated with memory impairments. Many facilities that specialize in Alzheimer's or related dementia disorders have building design features that assist with the problems associated with this disease: color-coded hallways, visual cues, and secure wandering paths for additional security.

Care. Similar to assisted-living communities, most provide assistance with dressing, grooming, bathing, and other daily activities. Assistance with medications differs according to state regulations. Meals, laundry, and housekeeping are usually provided within private and semiprivate rooms in a residential-type setting.

Before you decide on an out-of-home situation, remember to explore other possibilities that might remedy the situation. There are many types of services available that provide help for people in their home. For example, visiting nurses and frozen meal deliveries—as well as adaptive equipment such as walkers and wheelchairs—are available options that can be brought directly to the home of the person in need.

Modifications to the home itself, such as ramps or grab bars, also can add ease and safety to the existing living environment. Contact your local senior center for specifics.

Before making an assessment of a potential adult family home, spend a great deal of time with the person you are assisting. Their wishes should play the central role in the decision-making process. If someone does not want to be placed outside of their home, they probably shouldn't be asked to make the move.

Discuss with other family members the needs of the person being placed. How much independence is needed for that person to be comfortable? What kind of help do they really need? Is help required even with minimal tasks? Most adult family homes are designed for people who are fairly physically able but who may have some memory loss or difficulty completing routine tasks on their own. There are some agencies that may assist with doing a comprehensive geriatric assessment, and while some are free, others must be funded privately.

Once a facility is chosen, make sure the new resident can bring along special furniture, books, photographs, or music (often known as "reference points") to the new residence. Personal mementos tend to help ease the transition. Ask for a written list of all personal possessions the new resident brings into the home and make copies for the resident and another family member. Once the move is complete, expect at least a two- to four-week adjustment period. There may be sleeping problems, anger, confusion, and homesickness—all normal reactions. Regular visits with friends and family will provide support and help ease the transition. After a reasonable adjustment time, follow up with the resident to consider if the move is working. Alterations may be needed in routine, medication, or diet. Speak with the staff and with family about how best to make changes.

In Part One, I have discussed a physical move to a different home and environment. In Part Two, I turn our discussion to what the typical senior Boomers will do for future housing—stay in their present home and make it comfortable for their future years. We'll address some remodeling issues, introduce applications that could make life more enjoyable, and deal with the decision of bringing a family member or friend to live with you.

AGING IN PLACE

7

WHAT, EXACTLY, IS UNIVERSAL DESIGN?

Home features that can benefit all persons

Aging in place simply means living in one's home safely, independently, and comfortably regardless of age, income, or ability level. In most cases, it provides the pleasure of remaining in a familiar environment throughout one's maturing years and the ability to enjoy the familiar daily routines and the special events that enrich lives. It also brings the reassurance of being able to call a house a home for a lifetime.

In this section, we explore some of the changes that need to be made in order for people to "stay put"—where greater than 50 percent of the aging population will spend the final years of their life. We'll start this section with a chapter on universal design, or UD, perhaps the ultimate goal of today's builders, designers, and local officials. Universal design is not about one amenity or concept. It is a building/remodeling philosophy that is being implemented in all regions of the country. The ideas are being tried and tested in many of today's new homes in an effort to capture and retain the huge Baby Boomer group as it seeks to move out of the traditional family home and into its next versatile, flexible shelter.

WELCOME H.O.M.E. IS QUITE A CONCEPT

Diane Miller believes everyone should have a place to go to take a break from the rigors of a daily routine. And she has spent much of her adult life building a retreat that's not restricted to anyone, especially individuals who are physically disabled.

"I had polio as a child and had to plow through life in a chair," Miller said. "So I had a good idea of what other people just might want in a getaway. We've tried to create that here."

"Here" is Welcome H.O.M.E. (House of Modification Examples, http://www.hnet.net/~welcomehome/) in Newburg, Wisconsin, about 35 minutes north of Milwaukee and 15 minutes from the western shore of Lake Michigan. The 3,700-square-foot bed and breakfast perched on 18 acres was formed for the purpose of improving the quality of life for persons living with physical disabilities. By designing, building, and maintaining a unique single-family home, Miller has created a vehicle for providing information and examples of barrier-free living, commonly known as universal design.

"I have heard someone refer to universal design as design features that are good for the least able of us and are also good for the best and rest of us," said Tracy Lux of Trace Marketing, a Sarasota, Florida-based company specializing in the "mature" market. "Consumers need to be educated so they don't see the features as handicap equipment but rather as an opportunity to age in place."

The Welcome H.O.M.E. house is more a demonstration home than a model home. It has three different kitchens all with distinctive appliances, bathrooms with diverse fixtures, countertops at varying heights, a large selection of light switches and door handles, lift assist devices, roomy hallways, and clever grab bars—all without an institutional feel. The guest wing of the house features two bedrooms. One has a queen-size bed plus a foldout twin, while the second offers a double bed, a twin waterbed, and a foldout futon. Both rooms have a door leading to a screened porch overlooking the prairie.

Welcome H.O.M.E. is a living laboratory providing visitors with a place to relax while affording remodelers and homeowners the chance to experiment with different applications, household devices, fixtures, and adaptive equipment. Guests can explore the entire home for a few days or quickly during one day to determine the design that will work best for them in their own home. The first sign is the no-step entry, making it easy to bring in luggage, a stroller, a walker, or a wheelchair.

"It's really impressive what Diane has done," said Chuck Russell, president and CEO of Woodinville, Washington-based Westhill, Inc., a homebuilder specializing in custom homes and remodeling, who spent several days gathering ideas at Welcome H.O.M.E. "A lot of builders are truly interested in helping people age in place; it's great to have a place you can see that's done right with so much variety."

According to the U.S. Bureau of the Census and the National Center for Health Statistics, the older population—persons 65 years of age and older—numbered 35 million in 2000, and most of them would like to stay in their home as long as possible. This age group represented 12.4 percent of the population, or about one in every eight Americans. In addition, the number of Americans aged 45 to 64—who will reach 65 over the next two decades—increased 34 percent from 1990 to 2000. In nearly ten years of studies before 2000, more than 80 percent of respondents expressed this preference to remain in their home. Since then, the American Association of Retired Persons (AARP) reports the number has reached 90 percent, but accommodating that preference and those numbers has been another matter.

Russell is a member of the country's first certified aging-in-place specialists (CAPS) who completed training for a new professional designation. The CAPS program is a three-day seminar that provides information about aging-in-place home modifications, including background on the older adult population, common aging-in-place remodeling projects, marketing to the aging-in-place market, codes and standards, common barriers and solutions, product ideas, resources, and communication techniques. The program is sponsored by the National Association of Home Builders (NAHB), a Washington, D.C.–based trade association representing more than 205,000 members involved in home building, remodeling, property management, and other services. The CAPS program was created by the NAHB Remodelers Council in collaboration with the organization's seniors housing council, research center, and the AARP.

According to Russell, an AARP study, "Fixing to Stay," was a wake-up call to the residential remodeling industry. The results sent messages loud and clear:

- Americans prefer to stay in their home as they mature rather than seek assisted-living and other arrangements.
- Older consumers want a reliable means of identifying the professionals they can trust to remodel their home.

"We are a genuine nonprofit and rely on volunteers and donations for everything," said Miller, who has been supported by national companies such as Kohler, Culligan, and Benjamin Moore. "We have kept it simple and inexpensive mainly because we can't afford many of the elite items that are available today. While an elevator is probably out of our reach, we hope to do more in the home with new hearing impairment applications and interior electric door openers."

Welcome H.O.M.E. is open to the public year-round, and summer is its busiest season. It features its own hiking trails, biking, and woodlands, and it is two minutes from fishing, cross-country skiing, tennis, canoeing in the Milwaukee River, and exploring the 350-acre Riveredge Nature Center. Also close by are three golf courses, downhill skiing, boat moorings, wine tasting, art galleries, antiques, and summer farmers' markets.

UNIVERSAL DESIGN HAS BROKEN THE "INSTITUTIONAL LOOK"

Tracy Lux said many universal design features have become known as designs for "easy living." Special-task lighting, well-placed ovens and microwaves, and elevated washers, dryers, and dishwashers are among the changes being refined. Christine Price, aging specialist with Ohio State University and assistant professor of Human Development and Family Science in the College of Human Ecology, agrees with Lux. According to Price, universal design is a movement that advocates all features and environments be not only accessible to people regardless of age, size, or physical ability but they be attractive and appear seamless to the design of the home.

For example, universal design features include installing lever-style doorknobs and faucet handles, providing kitchen counters with different heights, placing electric outlets higher and light switches lower on walls, and creating at least one no-step entry into the home.

Why now? Why all the bother with a one-design-fits-all theory for living? First, GI generation members not only need these changes now but they are also expected to stay in a universal design home longer and therefore save on medical costs. An AARP study compared seniors living in universal design houses with seniors in traditional settings. The study found significant cost differences for health care—those in universal design settings paid less than half the amount paid by those living in regular designs. The study pointed to savings garnered by "undergoing less physical decline." For example, by providing at least one no-step entry to homes, the likelihood of falls and injuries is reduced as well as allowing safer exits during a fire or other emergency. Other products, like the elevated dishwasher, can be therapeutic in helping to use muscles and maintain wellness.

Second, the Boomer group is the largest, healthiest, and wealthiest group ever seen on the American landscape. Its passage into retirement years will have an equally profound effect on the types of housing in demand. Boomer homes will typically be one-story houses with three bedrooms—not apartments or condominiums.

"Seniors and Boomers are so active now that some of the activities are clearly putting stress on their bodies," said Susan Mack, a California-based occupational therapist and president of Homes for Easy Living Universal Design Consultants in Murrieta, California. "I've got people who are getting hip and knee replacements in their 60s and people in their 40s getting their knees scoped. This did not happen with previous generations because they didn't live as long or put this stress on their bones so soon. If you've got a sports injury, do you want to come home to a house that is fraught with hazards and barriers? These are not just designs and ideas for the frail elderly. We are also providing solutions for people who never thought they were going to get old—at least not this quickly."

Nearly a quarter of Americans aged 45 or older say they or someone they live with will have trouble maneuvering around their home in the coming years.[1] Fewer than 10 percent of the nation's 100 million housing units have features to make them universally accessible.

More important, U.S. builders and remodelers have anticipated the huge need—and the financial rewards resulting from it—and jumped on board. Projects for the aging-in-place remodeling segment range from installation of bath and shower grab bars and adjustment of countertop heights to the creation of multifunctional, first-floor master suites and the installation of private elevators. CAPS training participants learn the mechanics and nuances of effective assessment of clients' needs and integrating myriad considerations into unified, aesthetically pleasing, functional solutions.

In addition, no one can deny that we now live in a more dangerous world. The desire to find safety, or experience the mere perception of safety, has kept many U.S. residents, especially seniors, closer to home since September 11, 2001—spending more time in the home itself. Retirees are not the only segment of the population looking at the possibilities of "cocooning." In fact, Americans are moving at some of the lowest rates in more than 50 years.[2] The 40 million people who moved between 2002 and 2003 comprised 14 percent of the population, down sharply from a rate of 20 percent in 1948 when the Census Bureau first began collecting information on movers.

Some seniors are just now beginning to think about ways to tastefully modify their home to enable them to remain living independently—and more safely and comfortably. Solutions often exist but people are not always aware of the products. For example, Lifease, Inc., based in New Brighton, Minnesota, charges a modest fee for its online questionnaire, LivAbility, which allows homeowners to assess their needs and abilities and then obtain personalized suggestions to improve their living environment. After the questionnaire is completed, the Lifease engine selects solutions based on the input. The resulting report includes ideas and products for safety, convenience, comfort, and independence in the home. Low-cost and no-cost solutions are listed. If the solution is a product, Web sites are given for the supplier with a range of prices. If appropriate, the rationale for listing the product is included. Another company, SAFE Aging, Inc., based in Tarpon Springs, Florida, has developed a paper questionnaire for older adults that identifies potential risks or hazards that can threaten health, safety, or function in the home. The Safety Appraisal for Elders (SAFE) can be completed privately at home, with or without assistance and at any pace, and is also modestly priced.

Households of all ages have roots in their community and strong emotional ties to their home. Few people want to move solely because their house no longer fits their needs. The problems faced by older individuals are compounded by the fact that they live in the oldest housing stock. These homes may have deferred maintenance, with roof or plumbing leaks, heating deficiencies, or dangerous electrical problems, in addition to a lack of adequate lighting, railings, storage, and other accessibility concerns. Modification needs may get lost among many other pressing maintenance items, prolonging dangerous arrangements that may lead to falls and malnutrition or isolation within the home or the community.

FALLS ARE A CONSTANT NIGHTMARE

According to the National Center for Injury Prevention and Control (NCIPC), falls are the leading cause of injury deaths among older adults and the most common cause of nonfatal injuries and hospital admissions for trauma. The Centers for Disease Control (CDC) reports that in 2001, more than 1.6 million seniors were treated in emergency departments for fall-related injuries, 373,000 were hospitalized, and over 11,600 deaths were reported in people aged 65 and older. Experts report that one-half to two-thirds of all falls occur in or around the home. Common environmental fall hazards include lack of stair railings or grab bars, slippery surfaces and rugs, unstable furniture, and poor lighting. Other older homeowners, with neither the means to modify nor the money to move, will live constrained and unsafe lives because of their home.

HEADING OFF COSTLY INJURIES

Backers of home modifications, or "home mods," believe that significant health care cost reductions are possible if home modifications become more common. These changes, some of which are shown in Figure 7.1, can help consumers avoid injuries and reduce their use of medical services or institutional care. Susan Duncan, a housing consultant whose Bellevue, Washington-based company, Adaptations, helps families with accessibility and design questions, was instrumental in organizing the annual National Aging in Place Week. She said the keys to having all age groups grasp universal design is to highlight the latest features and remove some of the outdated terms in building and remodeling.

Figure 7.1 *Helping at Home: Basic Home Modifications*

ACTIVITY	COMMON HOME MODIFICATION
Using the bathroom	• Install grab bars, shower seats, or transfer benches • Place nonskid strips or decals in the tub or shower
Turning faucets or doorknobs	• Install faucet or doorknob adapters
Getting in and out of the home and narrow doorways	• Install permanent or portable ramps • Widen doorways or install swing-clear hinges
Climbing stairs	• Install handrails on both sides for support • Install a stair glide • Increase lighting at the top and bottom of stairway

Source: National Resource Center for Supportive Housing and Home Modification

"The two most important terms we need to keep explaining and re-peating are 'universal design' and 'visitability,'" Duncan said. "The terms we absolutely no longer want to use are the cutesy phrases like 'physically challenged.' And, if you are going to use 'disabled,' you al-ways need to attach people to the term—such as a 'person with a disabil-ity' or the 'disabled population.' The language landscape has really changed with civil rights laws."

Representatives from regional departments on aging and disability services have led the movement to eliminate the word *handicapped* from directional signs and even casual conversation. *Accessible* is now the ac-ceptable term for easier access (a building is "accessible"; not "handi-capped" parking).

"People who are older grew up with the word 'handicapped' and it became part of their culture," Duncan said. "But the Americans with Disabilities Act of 1990 started to change the landscape and how we identify people and places."

Duncan and other independent counselors are campaigning to make all homes—not just those hosting a party, meeting, or reunion—"visitable." According to Concrete Change, a nonprofit, Decatur, Georgia-based company, the essentials for visiting—and for surviving in your house with a temporary disability—are simply to be able to get in and out of the house and be able to use the bathroom. Steps at most entrances of a home stymie people who use wheelchairs or walkers or who are impaired by stiffness, weakness, or balance problems. Wheelchair users often are stopped—by inches—from fitting through the bathroom door in a friend's or relative's home.

Recent trends indicate that individuals return home from the hospital with more acute conditions than in the past. Accessible, safer homes make it possible for some to leave rehabilitation or nursing settings sooner to return to a home that supports their recovery and lessens additional injuries or secondary disabilities.

"When did we start making doorways so tiny?" Easy Living Universal Design Consultants's Susan Mack asked. "I know friends in wheelchairs who simply will not attend holiday parties because they don't want to be lifted into the home. It's simply embarrassing for them. And if they do attend, there's a 99.9 percent chance they won't drink anything because they know they'll never be able to get into the bathroom."

Home modifications refer to adaptations to homes that can make it easier for someone to carry out daily activities, such as preparing meals, climbing stairs, and bathing, as well as changes to the physical structure of a home to improve its overall safety and condition. These project designs have come a long way. They are custom, attractive amenities that no longer sing out "an old person lives here," and that also can enhance the resale value of the home. Because these improvements and alterations can serve all ages, hence the name "universal design."

MINOR HOME REPAIRS ARE OFTEN MAJOR FOR SENIORS

The attractive poster on the wall of a local senior center hit too close to home—mainly because it was all about home. More than a decade ago, we had faced a similar situation:

"At 71 years old, Claire lost her husband. Her children encouraged her to move, but she felt differently. This was the house where she and George had raised three children, planted their annual garden, and entertained friends and family. It was home. She missed George and especially felt afraid at night. The loose latch on the door never bothered her until now. She called the Minor Home Repair program and they sent a Repair Specialist who installed a new lock. He even added a dead bolt and installed bars on the basement windows. For a small labor charge and the cost of materials, the job was done. Pleasant dreams, Claire."

The only difference between Claire and George's story and my parents' situation was the solution: There was no reliable home repair specialist in the huge metropolis in which my parents lived that they trusted with the job. The Kelly kids had moved away and my parents constantly struggled with finding a competent handyman who would appear when promised to maintain the critical systems of an 80-year-old home. Once, after the family home was burgled and my mother's car stolen, my folks installed new locks, bars on first-floor entry windows, and a huge, wrought iron gate in the driveway. The cost was stunning—especially for persons on a fixed income. And I never felt the heavy gate was installed properly. It needed an extra push and lift to settle in place so that the tiny, drilled holes would properly align and accept the arm of the small padlock.

"That gate would work fine," my Dad would say, "if you clowns would stop riding it when it swings!"

There are a variety of senior home repair services, both public and private, in many cities across the country. The U.S. Department of Housing and Urban Development (HUD) has provided some of the greatest assistance by helping to alleviate some of the cost and reliability issues involving minor home repair for seniors. For example, the Senior Services Minor Home Repair Program (http://www.hud.gov/) has been serving older clients in many cities since 1974. Services range from senior chore services to painting programs that help seniors spiff up their home.

"Some of our seniors have let things go in the past because they know what it costs to call an electrician or a plumber," said Margaret Strachan, deputy director of Seattle's Senior Services. "It is exceedingly difficult for people to understand the different alternatives and options when they are feeling forced to make changes."

The minor home repair program also provides critically needed plumbing, electrical, and carpentry repairs or modifications for low-income homeowners and disabled renters. According to the agency, the need for repair is related to preventing harm to the security, safety, or health of the resident.

In one case, a client had fallen twice while going down the back stairs. The steps to the back door were rotten and the railings unstable. A prowler twice had entered her house through the back door. Not only did she feel unsafe in her home at night, she also could not rely on safe footing, especially if she had to exit in a hurry. A program contractor replaced her ten-foot stairway and installed new railings. The contractor also bolstered the back door and provided a new security lock.

Materials are provided at cost and there is a small charge for labor. Applicants must meet specific income-limit guidelines. Job estimates are free, yet repairs can be made to the primary house structure only and include:

- **Plumbing**
  - Fix leaking pipes and faucets
  - Clear clogged drains
  - Replace defective toilets and sinks
- **Electrical**
  - Replace broken switches, sockets, and fixtures
  - Install smoke detectors
- **Carpentry**
  - Rebuild broken steps
  - Repair rotted and unsafe porches
  - Replace broken doors and window panes
  - Install locks and deadbolts
- **Special aids for disabled access**
  - Build wheelchair ramps
  - Install grab bars and handrails

PAYING FOR HANDRAILS . . . WHEN OTHER LOANS ARE NOT AVAILABLE

While many homeowners will be able to pay for a home remodel with savings or a home equity loan, other seniors may not have the cash or enough home value to do the work. FHA Title 1 (800-767-7468 or visit http://www.hud.gov) may not be the perfect way to finance a home improvement project, but it could be the only way for some people. These loans of up to $25,000 are available to owner-occupants who want to repair or improve their property. Up to $15,000 can be obtained regardless of home value. And if you need $5,000 or less, no security is necessary.

To obtain the loan, you need to own the property or hold a long-term lease to it. Borrowers have to execute a note agreeing to repay the loan and meet very lenient qualifying guidelines. Total debt (including present home loans) may not exceed 45 percent of monthly income. The loan is great for people who can't borrow any more money in the conventional market. The Title 1 loan fills a need, but the loan is not inexpensive. Fees vary from lender to lender but can be 10 percent of the loan amount for loans up to $20,000 ($1,000 for a $10,000 loan; $2,000 for $20,000) with interest rates in the 10 percent to 12 percent range. Obviously, these loans are significantly more expensive than home equity loans. In fact, the interest rate can be double of what can be obtained in the conventional market. But some people don't have the luxury of qualifying for the best loans available and need "unconventional" financing just to get along with their life. Banks and other qualified lenders make these loans from their own funds; HUD then insures the lender against a possible loss. The loan insurance program is authorized by Title 1 of the National Housing Act, thus the loan name.

For example, a couple who had purchased a home for $220,000 received an appraisal for $205,000 three years later. They desperately needed to borrow some money to make repairs, but they owed as much on the home as the appraised value. The Title I loan turned out to be a real benefit to them. Because Title 1 guidelines do not require borrowers to have equity established in the property for amounts less than $15,000, new homeowners or individuals who have recently refinanced have a chance to make improvements on their home right after they purchase—something virtually impossible under conventional guidelines.

According to HUD, Title 1 loans may be used for any improvements that "will make your home basically more livable and useful." Therefore, you can use Title 1 cash for built-in dishwashers, refrigerators, freezers, and ovens. However, the loans cannot be used for "certain luxury-type" items such as swimming pools or outdoor fireplaces. Title 1 money cannot pay for work that has already been done. Improvements can be made by the homeowner or through a contractor or dealer. Your loan can be used to pay for materials and labor. In addition, the cash from the loan can pay for architectural and engineering costs and building permit fees. The federal government requires an inspection for loans greater than $7,500. When the work is finished, you must furnish the lender with a completion certificate.

NEW DESIGN CONCEPTS WILL CONTINUE TO EMERGE

As mentioned earlier, the aging Baby Boomers will continue to re-define home design, both new and existing. In this decade and the next, builders and developers will build the homes and communities that allow retirees to reconnect with their friends and family. Current and future retirees do not want a house built for old people. They want an easy-living home that a world-class athlete would also enjoy, and their preferences will vary greatly based on their socioeconomic status and their values. Here again are the key features about the future of new home design for retirees:

- Inexpensive, commonsense universal design concepts that are de-signed to make life more enjoyable will grow in popularity.
- Retirement home segmentation will occur, allowing developers to maximize absorption by building multiple types of homes and neighborhoods that appeal to different psychographic categories of retirees.
- Home designs will vary dramatically based on the socioeconomic conditions of local retirees and their psychographics.

Inexpensive Universal Design Concepts

Here are some of the inexpensive universal design features desired as much by families with small children as by senior citizens: [3]

- General Design
  - At least one single-level floor plan, if possible
  - At least one full bedroom downstairs
  - In two-story plans, one hall closet on each floor designed in a manner that an elevator/lift system can be installed as an upgrade opportunity. Elevators are less expensive than you think, and the elevator industry is booming.
  - At least one level entry with a ½ inch or less threshold
  - 32- to 42-inch wide interior door openings versus the current 28-inch standard
  - Lower-height doorbells and front-door viewers
  - Light switches and easy to read and adjust climate controls that are 48 inches or less off the ground
  - One electrical receptacle 15 to 27 inches above the floor in most rooms
  - Rocker light switches
  - Higher-wattage light fixtures (the latest fluorescent technologies allow for better lighting at a lower cost)
  - Built-in night lighting
  - Outdoor lighting
  - Easy-open crank windows that are no more than 30 inches off the ground
  - Lever door handles
  - Adjustable-height closet rods
  - Visual smoke detectors/fire alarm
  - Front-loading washer/dryer

Inexpensive Universal Design Concepts (continued)

- Kitchen
  - One area with under counter knee space
  - Variable-height countertops
  - Pull-out cabinet shelves
  - Plenty of low-level storage
  - Foldout steps to reach cabinets at moderate heights
  - Lever-handle faucets
  - Dishwashers and ovens at raised heights
  - Refrigerators with adjustable and easily pulled out shelves (typically side by side)
  - Cooktops/ovens with heat indicators, automatic shut-off, and controls within easy reach
- Bath
  - At least one full bath downstairs
  - A ledge surrounding the tub
  - Room to maneuver
  - Ease of access
  - Accessories (such as a toilet paper holder) placed for ease of use
  - Towel rods that double as safety bars
  - Easy-lever fixtures
  - Walk-in shower
  - Adjustable-height shower fixture with handheld shower head
  - Antiscald devices
  - Nonskid flooring
- Technology Options
  - Keyless entry (option)
  - Emergency response system (option)
  - Intercom/video system for front door (option)
  - Security system (option)
  - Power backup system (option)
  - Upgraded wiring to handle multiple computers, home network, broadband communications, entertainment centers, video security system, etc.

*Inexpensive **U**niversal **D**esign **C**oncepts (continued)*

- Television-based system controls (heating, air-conditioning, key appliances, etc.)
- Computerized feedback system (Is furnace running? Is garbage disposal on? Audio feedback and visual display.)

In this chapter, we've addressed some of the basics of aging in place. In the next chapter, we will consider some creative applications and fairly significant remodeling projects—beyond the basic "home mods"—with planning and renovation ideas followed by some cost estimates of the more popular and necessary aging-in-place jobs. We'll also take a look at average returns nationally for typical improvements. That way, you'll get an idea of what sort of return you could receive on your investment down the road should you choose to spend those dollars to be more comfortable in your home today.

8

PROJECTS AND COSTS FOR EASIER LIVING AND PEACE OF MIND

Choosing where to spend to net comfort and a favorable return

If you decide to stay in your own home—and an overwhelming number of seniors would prefer to stay put—what will you do to make it work? Or, more pragmatically for GI generation "make-doers," what changes offer the best potential for making it comfortable for you?

This chapter provides you with a capsule guide for deciding on and executing the typical major renovations—roof, bathroom, and kitchen—plus some other creative applications that are often needed to age in place. Any renovation will cost money, and all dollars are precious, so it's important to spend them wisely. This chapter also contains some of the latest useful gadgets, including one that could really

HARRY'S BECOMING PARANOID ABOUT CRIME IN THE NEIGHBORHOOD.

make seniors living alone—and their adult children—feel safer and more confident.

As with any expenditure, you ought to work through a decision process before the project starts. No matter what it is that you will be doing to the house, ask yourself the following four questions:

1. *How long do I realistically intend to stay in this house?* While the answer is often difficult to figure out, give some thought to a best guesstimate. Minor home modifications are fine for the short term, but it's usually not advisable to go through the anxiety of a major room remodel if you definitely will move out in a few months. Roofs are a different story because they often are mandatory.

2. *Who will do the work?* When you employ construction help, it's important to find efficient and honest workers. If you have used contractors in the past, you probably have a roster of dependable helpers.

3. *How do you find contractor referrals?* Your primary source is friends who may have used others in the past, or the local senior center can help. Also, ask the local homebuilders association about its certified aging-in-place specialists (CAPS).

4. *How will you pay for the remodel?* If you are using a reverse mortgage (discussed in Chapter 11 and in detail in Part Three) for all or part of the remodel, consider a program that features a line of credit. That way, you will only pay interest on the funds you actually use and the remaining balance can increase over time. For example, you could pay one lump sum for a roof replacement, then wait until other remodeling bills, or maintenance receipts, are sent to you before drawing on your credit line.

Before viewing the statistical results for the return on home improvements, understand that seniors often don't really care if they recoup their investment. Others simply want the peace of mind of knowing that their children might recover a portion of the remodeling costs if or when the house is eventually sold. The chart in Figure 8.1 shows the national averages for the rate of return for the most popular remodels and additions as gauged by *Remodeling* magazine in 2005. A value of 100 percent means that the investment is fully recouped in the sales price. However, the table is merely a gauge and does not reflect only "aging" projects. The same project done in two different areas may cost different amounts. The impact of any home improvement on the ultimate sales price is not the same in all cases and usually depends on the location and condition of the overall house and the market demand at the time the home is marketed for sale. The numbers presented in the chart are reference numbers only, and they are intended for comparison purposes. They do not represent amounts that actually must be spent, but they give you a good idea of what to expect..

Figure 8.1 *Remodel/Additions–2005 National Averages*

Job Description	Job Cost	Resale Value	Cost Recouped	Variance vs.		Rank		
				2003	2002	2004	2003	2002
Siding Replacement Upscale	$10,393	$10,771	103.6%	n/a	n/a	n/a	n/a	n/a
Bathroom Remodel Mid-Range	10,499	10,727	102.2	0.9%	3.0%	3	6	3
Minor Kitchen Remodel, Mid-Range	14,913	14,691	98.5	n/a	n/a	1	n/a	n/a
Siding Replacement Mid-Range	7,239	6,914	95.5	-5.4	17.3	2	2	7
2-Story Addition, Mid-Range	80,123	75,831	94.6	n/a	n/a	n/a	n/a	n/a
Attic bedroom, Mid-Range	39,188	36,649	93.5%	10.9	n/a	9	4	n/a
Bathroom Remodel, Upscale	26,052	24,286	93.2%	-7.6	-6.0	10	9	4
Major Kitchen Remodel, Mid-Range	43,862	39,920	91.0	6.0	19.4	15	15	14
Deck, Mid-Range	11,294	10,196	90.3	16.8	n/a	4	1	n/a
Basement Remodel, Mid-Range	51,051	46,010	90.1	-4.0	-3.2	17	12	8

Figure 8.1 *Remodel/Additions–2005 National Averages*

Job Description	Job Cost	Resale Value	Cost Recouped	Variance vs. 2003	Variance vs. 2002	Rank 2004	Rank 2003	Rank 2002
Window Replacement, Mid-Range	9,684	8,681	89.6	0.3	14.6	7	8	12
Window Replacement, Upscale	16,096	14,259	88.6	-3.7	8.7	8	7	9
Bathroom Addition, Mid-Range	22,977	19,850	86.4	-9.0	-8.3	5	3	1
Roof Replacement Upscale	16,453	14,141	85.9	n/a	n/a	n/a	n/a	n/a
Bathroom Addition, Upscale	47,212	40,488	85.8	-3.7	-0.3	10	9	4
Major Kitchen Remodel, Upscale	81,552	69,194	84.8	0.8	0.6	13	11	5
Roof Replacement, Mid-Range	11,164	9,456	84.7	n/a	20.6	11	n/a	13
Family Room, Mid-Range	54,773	45,458	83.0	-0.1	1.4	12	10	6
Master Suite, Mid-Range	73,370	60,460	82.4	4.9	6.6	14	14	11
Master Suite, Upscale	137,891	110,512	80.1	0.8	1.0	16	13	10
Sunroom, Mid-Range	31,736	23,643	74.5	n/a	n/a	18	n/a	n/a
Home Office Remodel, Mid-Range	13,143	9,569	72.8	n/a	n/a	n/a	n/a	n/a

The process of altering a home to age in place is often complicated by the limited dollars you have. Every dollar of your hard-earned cash can easily be spent elsewhere, so it's always important to plan before you remodel. Renovating your house is not an all-or-nothing process. Every area offers a lot of possibilities to spend more or less. However, if you are spending money to become more comfortable and be safer as you age, do your best to get what you pay for.

"The probability of being poor at some point in old age remains very high, and many people underestimate the costs associated with aging," said Tony Copeland, counselor for the American Association of Retired Persons (AARP). "Seniors often have unrealistic expectations about their physical abilities as they grow older."

My mom is a good example. She, like many widows and widowers, lives alone and lost her ability to climb steps long before anticipated. Disabilities typically mean home modifications or a move to another place. Most people, however, would prefer to stay put.

What adjustment do you make first? How do you judge need versus want? Most of the time, you start with the roof over your head. One of the first places seniors plop down money is to repair or replace the roof of their longtime home. When asked how they are going to spend their funds, they often say something similar to: "After I get a new roof, I'm moving to Maui for March." or "I need a new roof before I do anything else." A bad roof will make even the best of houses unlivable. So it is a necessary evil that the owner cannot do without.

Kitchens have become more than just for cooking and eating. They are gathering places where entertainment accompanied by food takes place. The category of small kitchen remodel (first introduced in 2004) came as no surprise nor did its return results. An out-of-date, 200-square-foot kitchen can return your investment quite easily given some fresh paint, new fixtures, and perhaps a new appliance or two. There has been a tendency in new construction to build the bathroom bigger and include more fixtures as well as more space. Bathroom remodels and additions historically have been some of the most profitable of all discretionary house projects. Returns tend to be higher in larger metropolitan areas, even though costs are seemingly unrelated to city size. In part, this is a result of higher prices in larger metro markets, where small percentage changes in value can result in large dollar returns. A midrange remodel updates and replaces the fixtures in an existing bathroom that is at least 25 years old. The upscale remodel expands a 5-by-7-foot bathroom to 9 by 9 and also includes new fixtures.

NAHB DOES ITS RESEARCH

The National Association of Home Builders (NAHB), through its research center, took a step toward increasing builder awareness of consumer need when it constructed four demonstration homes in Bowie, Maryland. Known as the MADE (Marketable, Affordable, Durable, Entry-Efficient) homes, the houses were built to showcase innovative building techniques and to provide an example of well-built, low-maintenance, affordable homes. They showcase larger, more extensive projects than the Welcome H.O.M.E. house described in Chapter 7 and have the benefit of additional sources of funding. One of them, the LifeWise Home, was developed through the efforts of the NAHB Research Center, the U.S. Department of Housing and Urban Development (HUD), the U.S. Department of Health & Human Services Administration on Aging (AoA), and the National Housing Endowment. The LifeWise Home has become the focus of seniors' housing research programs offered by the NAHB Research Center, because it has been designed to accommodate the changing needs of the homeowner over the course of a lifetime. It exemplifies features of universal design, technology, durability, and energy efficiency, all of which affect a person's ability to remain in his or her home with safety and independence as he or she grows older. The NAHB Research Center has placed additional emphasis on the development and incorporation of new technologies into the home and on addressing increasingly important aspects of energy efficiency and its impact on seniors.

A significant level of technology was originally incorporated into the LifeWise Home, including a Polara Range, which acts as a stove and refrigerator; a tankless water heating system; ENERGYSTAR-rated appliances; and a computer-controlled home automation system. A new radio-controlled monitoring system developed to monitor the risks involved with aging in place was installed in the house as well. This system, developed in the United Kingdom by Tunstall and distributed in the United States by Health Watch, will support up to 25 individual sensors that call a control center for assistance when activated. Devices include an excessive heat and cold sensor that can detect if a pan has been left on the stove too long or if the heating system has stopped working when temperatures drop; a flood detector; a fall detector; and a "wandering client" sensor that provides an early warning if the user has left the home and not returned in a predetermined time. Systems such as these can help to extend the time that a person can remain in his or her home with greater safety, security, and independence, plus they provide some peace of mind to family members who may not live nearby. Recognizing that many new technologies similar to the one just described are being developed at a rapid pace, the AoA joined with the Research Center to develop a grants program known as Assistive Technology and Aging in Place (ATAP). ATAP is a demonstration program to help develop, identify, and promote the use of innovative assistive technologies through community partnerships, which may include manufacturers, academic institutions, and technology experts.

PROMOTING ENERGY EFFICIENCY

Many homes in which seniors live are older and lack energy-efficient features. Through a grant from the U.S. Department of Energy's National Renewable Energy Laboratory, the Research Center joined recently with Rebuilding Together, the nation's largest volunteer home rehab organization, to improve the energy efficiency and weatherization of a home that will serve as a national model for rehabilitation and/or modification of homes to obtain maximum energy efficiency. The house, located near Annapolis, Maryland, is occupied by a couple in their 60s who are financially and physically unable to make needed repairs and modifications. During past winters, the homeowners reported having to turn up the heat and burn twice as much oil as a similar house in the area in order to stay comfortable. The couple also tried to weatherproof the house by stuffing rags into openings around windows and doors. In February 2003, Rebuilding Together volunteers installed fiberglass wall insulation; attic, floor, and water heater insulation; exterior doors; high-efficiency replacement windows; a new heating and air-conditioning system; a new furnace; and duct work. The homeowners are expected to save more than $1,000 a year in utility charges.

In a second project with the Department of Energy, the Research Center worked with builders to introduce the Zero Energy Home concept into the single-family, new home construction industry. Zero Energy Homes (ZEHs) combine state-of-the-art, energy-efficient construction and appliances with commercially available renewable energy systems. The homes, like most other homes in the Tucson area, are connected to the utility grid. However, their sun-generated electricity systems reduced energy needs and produced enough power to rely solely on the sun's rays.

PORTUGAL PITCHES IN WITH IDEAS

The idea house concept is also being explored by other countries. For example, a model house on display in Portugal is providing a public showcase for the latest technology aimed at helping elderly or disabled people live independently. The "House of the Future" occupies about 1,600 square feet of Lisbon's Museum of Communications and features items made by multinationals as well as prototypes still in development by local universities. Displays range from the simple, such as a telephone with easy-to-read, extra-large buttons, to the high-tech, such as a talking kitchen scale. Other technologies include a computer that transforms text into a digital voice, fingerprint scans that open doors, and several voice-activated appliances. The house also features ramps instead of stairs and has no doors separating rooms to make it easier for people with special needs to get around. The surface of the dining room table can change color at the press of a button to create a different mood, while electronic artwork hanging on the walls can be changed just as easily to match new furniture. A robotic dog that dances, takes pictures, and can play with a ball is popular with visitors, as is a virtual garden where electronic flowers bloom and butterflies and rabbits appear when visitors step on its plasma screen floor.

Here is a Top Ten sampling of some of the newer furnishings and applications approved by the NAHB, without the butterflies and rabbits:

1. *Moen Handheld Shower.* Home Care by Moen offers a new handheld shower with a convenient push-button pause feature (on the handle) and removable safety strap. Featuring an ergonomic handle and an oversized lever that controls three comfort spray settings, the product suits those with

Throwing Mom a Lifeline

A gathering of my local and out-of-town siblings usually produces three things: a complete analysis of the Seattle Mariners, a comical story involving a teenage child, and several individual evaluations on how my mother "is really doing" living by herself.

That third piece is the result of personal visits and experiences or telephone conversations with the 86-year-old, independent individual who seven of us call "Mom." She's in marvelous shape and still drives herself to church and the bridge club, yet a curious, recent dizzy spell had us all wondering how any new episode would be handled.

"We should just get her a Lifeline, so that she can get help if anything happens," said Jim, my brother-in-law. "She can wear the thing around her wrist or around her neck so that nobody can see it. We should think about giving it a try."

The Lifeline program (http://www.lifelinesys.com; 800-380-3111) is one that several national monitoring companies offer for personal response services designed to provide immediate assistance in an emergency. The subscriber wears a waterproof pendant or wristband, which displays a "personal help" button. Should the subscriber require assistance (e.g., in the case of a fall, household accident, or the threat of an intruder), he or she simply pushes a button that sends a signal to a central communicator. The communicator dials a toll-free number and puts the subscriber in contact with the 24-hour monitoring staff.

"As people age, their number one concern is having to go into a nursing home," said Susan Gregory, executive director of Club 24 Senior Living at Home, a Northwest senior services company that evolved from Columbia Lutheran Ministries. "They don't want to leave their home and lose their independence. Products like the Lifeline help these people to stay in their home longer while providing some peace of mind for family and friends."

Club 24 is a good example of a membership organization that has a group Lifeline program yet is not linked to one specific church or community center. Often, church groups will begin a service in a neighborhood—for seniors, physically challenged individuals, or others with special needs—and the program will soon expand to the entire area.

Throwing Mom a Lifeline

Club 24 offers a Lifeline program plus light home maintenance and repair, hot meal delivery, shopping and errand service, lawn and yard work, in-home rehabilitation, and companionship and housekeeping.

"You sometimes hear about older friends who might have fallen and suffered a broken hip," Gregory said. "If the fall takes place in the home and nobody else is around, that person might not be able to move and get to a phone to call for help. Not only are they in a lot of pain, but they also have no way of telling anybody else about it to get help.

"As much as some older people want to be alone and 'out of everybody's way,' a monitoring device still lets them do that while providing a safety net in an emergency."

Lifeline units have voice capacity, allowing the monitoring unit to speak directly with the subscriber to determine what assistance is needed. If the subscriber is unable to answer, help will be summoned. In the event a user does not respond when summoned and an actual emergency is determined, the monitoring center will summon help from the appropriate local emergency response agency, such as the fire department. Most portable monitoring units contain a self-charging battery in the event of a power outage. Many programs also have the option of activating a series of messages from a Touch-Tone telephone to help remind users of medications, appointments, exercise, birthdays—and even favorite television shows. The messages can be programmed to play daily, weekly, or only once. When it is time for a reminder message to play, the telephone will chime, announce the time, and instruct the subscriber to press a button to hear the personalized reminder.

Costs of in-home monitoring packages vary. The price for the Lifeline service is about $40 for one-time installation, plus $35 a month ($45 for those with the reminders option).

arthritis. With an 84-inch, flex-soft hose, it is also helpful for those who find it necessary to sit while showering. Home Care by Moen also offers products such as grab bars, shower seats, and transfer benches. (http://www.moen.com)

2. *WarmlyYours Floor-Heating System.* WarmlyYours electric radiant floor-heating system is one of many now on the market that are designed to be energy efficient and maintenance free for the life of the system. These systems add warmth to bathrooms, kitchens, sunrooms, and any room where friends and family gather. The ultrathin floor-heating units are designed for convenient, invisible installation under tile, natural stone, hardwood, carpet, and floating wood floors. (http://www.warmlyyours.com or 800-875-5285)

3. *TimberTech® Decking Products.* All TimberTech planks are Americans with Disabilities Act (ADA) compliant and are maintenance free. TimberTech composite decking products, a wood alternative, feature engineered color technology and contain special additives to guard against harmful U.V. weathering to ensure maximum color with minimal fade. They also contain highly reflective, inorganic color pigments to ensure each board is comfortable to touch, regardless of sun intensity or air temperature. (http://www.timbertech.com or 800-307-7780)

4. *GE Profile™ Built-In Side-by-Side Refrigerators.* These refrigerators are good examples of the units now available in ADA-compliant and universal design models. The ADA models feature controls that are positioned within arm's reach (between 15 and 48 inches above the floor) and allow easy, one-hand operation. Shelves are easily accessible, with half of all freezer and fresh food space within comfortable reach. The universal design models have several easy-to-use features such as slide-out, spill-proof shelves, adjustable door bins, up-front electronic controls, and a tall LightTouch! dispenser with a child-lock option. Also available is a top freezer or CustomStyle™ side-by-side with a near-flush design that saves up to seven inches of floor space. (http://www.geappliances.com)

5. *Wellborn Accessible Cabinets.* Wellborn is one of many quality providers offering a comprehensive line of accessible cabinets to promote independent living and accommodate people with special needs. The base cabinets are 32½ inches high and include an 8½ by 6-inch toe kick, allowing for wheelchair access. This design offers full access to countertops, the convenience of a pull-out table, and easy-to-reach storage options. Wellborn also offers vari-

ous door styles, finishes, accessories, semicustom options, and other product lines for other rooms. (http://www.wellborn.com or 800-336-8040)

6. *Pedal Works Hands-Free Faucet Controller.* This application helps simplify time in the kitchen and save water and energy. The device allows people to turn faucets on and off without using their hands, making it possible to wash hands or food faster. When continuous flow is needed, such as when filling a sink or running the garbage disposer, just engage the latch. When doing dishes, step on and off the pedal to control water without waste. (http://www.activeforever.com or 800-377-8033)

7. *GE Monogram Outdoor Cooking Collection.* Consumers can take their pick of a wide variety of combinations of powerful burners and accessories. Burner controls are mounted on durable brass valves, ensuring long life in an outdoor environment. Burner igniters produce multiple sparks that fire up the grill quickly and dependably. Grill configurations range from the simple to the sophisticated—from the 24-inch, two-burner grill to a complete 48-inch cooking center that joins three grill sections with a rotisserie, a smoker, and two powerful side burners. GE's line includes a full selection of stainless steel gas cooking products designed for built-in or freestanding applications. The collection features a choice of natural gas or liquid propane gas models. (http://www.geappliances.com)

8. *Residential Elevators Luxury Lift Elevators.* Residential elevators promote accessibility and eliminate the need to move if the residents' needs or lifestyle changes. Residential Elevators, Inc., is one of several manufacturers with a wide range of elevators for the home. The company's Luxury Lift residential elevators are built using the same criteria used in the commercial elevator market. Buyers can select from a variety of elevator cabs and take advantage of many custom options, such as ceilings, fixtures, handrails, lighting, and automation features. (http://*www.residentialelevators.com* or 800-832-2004)

9. *Andersen Windows & Doors.* Andersen is one of several quality window and door manufacturers. The company has created a new line of architecturally styled products to complement its 400 and 200 Series. Buyers can choose from inspiring shapes, such

as radius-top casements, double-hungs, and French patio doors. Other product lines include the new KLM by Andersen Entranceways, the Andersen 400 Series Woodwright Windows, the Andersen Hardware Collections for Patio Doors, and more. (http://www.andersenwindows.com)

10. *AD-DS Approach Kitchen Line.* This is a line of universal design kitchen cabinetry and counters that has merged accessibility with style and smart-looking design. Sinks, cooktops, and other cabinets can be ordered with an adjustable-height feature that is operated by a conveniently placed push-button control. Sinks and cooktops are designed with ample knee space and clearance to sit while you work. The company also sells Approach products for the bath, including universally accessible sinks and vanity storage. (http://www.ad-as.com or 800-208-2020)

In this chapter, we've considered some of the projects and items that make aging in place easier and safer for many older consumers. In the next chapter, we will discuss the possibility of a parent moving into an adult child's home. It typically takes much more patience (and money) than anticipated, but that's why you included that extra room. Right?

9

WHEN MOM COMES TO LIVE

Responsibilities go well beyond adding a space

When a parent loses a spouse, the surviving spouse often will look to moving near, or in with, an adult child. Sometimes, there will be an interim stop—much like my mom's condo experience before she suggested a possible move closer to my sisters. My mom was fortunate to have a terrific group of friends in the neighborhood ("The White Haired Widows") that shared driving chores, meals, cards, and stories and pictures of their grandchildren and great grandchildren.

Knowing and accepting that a parent or older (perhaps disabled) family member is coming to live with you is one thing, finding a way to finance that accommodation is a totally different matter, as is attempting to predict emotions and expectations. In this chapter, we'll explore some of the realities of having an elder, or a person with a disability, come to stay in your home. It often results in more time and care for the older person than expected, and that care can alter the livelihood of everyone in the family, especially the caregiver. The Boomers, unlike their parents, have actually begun considering the possibilities. An example of this is the demand for an extra room on the main level of a new home to help accommodate parents. Susan Duncan, a housing consultant whose company, Adaptations, helps families with accessibility challenges, said more adult children are now looking at their own home with caregiving in mind.

"People are now looking at homes and saying to themselves, 'This type of home did not work for my mom, so let's solve the problem now,'" Duncan said. "This would not necessarily be a larger home but one that could support an aging family member. For example, if a bedroom and bathroom were on the main, or accessible, floor, where someone could live at least temporarily, it often is better than trying to convert a dining room into a bedroom."

Duncan added that many consumers are now asking about wider hallways and level access, hoping to add the potential for easy wheelchair movement in the future. "We have always looked for the pretty kitchen that seems to be very functional," Duncan said. "Now, many people are checking to see how easy it would be to maneuver a wheelchair up to a counter or reach a set of drawers."

There is a tendency in human nature to freeze family members at the age they had the most influence on our life. For acquaintances, the freeze time is often when we first encountered them. It helps us place perspective on our own life. So we hardly see the aging of those who are close to us but do not live close by until it's too late. Mom and Dad, though, did not see themselves as getting significantly older because they experienced each other every day.

The cost of adding a room or wider hallways can be expensive, especially when other hard-earned available dollars have already been spent on another project or emergency. Typically, homeowners dip back into the value of their residence via a home equity loan to perform the remodel. However, some low- and moderate-income borrowers are not able to come up with the required cash or eke out any more equity for still another expenditure. Now, companies like Fannie Mae are helping families finance the remodel. In some cases, the loan can also help individuals qualify for a home purchase of their own. The HomeChoice Program provides both options—two avenues that could make a difference and solve stressful situations. On the remodel side, the "retrofitting mortgage" helps older or disabled individuals shift to a family member's home rather than move to an institutional setting. This option combines a conventional first mortgage loan with a specialized second mortgage, often at a lower-than-market interest rate. The HomeChoice

Community Living option differs from traditional, single-family loans because qualifying borrowers do not have to be individuals. Borrowers can also be legal entities, including limited partnerships, government agencies serving adults and children, or nonprofit corporations. Group homes typically serve three to six persons and involve an independent coordinator to organize the financing.

There are income limits and home price limits on most of the HomeChoice programs, so consumers should check with local lenders and housing agencies for guidelines in specific regions. Eligible borrowers include persons with a disability, as defined by the Americans with Disabilities Act of 1990, or with a handicap, as defined by the Fair Housing Amendments Act of 1988. These include persons with physical or mental impairments that substantially limit their ability to perform basic functions (functions the average person can perform with little or no difficulty).

The National Home of Your Own Alliance approached Fannie Mae to create and assist in developing HomeChoice. The program considers the sometime complex income structures received by some people with disabilities. Fannie Mae designed the program as a three-year experimental pilot program in many states. The mortgage offers a down payment as low as $500, the acceptance of nontraditional credit histories, and greater flexibility in qualifying and underwriting standards.

OUT-OF-POCKET COSTS CAN BE OVERWHELMING

Regardless of how the home modification is financed, just about everyone overlooks the day-to-day costs far beyond those brought by the physical changes of a home. A U.S. census report estimated that caregivers of older family members or friends can spend approximately $20,000 out of their own pocket over a four-year period to help offset an elder's care costs. Most of the time, these adult children (nieces, nephews, grandchildren) have children of their own and lose income for taking time away from their primary job. A study by the American Association of Retired Persons (AARP) found that most 45- to 55-year-old Americans are not overly stressed during their actual caregiving time, and they received satisfaction in providing care for loved ones. However, care helpers, especially those with lower incomes, eventually tended to struggle, and the continual juggling of caregiving, children, and employment began to raise stress levels. [1]

A 2004 survey funded by the MetLife Foundation estimated there were 44.4 million caregivers who provided unpaid care to another adult. Almost six in ten (59 percent) of these caregivers either work or have worked while providing care. Approximately 62 percent had to make some adjustments to their work life, from reporting late to work to giving up work entirely—surprising not only their employers but also the federal government. [2]

The number of male caregivers was surprisingly high, the study revealed. Nearly four in ten (39 percent) caregivers were men, and 60 percent of them were working full-time. Caregivers are defined as people age 18 and older that help another person age 18 and older with at least 1 of 13 tasks that caregivers commonly do on an unpaid basis. Nearly eight in ten people who need care are age 50 or older (79 percent). Caregivers say that older care recipients' (ages 50 and over) main problem is aging (15 percent), and their main health problems are heart disease, cancer, diabetes, and Alzheimer's or other mental confusion. Caregivers say that younger recipients' (ages 18 to 49) main problems are mental illness and depression (23 percent).

Some key highlights of the MetLife Foundation report include the following:

- The value of family caregiving to society is estimated at $257 billion annually.
- A typical caregiver is female, 46 years old, married, has some college experience, and provides care to a woman age 50 or older.
- More than eight in ten (83 percent) caregivers say they assist relatives.
- A typical care recipient is female and widowed.
- The average age of care recipients ages 50 and over is 75.
- Among caregivers who are caring for someone other than a spouse, the most burdened caregivers say they make an average monthly financial contribution of $437.
- Almost one in five (17 percent) caregivers say they provide 40 or more hours of care per week.

In this chapter, we touched on the ramifications of housing a parent. Most of the time, parents want to stay longer in their home and neighborhood than they physically can manage. If Mom and Dad didn't want to leave the old neighborhood and move in with one of their children, chances are their children may struggle with eventually leaving their own neighborhood as well. In the next chapter, we will explore what it will take for some communities to retain their residents.

10

NOTHING BEATS THIS NEIGHBORHOOD

What once worked often needs easier access

Ah, the conveniences of the old stomping grounds! Jump on your bike and head to the local drugstore to buy penny candy. Or jump on your bike and pedal to the double feature (with cartoon) at the local movie theatre. Or jump on your bike and meet the gang for baseball at the park . . . . Wonderful, exciting times and memories that will never be forgotten.

But, oh, how times have changed. There is no more penny candy, no more double features with cartoons, and few of the gang want to spend more than 15 minutes playing baseball. And those of us who have aged in the suburbs no longer are able, or want, to jump on our bikes or in our cars as the prime mode of transportation. We'd prefer to walk or take easily accessible public transportation.

Patrick H. Hare, a Washington, D.C., author and land use and transportation planner specializing in accessory apartments, has referred to traditional suburban single-family homes as "Peter Pan" housing, designed for people who will never grow old. In this chapter, we will explore what a majority of older Americans want as they age—a community that ages with them. We'll discuss some of the changes that need to be implemented plus offer some alternatives to staying in the neighborhood yet leaving the family home.

A 2003 study by the American Association of Retired Persons (AARP) revealed that while seniors and Baby Boomers say they are very optimistic about their future living conditions, a substantial number may have unrealistic expectations and also don't know if their community offers the services they deem important. A subsequent report, released in 2005, established a link between the qualities of livable communities and Americans' ability to age successfully. The purpose of both studies was to examine people's expectations regarding their home, the community in which they live, and the services that are now available within their community that could help them remain independent, comfortable, and safe as they grow older. While it is encouraging that people 50 and over have an optimistic view of the future, there may yet be cause for concern.[1]

"There's a real need to educate the over-50 population about the availability of services in their community—and the home features now available—that can help them remain independent as they age," said Tony Copeland, an AARP counselor. "That way, when the need arises, they'll know where to turn."

Copeland's comments reflect the fact that while almost all respondents in the AARP report want to stay in their home for the rest of their life, many do not envision making changes to their home unless a specific need arises. Curiously, a previous AARP housing survey showed that nearly 25 percent of Americans age 45 and over say they or someone they live with will have trouble maneuvering around their home in the coming years. The majority of respondents considered themselves to be "planners" and respect the importance of planning for the future. Significantly fewer, however, have given a great deal of thought to the home features or community characteristics they will need in their later years, the study revealed.

"Some of the questions mean different things to different people," Copeland said. "For example, 'in their home' may be taken to mean the home they are presently in or the home they see themselves living in at some future date. The difference can be subtle but very significant."

Most respondents acknowledge and value home features that can help ensure they have a safe and comfortable home environment. However, while they recognize the value of these features, many lack them in their current home. Gopal Ahluwalia, a research specialist from the National Association of Home Builders (NAHB) economics department, noted that the amenity gaps (features seniors say they want that developers are not providing) common to both the NAHB and AARP research are grocery stores and drugstores within a planned community. Other wants and needs that are not being met are sidewalks, better transportation, and in-home meal service.

"Do you ever feel stuck in this neighborhood?"

"Builders have done a good job in some areas in providing what the 50-plus market wants—including wider streets, grab bars in hallways and bathrooms, and a master suite on the main floor," Ahluwalia said. "But we need to continually take into consideration more services in our planning. It's not feasible to have drugstores, grocery stores, and hospitals in every neighborhood, but better public and private transportation would go a long way to solving this."

When older people are not engaged in their community, they have lower feelings of self-control, less success dealing with aging issues, lower life satisfaction, and a poorer quality of life.[2] Today's shortcomings will be compounded as the number of older Americans swells in the next three decades. Only 56 percent of those who report low engagement in their community said they were satisfied with their life compared to 87 percent of those who were highly engaged.

"Each time an older person finds it is no longer reasonable to live in his or her home or community, it is a crisis on an individual and family level," said John Rother, the AARP's Director of Policy and Strategy. "Community features can enhance the lives of older residents... Public officials need to seek out and engage residents."

The AARP's work on Livable Communities is initially focused on housing and mobility issues. Older people feel more isolated when their home doesn't meet their physical needs, the report finds. A lack of affordable housing can force older persons to move. In an ideal situation, planning during an original design phase or making modifications to an existing structure can make homes suitable for people to age in their community if they wish or provide them alternatives in other communities where they want to live. This can reduce the number of people feeling forced to move into assisted-living facilities or nursing homes while they are still capable of living independently. Older Americans who don't drive make many fewer trips and frequently miss doing things because of insufficient transportation options. Public transportation can be a critical source of mobility for this population (one-sixth of medical trips for those over 50 are made on public transportation). Other mobility options, including safe walking options, taxi services, and human services transportation, can reduce reliance on private cars and increase opportunities for community involvement. A safe pedestrian environment with good sidewalks and easy access to grocery stores, health centers, recreational facilities, and other services can also have a positive effect.[3]

The concept encourages community leaders and civic groups to facilitate social involvement, including organizational membership and volunteering, and actively solicit contributions by persons of all ages and abilities in community decision making. It promotes the design and modification of homes to meet the needs of older residents and encourages stability through an adequate supply of diverse, affordable housing options. The plan also recommends that the transportation environment be improved to benefit older drivers (wider streets, parking spaces) while endorsing safety efforts and older driver education. Mobility options, including public transportation, walking and bicycling, and specialized transportation are critical for people with special needs.

To help community leaders and civic groups implement its recommendations, the AARP's Public Policy Institute has developed "Livable Communities: An Evaluation Guide." It includes a community evaluation tool, resources, tips, and innovative ideas and success stories. The AARP has also developed a ten-point community self-assessment checklist that can be used to evaluate and assess a community's livability.

STAYING IN THE NEIGHBORHOOD
BUT NOT IN THE SAME HOUSE

What's an attractive living option for an elderly homeowner who is house rich and cash poor yet cannot afford to sink all of the equity of the family home into a newer, maintenance-free house or condominium with people his or her own age? Builders and developers in many areas of the country have begun to explore Active Living Rental Communities (ALRCs), upscale apartment buildings with elegant entries and comfy common sitting areas in neighborhoods where rental housing would accommodate longtime local residents who no longer choose to own.

"There are a lot of people out there who want to move out of the responsibilities of maintaining the home they have lived in for decades," said John Rhoad, president of RMJ Development Group, LLC. "They want to move and they feel they are still young enough to move—maybe even more than one or two more times. They want to stay close to their familiar surroundings but they don't want to take all their money and sink it into a home that costs as much as the one they left. That's one of the downsides of home-price explosion."

The typical client would be a single man or woman in his or her late 60s who has lived in their home for 30 years. Other than the home that was bought for $30,000 that's now worth $350,000, these people don't have significant additional assets. A small pension, Social Security benefits, and minor stocks and bonds provide steady, yet not exorbitant, income of $4,500 a month. About 30 percent continue to work full-time or part-time, and many are involved in volunteer projects within the community. The targeted customer would be much like a reverse mortgage candidate who no longer wishes to stay in the home yet wants to remain in the immediate area. Perhaps the memories of a loved one are simply too constant, too close in every room of the family home. Maybe they have always wanted to move into a brand-new space with fresh paint and appliances where persons their own age consistently gather for a card game downstairs in a warm, cozy den where hot tea is available at any time. Such persons desire the flexibility to invest the equity of their current home and maintain liquidity for future health-related needs. In addition, the rising costs of homeowners insurance, property taxes, and condominium association fees have sparked a search to alternative living possibilities.

"There is a market for this sort of rental apartment because of the changing demographics," said Robert M. Lefenfeld, principal in Savage, Maryland-based Real Property Research. "There are also more and more people who prefer not to deal with condominium associations. A couple of people in board positions can make a real difference in how other people live."

The ALRC idea is to load resort-style amenities in neighborhoods that can support rents at $1.45 per square foot per month. (A 1,000-square-foot-unit would cost approximately $1,450 per month.) The building would have high-quality architecture, extensive landscaping, and a variety of exterior features, such as a heated pool, spa, walking trails, greenhouse, gate-controlled access to parking, and a covered entry. Interior common areas would include a business center, fitness center, catering kitchen, clubroom or library, and a game room. Individual living units include large bedrooms, crown moldings, nine-foot ceilings, maple cabinets, ceramic tile floors, a granite breakfast bar, seated shower with grab bars and glass enclosure, an all-electric kitchen with a built-in microwave over the range, lower-height wall switches, lever handle door hardware and faucets, and full Internet access. Ed Hord, a Baltimore-based architect, said activity, convenience, and entertainment will be the atmosphere to draw active adults to upscale rental housing. Rocking chairs, tiny apartments, or any clue the place says "retirement" will incite a stampede to the parking lot.

"The current multifamily seniors' rental product is typically focused on affordability and services for frailty," Hord said. "The average age of the resident is about 75 and the building was financed by low-income housing tax credits. This model has absolutely changed and we are just now seeing the demand in the past 18 months that stresses activity for persons who are much younger or feel much younger."

The ALRC model, with floor plans ranging from 710 to 840 square feet for one-bedroom to two-bedroom, two-bath, den apartments at 1,150 to 1,300 square feet, will also be promoted to "snowbirds" who prefer to spend the colder months in warmer climates.

"It's easy to just lock the apartment and go," Rhoad said. "The place will be safe and secure when they are gone. It's a huge factor for someone getting along in years."

EAST COAST METHOD NOT OFTEN FOUND ON THE LEFT COAST

Elaine Anderson, 73, was seeking an apartment building in which she could purchase shares.

"Things are so different here," said the New York transplant who decided to move to San Francisco to live closer to her children. "Everybody thinks I want to buy a building. I don't want to buy a building. I want to buy some shares in a unit."

It's not true that most westerners look at the word *co-op* and think about a chicken coop. However, the housing situation described by that four-letter word separated by a hyphen is certainly not as familiar to left coasters as it is to big-city easterners. Cooperative ownership of an apartment unit means owners have purchased shares in a corporation that holds title to a building. In return for the shares, owners receive a proprietary lease entitling them to occupy a specific area of the building. It can be thought of as a huge time-share with the right to use a unit but not actually own it. In a condominium, each unit is individually owned. Homeowners pay monthly dues to maintain the community property on the grounds (pool, gardens, etc.).

There are a few co-ops in San Francisco, Portland, and Seattle, but the alternative to home ownership in the West never blossomed as it did on the East Coast where "market-rate" co-ops thrive and units appreciate at market values. The alternative concept, one that is catching on in states like Minnesota, is the "limited equity" plan whereby shareholders make a smaller down payment and participate in a 40-year FHA-insured mortgage. Members accrue equity, perhaps at the rate of 1 percent a year. This arrangement attracts seniors who no longer want to tie up a significant portion of their assets in their home. In both plans, the stock certificate reflects the value of the home at move-in, and people participating in mortgages can deduct interest,

"We had more co-op ownership in the West prior to having condominium legislation," said Alan Tonnon, a Bellevue, Washington-based attorney specializing in real estate and a charter member of the Washington State Real Estate Commission. "But condo ownership became preferred because lenders feel more comfortable lending for a condo, and people like owning the place they live in. This is not the East Coast.

The psychological preference here has always been for single-family detached homes—something the condo has fought."

Real estate professionals with co-op backgrounds say the concept is not popular because lenders are reluctant to make loans. Initially, the underwriting did go along with what co-op owners wanted. Often, in a case of foreclosure, the underwriter wants the ability to rent the unit. Many co-op owners will not accept that. Therefore, most of the co-ops around here are seller financed. Cooperative housing can be any type of residential building, such as town houses, detached single-family homes, conventional apartments, manufactured housing, or highrises. Generally, the cooperative corporation owns the property including the buildings, amenities, and land. The corporation typically obtains a loan, known as a "blanket mortgage," that finances the whole property. The blanket mortgage generally has a first lien on the property.

The market-share homeowner's cost of buying the stock or shares is similar to the purchase price of the home. A co-op homeowner finances the purchase of stock with a co-op unit "share loan" that is generally secured by a pledge of the purchase of stock or shares.

The basic liabilities of blanket (group) and share (individual) co-op loans differ. Because condominium owners obtain their own financing and are responsible for individual property tax assessments, they are not responsible for any default on another owner's loan or property taxes. In a co-op, when an owner defaults under a blanket loan, the other shareholders generally must cure the default or they could risk foreclosure of the entire project.

If an individual obtains a share loan from a lender to purchase a certain portion of the co-op, the lender will seek the borrower's other assets if the borrower defaults on the loan.

When a co-op homeowner moves, the equity and appreciated value of the property is generally reflected in the price of the co-op owner's stock or shares. However, some co-ops are set up with "limited equity" arrangements in an effort to keep housing more affordable. By agreeing to freeze the price of moving into their co-op, residents could curtail speculating investors.

Why don't co-op owners jump at the chance to have a renter in their building if it would help with fees? Some folks feel there's a big difference between renting a house or condominium and owning one. Seniors will tell you that a reason they buy into anything as they age is security, not just from crime but from unpredictability. Having something to say about your neighbors is a big deal, and that is not available in a condominium.

Before leaving your longtime neighborhood and moving into any community new to you—older neighborhood, new planned-unit development, urban highrise, rural farm, age-targeted winter home—take the time to do the research. Compare the list below with what you already have in your home. If where you're headed is not a significant improvement over your present property, maybe it's time to see what you need to do to comfortably age in place.

- *Housing.* What types of housing are available? What are costs for small, detached, single-family homes? Are views attainable? What type of maintenance is required for quality rental homes? Do apartments and condominiums restrict young people? Does the condominium association permit subletting a bedroom? Are there special security provisions for owners who choose to live elsewhere part of the year? How are most homes in the area heated? What is the representative heating cost per year for an average home or apartment? Are electric rates favorable and predictable? How do they compare with major urban cities? Are there special programs for seniors?
- *Health care.* What level of emergency service is already in place? What is planned for the future? Are competent doctors, nurses, and clinic specialists available and accessible? If not, how close are they in terms of miles and time? Where is the nearest "full-service" hospital, and what are its latest technologies and specializations? Is there a high-standard, long-term care facility in the community? Are pharmacies and emergency clinics available at all times? Are local hospitals full or underutilized? Would projected growth cause an overload that might jeopardize other citizens' health services? Is special care for the handicapped available? Are visiting nurses or in-home services easy to arrange?
- *Climate.* What is the truthful definition of local climate? What are the average temperatures in summer and winter? What are the wind conditions (how will it affect golf shots?), and how much rain falls in specific months? When does the snow arrive, how long does it stay, and is it a limiting factor on the movement of

persons and vehicles? What is the humidity? Is the area affected
by dust, pollens, or industrial discharges?

- *Public safety.* Is the community adequately policed? What is the response time for police or fire calls? Does it boast a low crime rate?
Are there specific records of house break-ins, assaults, purse
snatchings, and car theft? Does the community have a 911 or similar response in place for police, fire, or medical services now?
What is the future probability of such a service online?

- *Government and taxes.* What local taxes exist in addition to federal
and state taxes? Are there any special tax exemptions for seniors?
What are property tax valuations? Are city and county offices
staffed by helpful people ready to provide quick answers? Are special taxes or levies likely? What has been the history of such taxes?

- *Utilities and services.* What is the quality of local land and mobile
telephone services? Do they offer any special benefits or pricing
for senior citizens? What is the quality of the television reception?
How many channels? What are the costs of cable services? Is there
sufficient programming information? Are Meals on Wheels, or
similar food services, available for the elderly?

- *Water/sewage.* Does the community provide clean and safe water?
What is the cost per year for a typical household, couple, or single
person? Is there a bottled water delivery service? How is sewage
and solid waste handled? Is there a nearby sewage treatment
plant? What percent of the homes in the community have individual septic fields? Have costs been stable? When are future assessments expected? Will they cover any specific problems?

- *Recreation.* What recreation opportunities exist for mature people?
What sports—besides golf and tennis—are emphasized? What kinds
of opportunities are available for fishing and hunting, and what
does licensing cost? Are there nice parks, sidewalks, and scenic
views that are safe at all times of the day? Is there an aquatic center?
Are there distinctive geological features in the area? How many
months a year is it possible to play golf? Are the greens fees expensive or affordable? Is membership in a club available? Does the club
restrict the number of rounds a guest can play? Does the club membership offer other benefits such as social events? Are organized
events such as ballroom or square dancing available? Do clubs,

hobby groups, and church organizations welcome newcomers and visitors?

- *Business.* Are new people made to feel welcome in the community? How does the community accept new business and new business ideas? Is there a local chamber of commerce or small business development center? What has been the history of consultants, antique shops, and small bookstores? Are there a variety of restaurants and food services that cater to seniors or offer senior discounts? Does the community offer shopping at retail establishments that are complete enough to save long trips?

- *Cultural amenities.* Is there a local symphony and nearby theatres with live stage productions? Is it easy for newcomers to participate in historical or art museums, bridge clubs, churches, lodges, and special interest clubs? What is the predominant entertainment outside the home? What types of films do the movie theatres present? Is there a special time for seniors? What types of newspapers serve the area? Can they be delivered to a part-time residence out of the area? At what cost?

- *Transportation.* Are there local bus, train, taxi, and van services available? How long a drive is it and how many miles are there to a major airport? Are flights reasonably priced? What are the conditions of local roads and highways? Are there freeways, or limited access, linking the community to any major urban centers?

In this chapter, we have pointed out that many of yesterday's neighborhoods need to be altered to serve the older residents of today. Because of the huge number of aging Americans, housing is not the only "shelter" issue that needs to be addressed. In the next chapter, we will dive into the larger question of long-term care, which has become as necessary for older adults as the roof over their heads. And just like the house, prices are going up every day.

11

CARING ABOUT LONG-TERM CARE

We are living longer but the needs often are greater

U.S. citizens are living longer and, for the most part, healthier lives. The risk of needing nursing home care before age 75 is relatively low, and most people will not need nursing home care for longer than a year. But down the road, there will simply be too many Baby Boomers and other seniors to be accommodated in nursing homes, not that they would want to be there anyway. Most members of this huge throng will have no other option than to age in place simply because there will not be enough nursing home beds to handle the load.

That would have been fine with my dad. My father, who died several years ago from Parkinson's disease, would have much preferred watching Notre Dame battle Southern California from the comfort of his own den on a football Saturday where he could shuffle to his closest bathroom in his favorite bathrobe and slippers without having to worry about how he looked in the hallway. He certainly would have enjoyed my mother's famous chicken and a cold beer from the kitchen refrigerator over a chance to eat institutional food in a cheerless cafeteria at an hour that interrupted college football. But we simply did not work fast enough to get the house, and my mom, ready for Dad's needs.

This chapter will address the underestimated and primary necessity most consumers are forced to face after the traditional working years—

health care and its costs—which is especially critical now to the GI generation. Most of this group did not have any form of long-term care insurance and are paying out of their pockets to balance the costs of health care, groceries, transportation, and property taxes. For many, these costs are a threat to their retirement years and the financial legacy targeted for their children. However, if younger generations save for retirement and/or invest in long-term care insurance now, part of the huge burden of health care costs would be lifted down the road.

The idea of entering a nursing home is appealing to very few. Seniors would much prefer to be treated in the comfort of their home and in familiar surroundings. A bulletin by the American Association of Retired Persons (AARP) observed that the state of Indiana once had 15,000 empty nursing home beds, yet older state residents preferred to be on a 30,000-person wait list for home and community care services.[1] In a capsule, long-term care threatens to bankrupt Medicaid and the states that pay for it. The best hope for a cure lies in cutting down on the need for institutional care. The least expensive, most acceptable alternative is simply keeping seniors in their own home as long as possible.

Perhaps the first major event to focus on a prime funding source for aging in place was the *Use Your Home to Stay at Home™* program initiated by the National Council on the Aging (NCOA) and commissioned by the Centers for Medicare and Medicaid Services (CMS) and the Robert Wood Johnson Foundation. The CMS grant totaled $295,000 and the Robert Wood Johnson Foundation grant $99,900. Dr. Barbara Stucki, PhD, a Bend, Oregon, researcher and consultant, was the project manager and lead author of the program's primary study, the *National Blueprint for Increasing the Use of Reverse Mortgages for Long-Term Care.* The goal was to begin work toward a public-private partnership to increase the use of reverse mortgages (discussed in detail in Part Three) to help pay for long-term care. The project combined research, consumer surveys, and discussions with analysts to identify cost-effective government interventions and other incentives that can facilitate the use of reverse mortgages. Stucki, a former senior policy analyst for the American Council of Life Insurance and an AARP employee, found of the nearly 28 million households with owners age 62 and older in the United States, approximately 13.2 million are "good candidates" for reverse mortgages.

"There is simply no other pot of funds sitting around that is going to solve the long-term care situation in this country other than home equity," Stucki said. "I just don't see any other way—unless people simply want to dig deep down and pay out of their pocket. The idea is to use your home to stay at home.

"These good candidates could get on average $72,128 on a reverse mortgage. That was the key for me," Stucki said. "It showed there was a significant chunk of change for millions of households. Although some homeowners have pulled equity out of their home to make improvements as they've aged, the concept of home equity to pay for health care is relatively new. Using reverse mortgages for many can mean the difference between staying at home or going to a nursing home."

Of the 13.2 million potential candidates for reverse mortgages, about 5.2 million are either already receiving Medicaid or are at financial risk of needing Medicaid if they were faced with paying the high cost of long-term care at home, Stucki reported. This group would be able to get $309 billion from reverse mortgages that could help pay for long-term care. In 2000, the nation spent $123 billion a year on long-term care for those aged 65 and older, with the amount likely to double in the next 30 years, according to NCOA. Nearly half of those expenses are paid out of pocket by individuals, and only 3 percent are paid for by private insurance. Government health programs pay the remainder.

NURSING HOMES COST MORE THAN MEETS THE EYE

Nursing home costs are even more severe for the average household. Individuals and their families pay one-third of all nursing home expenses. To pay these bills, they often use savings or sell assets such as stocks, bonds, or their home. State Medicaid programs pay for almost half of all nursing home care, but consumers get no assistance from Medicare, Medicare supplemental insurance, or Medigap for long-term care. For example, Medicare beneficiaries who meet strict eligibility criteria are covered for 100 days of skilled nursing home care and must make a copayment after the 20th day. Though Medicare may pay for some at-home assistance for beneficiaries who meet certain conditions, the program does not cover custodial or intermediate care or prolonged home health care. Medicare supplemental insurance, or Medigap, does not cover long-term care either. Some standardized Medicare supplement policies contain an at-home recovery benefit that may pay up to $1,600 per year for short-term assistance with daily activities but only for those recovering from an illness, injury, or surgery.

Stucki contends that reverse mortgages could play an important role in helping more seniors—affluent, modest, or poor—to pay for services and improvements in their home, such as adding bathroom grab bars, which would help keep them accident free and healthy, and pay for getting part-time professional help.

"Ultimately, it's really got nothing to do with money," Stucki said. "It's keeping individuals from working themselves into an early grave trying to take care of Dad. People can look at their home as an insurance policy. Let's turn to it to get the help we need. And that help can mean everything . . . whether it's a part-time aide to come for a few hours a day just to be around so Mom isn't so dependent on the kids. That is the message. Look at what's possible with this home."

The home is an exempt asset for purposes of calculating Medicaid eligibility, which means a person who needs nursing home services and who has no other significant source of revenue is likely to qualify for Medicaid services without the need to reduce the value of that asset. On the other hand, because many home and community services are not covered by Medicaid, a low-income older person who is trying to remain at home for some period of time prior to a nursing home admission could use cash generated from a reverse mortgage to buy that time. There are a variety of other complex issues related to the interplay of Medicaid eligibility and reverse mortgages.

Stephen A. Moses, president of the Seattle-based Center for Long-Term Care Financing, is obviously a proponent of long-term care insurance policies. He believes that the average family waits too long to discover how inadequate nursing home care can be. Once an insurable health care risk occurs, it's too late to buy long-term care insurance that would cover extra professional assistance and care in the nursing home. See Figure 11.1 for the opportunities and limits to a long-term care insurance policy.

"You can't buy fire insurance when the house is up in flames," Moses said.

What usually happens to Mom and Dad is the least preferred option, according to Moses. Most of the time the family depends on Social Security and Medicare only to discover any benefits are short-term. Finally, they end up considering Medicaid, a government program that does pay for custodial nursing home care for as long as needed.

"Medicaid is a means-tested, public-assisted program," Moses said. "It is welfare. It has a dismal reputation for problems associated with access, quality, low reimbursement, discrimination, and institutional bias. Nevertheless, because of its generous and elastic eligibility rules, Medicaid has become the primary third-party payer for long-term care in the United States. It's the path of least resistance for people who did not save or insure for long-term care. But if you end up on Medicaid, you'll most certainly end up in an underfinanced nursing home that is struggling to provide low-cost care of uncertain quality."

For years, Moses has floated the controversial idea of eliminating the home from the Medicaid component. That way, consumers would either have to buy long-term care insurance policies or spend home equity (via a reverse mortgage) before qualifying for Medicaid.

"It would go a long way to solving the health care mess in this country," Moses said. "It would improve the quality of care and reduce the enormous amount of money the government pays to health care while retaining Medicaid for the poor."

The AARP, a nonprofit membership organization that addresses the needs and interests of persons age 50 and older, was founded in 1958 by a retired California educator, Dr. Ethel Percy Andrus, and represents more than 35 million members. About half of its members are working, either full- or part-time. Nearly a third of its members are under the age of 60. The 60 to74 age bracket comprises 46 percent of membership, whereas 21 percent are age 75 and over. The organization, which estimates about half of all U.S. homeowners 65 or over have lived in their house for 25 years or more, has long been opposed to seniors taking out reverse mortgages solely to purchase long-term care insurance policies—especially if all of the reverse proceeds were used for insurance premiums. Obviously, the older the person, the more expensive the policy, as you will see in the section to follow.

Even in 2000, the number of Americans over 55—comprised mostly of GIs and Silents—constituted more than a quarter of the population. By 2020, when the Baby Boomers reach 65, that percentage will reach

FIGURE 11.1 *Opportunities and Limits of Long-term Care Insurance*

Long-Term Care Insurance Opportunities	Long-Term Care Insurance Requirements/Limits
Long-term care insurance gives you financial protection against the cost of long-term care services.	If you don't buy a long-term care insurance policy from a reliable insurance company, you might not get the coverage you need in the future.
It helps give you more control and choices over your long-term care coverage. You are able to choose the types of services and customize your care based on your financial and social needs.	Make sure you buy the long-term care insurance policy that is right for you. Some policies offer more coverage than other policies. You may have to pay additional long-term care costs. Read the policy carefully to see what is and what isn't covered.
You won't have to use your savings or life insurance to pay for your health care needs. This will allow you to leave money or other items to your heirs (family and friends).	Some people might not be able to get a long-term care insurance policy because they have a preexisting condition. A preexisting condition is a health problem you have before getting a new insurance policy.
The Federal Long-Term Care Insurance Program offers long-term care insurance at a group rate for federal and U.S. Postal Service employees and annuitants, members, and retired members of the Uniformed Services.	Long-term care insurance policies can be expensive. You might not be able to continue to pay the monthly premium. Remember, it is better to buy a long-term care insurance policy at a younger age when premiums are lower. If this is done, a periodic review is advised to make sure your policy covers your current and future long-term care needs.
Your family or friends won't have to worry about how you will get or pay for your long-term care.	Generally, if you buy a long-term care insurance policy without a nonforfeiture benefit and don't use it, you won't get your money back for the policy.

Source: Centers for Medicare & Medicaid Services

nearly one-third. By 2050, it will be over 40 percent. This is a major and growing market for reverse mortgages, not only in the future but also now. If the recent numbers are any indication, the number of reverse mortgages made each year should continue to double the previous year's volume for the foreseeable future. It's simply a matter of numbers. Like all projections, reverse mortgages depend on a lot of "ifs." While the census numbers appear to be reasonable and reliable, the market projection will be affected not only by demographics but also by interest rates, prices, and alternative choices. The reliability of any projection over time will be subject to prevailing conditions. That said, the underlying base of demand for a reverse mortgage product simply to age in place—established by the structure of the population—is very strong.

"The reverse mortgage may not be the silver bullet everyone is looking for, but it certainly is part of the pie," said Don Redfoot, AARP senior policy advisor. "It will be very useful to people who are 'self-insuring,' using the funds to supplement the services they already will be receiving with other quality care. It also will be used to make the home modifications that will be needed for people to be more comfortable at home for a longer period of time. And that's important....For an older person, a home represents their life story."

The debate over long-term care insurance and how to pay for it will continue for decades. The AARP is not eager to see seniors take out a reverse mortgage for the sole purpose of purchasing a long-term care policy. But a reverse mortgage borrower who would use at least a portion of those funds to offset the cost of a long-term care policy could be well served.

"People who purchase long-term care insurance and those who take out a reverse mortgage are very different segments of the population," Redfoot said. "Reverse mortgages can be a very expensive proposition for people using the funds only for insurance products. Most of the time, they would be better served by borrowing on other terms."

So who actually needs long-term care insurance? The main reason people buy private insurance is to avoid being financially wiped out by long-term care costs. Thus, long-term care insurance is really a wager on your health. That risk can pay off, and there is also a chance that you'll pay premiums year after year and never need the coverage. That's what opponents to long-term care plans say.

Agencies differ on the chances of consumers ending up in a nursing home or needing in-home care. It's a big, fat Catch-22. If you don't have coverage, you could blow your life savings on two years in a nursing home. If you do have it, you could stretch your budget to make the payments on the premiums and then never need the coverage. However, if you purchase long-term care insurance and you eventually require the coverage, you will have better-quality care and a greater chance of leaving your assets to your estate while easing the burden on Medicare and Medicaid. Couples typically get a much better rate than two single persons.

According to the United Seniors Health Cooperative, a nonprofit organization based in Washington, D.C., people should consider long-term care insurance only when they have at least $75,000 in assets (excluding home and car); an annual retirement income of at least $35,000 (depending on costs in the state where they live); the ability to pay premiums without making any lifestyle changes; and the ability to afford the policy even if premiums increase during their lifetime. These are only general rules of thumb. However, if you don't fall within these guidelines (the AARP would argue that today's reverse mortgage borrowers do not), you would be better off letting your money earn interest, paying for care as the need arises, and relying on Medicaid if long-term care becomes necessary. However, remember if you do plan to rely on Medicaid, care will be minimal and probably not what you anticipated. Private long-term care would be a welcome supplement. Even if you do fit the above profile, be sure to consult a financial advisor, a life or health insurance counselor, or an attorney about all your options.

Each long-term care policy has its own eligibility requirements, benefits, costs, and restrictions. Policies are not standardized, so the services covered by different companies vary greatly. Services generally covered include nursing home care (skilled, intermediate, and custodial), care in your own home and in adult day care centers, assisted living, personal care, hospice care, and care for people with cognitive disorders such as Alzheimer's disease. Services generally excluded include psychological disorders, such as anxiety or depression, alcohol or drug addiction, illness or injury caused by war, attempted suicide, or intentional, self-inflicted injuries. Annual premiums for long-term care plans vary depending on the company, the comprehensiveness of the coverage, and the date the plan was purchased. Here are the approxi-

mate annual costs for long-term care insurance followed by some elements to consider:

Age at Time of Purchase	Cost Range: Nursing Home Only	Cost Range: Nursing Home and Home Care
55	$250 to $1,100	$300 to $1,500
65	$450 to $2,000	$600 to $2,600
75	$1,100 to $3,000	$1,170 to $5,000

- *Periodic increases.* Often, insurance agents promise that there will be no rate hikes. However, make certain your policy clearly states your premiums will not be raised. The brochure might say the insurer won't raise your rates unless it raises them for your entire "class," yet what constitutes your class?
- *No total package.* Even with private coverage, your health care needs will not be completely met because most policies do not pay for everything you require. However, it's best to gauge your choice of daily benefits on how much nursing homes in specific areas charge. Home care benefits are usually 50 percent of nursing home care benefits.
- *Identify facilities.* Make sure you understand exactly what kind of facilities the policy will cover before you buy it. There are no national standards on what counts as a long-term care facility. For example, an "adult day care center" or "assisted-living facility" can vary widely from state to state and company to company. So if you buy a policy in one state and then retire to another state, there might not be facilities in your new state that match the definition in your policy.
- *Auxiliary coverage.* Life insurance companies also offer policies with long-term care riders on many whole life or universal life products. Some customers choose riders because they gain the security of knowing they have coverage for long-term care. However, check on how the rider handles the rising cost of care. Consumers may best be served with a separate and independent long-term care policy.
- *Discount for spouse.* Most companies give a spousal discount only if you and your spouse purchase identical policies. But purchasing

identical policies might not be a good idea because women tend to live longer than men and are more likely to live alone in their later years, resulting in different long-term care needs.

The older the individual covered, the higher the premium. For instance, premiums for coverage on a 70-year-old individual are about three times those for a 50-year-old.

Most long-term care policies are indemnity-type policies, meaning they will pay you for actual charges by the care provider (up to the policy's limits). Other long-term care policies, instead of being based on indemnity, pay daily benefit amounts to the insured rather than paying for actual charges. The latter type of policy offers insurers greater flexibility (e.g., allowing them to pay for home care) and less paperwork. For example, let's say you choose a policy that pays $160 per day for five years. The maximum that policy will pay is $292,000 ($160 per day, times 365 days, times five years).

PLUSES AND MINUSES OF LONG-TERM CARE INSURANCE

On the Plus Side

- Although expensive, long-term care insurance may provide protection against costly care. If other options are not viable, it may be the way to meet your goals. Even though policies remain a low-value product, they are better than nothing.
- If you have family caregivers, the extra home care coverage in long-term care insurance might make it possible to remain at home longer.
- It is better to buy long-term care insurance early when premiums are lower. Once you develop a serious medical condition, you probably will not qualify for coverage

On the Minus Side

- You may never use the coverage that you paid for.

- Most policies lack sufficient home care coverage to keep an individual out of a nursing home unless family members or informal caregivers are available to help in providing care.
- Policies typically return from 60 percent to 65 percent of total premiums paid in benefits.

In Part Two, we explored the concept of aging in place and making older homeowners comfortable in their present home. Some potential buyers simply can't afford to move whereas others want to tweak their longtime home to accommodate future needs. In Part Three, we will consider some of the alternatives to funding future years. Even though many avenues, such as conventional annuities, have been around for decades, we will begin with the unconventional—a detailed look at reverse mortgages, mentioned above as one of the key potential ingredients to aging in place.

FUNDING FUTURE YEARS

12

REVERSE MORTGAGES CAN BE A VIABLE OPTION

Underestimated tool taps home equity for consumers over age 62

The number of Americans over the age of 65 who continue to work has risen in the past decade. This unexpected rise can be traced to a variety of factors including shell-shocked retirement accounts, falling interest rates on savings tools, fewer company pension plans, and the inability to save. In 2000, the Social Security rule that reduced the benefits of those seniors who continued to work once they reached age 65 was eliminated, thus propelling many interested seniors back into part-time employment—just check any baseball spring training facility. There are seniors selling tickets, programs, hot dogs, and popcorn, plus acting as ushers and parking lot directors.

In Part Three, we will explore some of the avenues that older consumers are taking to fund and offset the growing costs of the next phase of their life, with some specific strategies regarding the family home. In this chapter, we begin with reverse mortgages, one of the most confusing, controversial, and misunderstood strategies that eventually could be the key to comfort for countless individuals over age 62.

Picture a fast-talking salesman who never had a bad day. Shiny polyester suit, white shoes, all smiles, and "yes ma'ams." He'd swindle your grandmother, take all of her money, and laugh all the way to the bank. For years, that was the reputation of anyone involved with the reverse mortgage industry. The loans were seen as evil, a windfall for any lender underwriting them, and a killer of family estates.

Today's reverse mortgages have been spiffed up and the rough edges filed. The most popular program is even insured by the federal government. While a few of the older loans giving lenders an "equity share" of the home's appreciation are still in place and causing irritation, the reverse mortgage now can be a viable option for persons over 62 who find themselves with significant equity in their home and little outside income. In this chapter, we explore the versatility and costs of reverse mortgages and how they will continue to fit into the financial possibilities of an aging population.

Reverse mortgages can be used for any reason, including paying for health care and home modifications (as discussed in Chapter 11), travel, real estate purchases, automobiles, or college education. Consumers can choose how to receive the money from a reverse mortgage. The options include fixed monthly payments, a line of credit, a lump sum, or a combination of the above. The most popular option, which is chosen by more than 60 percent of borrowers, is a small lump sum combined with a line of credit that allow the consumer to draw on the loan proceeds at any time. The size of the reverse mortgage depends on age at application, the loan type, home value, and—sometimes—location. In general, the older the consumer and the more valuable the home (and the less the amount owed), the larger the reverse mortgage.

The costs associated with getting a reverse mortgage include the appraisal fee, origination fee (which can be financed as part of the mortgage), and other charges similar to those for regular mortgages. One of the most confusing fees involved is the mortgage insurance premium. Seniors are usually flabbergasted when they find the amount is 2 percent of the appraised value of their home. Couple that cost with a loan origination fee and standard closing costs, and a borrower can easily spend $5,000 to borrow $279 a month for life. Why should a senior who owns his or her home free and clear have to pay for mortgage insurance? Unlike typical mortgage insurance that protects the lender if the borrower defaults, mortgage insurance on a reverse mortgage insures that the borrower (or the borrower's estate) will never owe more than the value of the home. That means other assets will never be used to repay the mortgage if the home's value turns out to be less than the loan balance. Today's reverse mortgage is a "nonrecourse" loan, and the mortgage insurance insures that component. However, unless there's an emergency, reverse mortgages should never be used for a short-term fix because of the loan costs. The term of the average reverse mortgage runs about 11 years.

DIFFERENT VARIETIES

There are three reverse mortgage products available to consumers in the United States and one product in Canada. In the United States, the most popular reverse mortgage is the federally insured FHA Home Equity Conversion Mortgage (HECM). The other major product is the Home Keeper reverse, developed in the mid-1990s by Fannie Mae. Financial Freedom Senior Funding Corporation offers a "jumbo" private reverse mortgage product, designed to accommodate seniors living in higher-priced homes. This is the Cash Account Plan. The HECM and Home Keeper products are available in every state, whereas Financial Freedom's product is offered in most states and the District of Columbia. In Canada, the reverse mortgage product offered nationwide is the Canadian Home Income Plan (CHIP).

Reverse mortgages require that all prior loans and liens must be paid off so that the reverse mortgage loan is in "first place," or in first lien position. Many times, the proceeds from the reverse mortgage can pay off the underlying loans. A person does not have to own the home "free and clear" to obtain a reverse mortgage.

SOME SENIORS ARE NOT CANDIDATES

Who should not, or cannot, get a reverse mortgage? For homeowners over age 62 with considerable assets other than the equity in their home or for those people whose goal is to leave all of the equity in their home to their children, reverse mortgage costs may not make sense. It also depends on the borrowing philosophy and need of funds of the homeowner. Sometimes there is not enough equity in the home to merit the cost of the loan. Or if taking money out of the home, especially after it's completely paid off, is adverse to one's investment philosophy, it's unlikely even an attractive program would alter that mind-set. However, before cashing in your stock, paying the capital gains tax, and handing the remainder to the kids for the down payment on their first home or other expenditures, take a peek at using the reverse mortgage as an alternative financing plan. Once a stock is cashed, it's gone. Some of the costs of the reverse mortgage and funds extended to the kids could be recovered in future appreciation as you remain in the home.

The goal of many GI generation members was to have their home completely paid off by the time they retired. They lived through the Great Depression and were trained to never leverage an asset unless absolutely necessary. Folks who had to take out a second mortgage usually were in dire straights. Now, this dim view of borrowing has changed with a rise in home values, lower interest rates, and the desire on the part of homeowners to do more in their later years.

There are also some absolute "need" households today where the cost to the homeowner of obtaining a reverse mortgage is not the most critical factor. What price do you assign to relieving the anxiety of a maxed-out credit card? How do you quantify the ability to purchase needed medications?

You cannot predict when you are going to die, but you can make an educated guess at how long you will stay in your home. Unless you are in a desperate situation and really need cash, it probably will not make sense to obtain a reverse mortgage if you are going to stay less than four years. That's because of the fees involved. If you plan to stay longer, and a growing number of people plan to do so, the reverse mortgage could be a viable option.

APPRECIATION FACTOR COULD BE HUGE

Potential reverse mortgage borrowers often underestimate the amount of appreciation they accumulate during the term of the reverse mortgage. Three-bedroom, two-bath homes containing 2,250 square feet in Las Vegas were selling for $185,000 in 2000 yet are back on the market in 2005 at $345,000—and heading higher. Although these soaring home prices are the biggest challenge to first-time buyers in this country, the increased values could be a boon to seniors who couldn't care less how much their home is now worth because they simply want to stay in it. By pulling out some of the newfound equity, seniors can live more comfortably while leaving much of the home's value to their estate, usually their children. Some of these people, needing to pay bills and wanting to help a grandchild with college tuition, are saying, "Kids, we intend to leave you the $185,000 the home was worth in 2000, but we'd like to spend the difference." By spending it via a reverse mortgage, seniors continue the potential for home appreciation, thereby offsetting the amount they spend.

The average price for a U.S. home increased 13.4 percent from the second quarter of 2004 through the second quarter of 2005, according to the Office of Federal Housing Enterprise Oversight. The four years leading up to 2004 had similar numbers. If you consider the astonishing appreciation in three of the four states that contain the most persons over the age of 65 in the United States—California, Florida, and New York—and compare the recent appreciation rates to the numbers used to calculate the future value on the nation's most popular reverse mortgage, a huge difference surfaces. That's because the standard appreciation index used on the FHA HECM remained at 4 percent. It has not changed. Granted, one year does not make a cycle, but the annual leaps in home values stated above are not unprecedented. Even if home appreciation slows considerably in the states with the greatest senior population, the amount of money remaining after utilizing a reverse mortgage would be far greater than the HECM estimates.

"He's so fat with equity it makes me sick."

SAMPLE OF THE LUMP-SUM OPTION

Let's suppose Tom Tuttle lost his job as a commercial painter and had little income, but his home, worth $150,000, was completely paid off. He did not want to relocate and eventually wanted to leave "something" to his one son, Fred. Tom, age 64, took out a reverse mortgage and was eligible to get $83,100 in one lump sum. After closing costs of $7,800 and servicing fee set-aside costs of $4,887, he was handed a lump-sum payment of $70,412 that he used to purchase painting equipment and a new truck. After ten years, Tom had a booming painting business and had plenty of cash in the bank to buy a new home with a swimming pool. He decided to retire and sell the business. Over the past ten years, some of the homes in Tom's area increased 12 percent a year, but his home increased 10 percent a year. Tom sold the home for its fair market value of $311,845 and paid off the loan balance of $158,471, leaving $153,374 to Fred—more than the value of the home when Tom was in desperate straights ten years earlier. Tom also made no mortgage payments for ten years. The amount of equity that Tom could borrow at the start of the loan nearly doubled over the ten-year term.

FEES CAN BE EXPENSIVE FOR SHORT-TERM LOANS

Were the loan fees expensive? Absolutely. In the first two years they would have cost 10.32 percent had Tom sold the home. In fact, the fees would have been even higher had Tom not chosen a lump-sum payout at the beginning. If Tom had selected monthly checks for life, his fees during the first one to two years of the loan would have been 59.51 percent. That's because Tom's $432.16 monthly check totals only contributed $14,096 to the loan balance. When you factor up-front fees of $7,800, Tom had better stay in the home a long time to make those monthly payments worthwhile. On the lump-sum program, however, Tom's total annual loan cost after the ten-year period was 5.71 percent. Was Tom's home appreciation rate too high to be realistic? Perhaps, but the expected interest rate, 6.25 percent, was also calculated at a higher than normal level. The intangible variable was Tom's need to begin work on his own and buy the painting equipment and new truck. How do you assign an interest rate, or loan fee, when there is no other way out? Plus, he left a considerable amount of money to Fred, again showing that seniors can spend all, or part, of their home's future appreciation and still leave the kids an inheritance from the home sale. The table in Figure 12.1 shows the difference a few percentage points in appreciation can make.

FIGURE 12.1 *Federal Housing Administration*

Home Equity Conversion Mortgage (HECM)
Amortization Schedule—Annual Projections

Borrower Name/Case	Tom Tuttle—Total Draw		Refinance: No
Age of Youngest Borrower:	64	Initial Property Value:	$150,000
Expected Interest Rate:	6.250%	Beg. Mortgage Balance:	$78,212
Maximum Claim Amount:	$150,000	Initial Line of Credit:	$0.00
Initial Principal Limit:	$83,100	Monthly Payment:	$0.00
Initial Draw:	$70,412.06	Monthly Servicing Fee:	$30.00
Financed Closing Costs:	$7,800		

NOTE: Actual interest charges and property value projections may vary from amounts shown. Available credit will be less than projected if funds withdrawn from line of credit.

		Annual Totals				End of Year				
Year	Age	SVC Fee	Payment	MIP	Interest	Loan Bal.	Line of Credit	Prin. Limit	Property Value @4%	Property Value @8%
1	64	$360	0	404	$5,055	$84,031	0	$88,886	$156,000	$156,000
2	65	360	0	434	5,430	90,255	0	95,075	162,240	168,480
3	66	360	0	466	5,831	96,913	0	101,694	168,729	181,958
4	67	360	0	501	6,260	104,034	0	108,775	175,478	196,515
5	68	360	0	538	6,720	111,651	0	116,349	182,497	212,236
6	69	360	0	577	7,211	119,799	0	124,450	189,797	229,215
7	70	360	0	619	7,736	128,514	0	133,115	197,389	247,552
8	71	360	0	664	8,298	137,835	0	142,384	205,285	267,357
9	72	360	0	712	8,899	147,806	0	152,298	213,496	288,745
10	73	360	0	763	9,542	158,471	0	162,902	222,036	311,845
11	74	360	0	818	10,229	169,878	0	174,245	230,918	336,792
12	75	360	0	877	10,965	182,080	0	186,377	240,154	363,736
13	76	360	0	940	11,751	195,131	0	199,354	249,761	392,835
14	77	360	0	1,007	12,593	209,091	0	213,235	259,751	424,261

FIGURE 12.1 *Federal Housing Administration (continued)*

Total Annual Loan Cost Rate				
Appreciation Rate (%)	Disclosure Period (Years)			
	2	10	20	28
0%	10.32%	5.70%	3.48%	2.47%
4	10.32	5.70	5.08	4.88
8	10.32	5.70	5.08	4.88

While the housing market has set record levels for sales activity in every year from 1996 to 2005, it will undoubtedly slow. That frenetic pace cannot be expected to continue indefinitely because the housing industry runs in cycles and interest rates fluctuate. But experts don't see any huge chuckholes in the road for home appreciation. There are simply no major negative indicators on the horizon.

Dr. James F. Smith, a professor of finance at the Kenan-Flagler Business School at the University of North Carolina at Chapel Hill, has been one of the country's top forecasters of interest rates and housing markets. In 2003, Smith believes the country entered a period similar to the one we experienced from 1953 to 1965 when productivity was relatively high and inflation was never considered a major factor.

"Housing values will continue strong because of the number of people who really want to buy a home," Smith said. "You have to understand the huge immigrant population that will help to drive the housing ladder. You might see a couple of time blips, but housing will absolutely remain strong and continue to gain in value. It would take a horrible spike in inflation for interest rates to throw the housing markets out of sync. I really don't see that happening. You've got every bank in this country trying to stamp out or keep inflation low."

Real estate prices don't crash like stocks do when the bull runs out of steam. Home prices move up and down but within a lesser range than stocks. And in most markets in this country, homes will be worth considerably more 11 years down the road, which is the length of the average reverse mortgage.

The amount of cash proceeds received in a reverse mortgage is based on a formula using age, home value, location, and interest rates as factors. Let's take a quick look at how each affects the amount borrowed:

- *Rate.* The lower the interest rate, the larger the reverse mortgage. This is because a current variable-rate interest benchmark is used to determine the initial size of a reverse mortgage. Because interest rates have been historically low since 2000, the combination of low rates and high home values made it an optimal time for seniors to obtain or refinance a reverse mortgage. The ability to get larger reverse mortgages recedes when interest rates rise.

- *Age.* The older the borrower at the time the reverse mortgage closes, the larger the share of home equity the borrower can borrow against. This is because remaining life expectancy decreases with age. The younger the borrower, the larger the percentage of home equity that is reserved to ensure future payment of the accrued interest on the loan. In the case of a couple seeking an HECM, the loan size is based on the age of the younger borrower.

- *Appraised value.* The higher the value of the home, the more a senior can borrow.

- *Location (HECM only).* The FHA single-family loan limit for the particular area where the home is located affects the size of the reverse mortgage that a borrower can get. The FHA loan limit varies by county and typically changes annually in an attempt to keep pace with rising home prices. Loan ceilings are lower for nonmetropolitan and rural areas and higher for higher-priced metropolitan areas. Some counties have FHA limits between these two extremes. However, once the value of a home exceeds the FHA loan limit for the area, the size of the HECM can't get any larger. What would significantly improve the product is a single national limit, enabling homeowners with expensive homes in low-cost regions the ability to tap as much equity as those in high-cost areas of the country. The ability to borrow should not be curtailed by geographic location.

- One common misperception of prospective borrowers is that they can qualify for a reverse mortgage equal to or close in size to the value of their home, or at least the local FHA loan limit. This isn't the case. The actual loan amount will be equal to a smaller amount than these two figures (but still a substantial fraction of the home's value) to ensure that there will likely be sufficient equity left in the home when the loan comes due and ensure full repayment.

RULE OF THUMB FOR LOAN AMOUNT

A very rough rule of thumb to estimate your maximum reverse mortgage loan amount is to use your age, minus five years, as the percentage you can take from your net equity. For example, if you are a 75-year-old person with a $200,000 home owned free and clear in a midexpense area of the country, the maximum reverse mortgage line of credit you could expect to receive would be $137,000 before closing costs (70 percent of $200,000 is roughly $137,000). And because of the complex formula of most of the reverse mortgage products, Mom and Dad probably will be unable to tap all of the equity in the family home anyway.

The size of a reverse mortgage is also affected by the type of loan chosen. In addition to the HECM, which accounted for 90 percent to 95 percent of all reverse mortgages made in 2004, there are two other reverse mortgage products (which were touched on briefly earlier in this chapter). One is the Fannie Mae Home Keeper loan, available in every state. The other is the Cash Account Plan, a proprietary "jumbo" reverse mortgage product developed by Financial Freedom Senior Funding Corporation of Irvine, California. Available in a majority of states, the Cash Account is usually taken out on more expensive homes because it permits a much larger reverse mortgage than the HECM or Home Keeper. The borrower has several choices on how to take out the funds from a reverse mortgage. The proceeds can be taken as a lump sum, a line of credit, a fixed monthly payment, or a combination (see Figure 12.2 for an example). For most lines of credit, an added benefit is that the unused amount of the line of credit grows automatically each year based on a formula. In some cases, the credit line grows at a rate half a percentage point higher than the interest rate on the loan.

Here is a capsule of the three programs for a $200,000 home that is owned free and clear. Financial Freedom's Cash Account is more suitable for more expensive homes. While there are many reverse mortgage calculators available on the Internet, one of the better ones can be accessed at http://www.financialfreedom.com. Click on "How Much Money Can You Get?" and then follow the steps and enter the basic information requested. The calculator will provide you with the amounts you can expect from the major programs and their options. Where you live is critical to the FHA HECM product.

Figure 12.2

Ms. Edith Frank, Age 75 Redmond, WA 98052	REVERSE MORTGAGE PROGRAMS		
Home Value: $200,000	**FHA/HUD HECM**	**Fannie Mae Home Keeper**	**Financial Freedom Cash Account**
CASH AVAILABLE Cash Available	$122,528	$73,808	$58,324
Monthly Income Available	$822	$638	N/A
or LINE OF CREDIT Credit line Available	$122,528	$73,808	$58,324
Annualized Growth Rate	4.12%	N/A	$5.00%
Credit Line Value in 5 Years	$149,904	$73,808	$74,438
Credit Line Value in 10 Years	$183,389	$73,808	$95,004
or ANY COMBINATION OF THE ABOVE For example: 50 percent cash, 25 percent monthly check, 25 percent line of credit.			

Source: Financial Freedom Senior Funding

Remember, seniors can "outlive" the value of their home without being forced to move. The homeowner cannot be displaced and forced to sell the home to pay off the mortgage, even if the principal balance grows to exceed the value of the property. If the value of the house exceeds what is owed at the time of the homeowner's death, the rest goes to the estate.

Let's look at the standard costs for the most popular reverse mortgage products. Many of the same costs that a borrower pays to obtain a home purchase loan or to refinance an existing mortgage also apply to reverse mortgages. You can expect to be charged an origination fee, upfront mortgage insurance premium (for the FHA HECM), an appraisal fee, and certain other standard closing costs. In most cases, these fees and costs are capped and may be financed as part of the reverse mortgage. Some proprietary loans have no fees but require the homeowner to take most of the amount of the reverse mortgage at closing.

MORTGAGE INSURANCE PREMIUM

The most confusing fee involved in a reverse mortgage is the mortgage insurance premium. Seniors are usually flabbergasted when they find the amount is 2 percent of the appraised value of their home or maximum claim value, whichever is less. (This up-front insurance is waived only if all of the loan is used to pay for long-term care insurance.) There is also an ongoing annual premium equal to 0.5 percent of the loan balance. Unlike typical mortgage insurance that protects the lender if the borrower defaults, mortgage insurance on a reverse mortgage ensures the borrower (or the borrower's estate) will never owe more than the value of the home. That means other assets will never be used to repay the mortgage if the home's value turns out to be less than the loan balance. That's why the new reverse mortgages are known as "nonrecourse loans."

ORIGINATION FEE

The origination fee covers a lender's operating expenses—including office overhead, marketing costs, and so on—for making the reverse mortgage. Under the HECM program, the origination fee is equal to the greater of $2,000 or 2 percent of the maximum claim amount (i.e., county FHA loan limit).

APPRAISAL FEE

An appraiser is responsible for assigning a current market value to each home that's used as collateral for a reverse mortgage. Appraisal fees generally range between $300 and $400. In addition to placing a value on the home, an appraiser must also make sure there are no major structural defects, such as a bad foundation, leaky roof, or termite damage. Federal regulations mandate that a senior's home be structurally sound and comply with all home safety codes in order for the reverse mortgage to be made. If the appraiser uncovers property defects that require repair, the borrower must hire a contractor to complete the repairs. Once the repairs are done, the same appraiser is paid for a second visit to make sure the repairs have been completed. The cost of the repairs may be financed in the loan and completed after the reverse mortgage is made. Appraisers generally charge $50 to $75 for the follow-up examination.

SERVICING SET-ASIDE

The servicing set-aside is an amount of money deducted from the available loan limit at closing to cover the projected costs of servicing the borrower's reverse mortgage account. The servicing set-aside is a calculation and not a charge. The only amount added to the loan balance is the monthly servicing fee, which ranges from $30 to $35. Federal regulations allow the loan servicer (which may or may not be the same company as the originating lender) to charge the $30 to $35 monthly fee.

TOTAL ANNUAL LOAN COST

Much like the annual percentage rate (APR) charged on "forward" loans, lenders are required to provide consumers considering a reverse mortgage with a total annual loan cost (TALC) statement. This is a single rate that would include all costs and generate the total amount projected to be owed on the loan at a future time when it is applied to all the cash advances the borrower will receive (not including any advances used to finance loan costs). Because this total annual average rate will vary with future changes in the home's value over time, the statute specified that TALC rates should be disclosed for "not less than three projected appreciation rates and not less than three credit transaction periods."

As Figure 12.3 shows, the costs of a reverse mortgage are very high if the homeowner moves out during the early years of the loan.

The cost of any reverse mortgage loan depends on how long you keep the loan and how much your house appreciates in value. Generally, the longer you keep a reverse mortgage, the lower the total annual loan cost rate will be. Figure 12.3 shows the estimated cost of your reverse mortgage loan expressed as an annual rate. It illustrates the cost for

Figure 12.3

Federal Housing Administration **Home Equity Conversion Mortgage (HECM) Program**	
TOTAL ANNUAL LOAN COST RATE	

Borrower Name/Case Number: **Edith Frank**	Line of Credit
LOAN TERMS	MONTHLY LOAN CHARGES
Age of Youngest Borrower: 63	Mo. Servicing Fee: $30
Appraised Property Value: $150,000	Mortgage Insurance: 0.5% annually
Initial Interest Rate: $3.570% Monthly Advance: $0.00 Initial $0.00 Line of Credit: $69,059.0 Length of Term: 4 TENURE	OTHER CHARGES: Shared Appreciation: None

INITIAL LOAN CHARGES
     Closing Cost: $4,800
     Mortgage Insurance
        Premium: $3,000
     Annuity Cost: None
	REPAYMENT LIMITS
	     Net proceeds estimated at
	     93% of projected home sale

Total Annual Loan Cost Rate	

Appreciation Rate (%)	Disclosure Period (Years)			
	2	10	20	28
0%	16.15%	6.71%	5.65%	4.93%
4	16.15	6.71	5.65	4.93
8	16.15	6.71	5.65	4.93

your age, your life expectancy, and 1.4 times that life expectancy. The table also shows the cost of the loan, assuming the value of your home appreciates at three different rates: 0 percent, 4 percent, and 8 percent. The total annual cost rates in this table are based on the total charges associated with this loan. These charges typically include principal, interest, closing costs, mortgage insurance premiums, annuity costs, and servicing costs (but not disposition costs, which are the costs incurred when you sell the home). The rates in the table are estimates. Your actual costs may differ if, for example, the amount of your loan advances varies or the interest rate on your mortgage changes. You may receive projections of loan balances from counselors or lenders that are based on an expected average mortgage rate that differs from the initial interest rate.

OTHER CLOSING COSTS

Other closing costs that are commonly charged to a reverse mortgage borrower include the following:

- *Credit report fee.* Verifies any federal tax liens or other judgments handed down against the borrower. Cost: Generally under $20
- *Flood certification fee.* Determines whether the property is located on a federally designated flood plane. Cost: Generally under $20
- *Escrow, settlement, or closing fee.* Generally includes a title search and various other required closing services. Cost: $150 to $450
- *Document preparation fee.* Fee charged to prepare the final closing documents, including the mortgage note and other recordable items. Cost: $75 to $150
- *Recording fee.* Fee charged to record the mortgage lien with the county recorder's office. Cost: $50 to $100
- *Courier fee.* Covers the cost of any overnight mailing of documents between the lender and the title company or loan investor. Cost: Generally under $50
- *Title insurance.* Insurance that protects the lender (lender's policy) or the buyer (owner's policy) against any loss arising from disputes over ownership of a property. Varies by size of the loan, though, in general, the larger the loan amount, the higher the cost of the title insurance.
- *Pest inspection.* Determines whether the home is infested with any wood-destroying organisms, such as termites. Cost: Generally under $100
- *Survey.* Determines the official boundaries of the property. It's typically ordered to make sure that any adjoining property has not inadvertently encroached on the reverse mortgage borrower's property. Cost: Generally under $250

In a traditional, "forward" mortgage, the borrower starts with little equity in the home and a large loan balance. The reverse mortgage's big picture begins the opposite way—the equity portion makes up most of the home's value and the debt portion, if any, is very small. The reverse mortgage borrower receives money from the equity in his or her home in the form of a line of credit, monthly check, lump sum, or a combination of the above. Because there are no monthly payments required on the reverse mortgage, the loan balance increases as funds are received and interest accrues on the loan balance. Therefore, the loan balance increases and the equity in the home decreases during the term of the reverse mortgage. The line of credit is different in that interest is not charged until the funds are actually used. The borrower's remaining credit line grows over time.

"This is what I believe to be the remarkable feature of the reverse mortgage," said Richard Garrigan, professor emeritus of finance at Chicago's DePaul University. "No other mortgage that I know allows this type of growth in a line of credit. It's going to make a lot of people feel better about paying the fees to obtain the reverse mortgage."

The interest rate on the reverse mortgage is determined either at the time of application or at the time the loan closes, whichever is lower. There are interest rate ceilings, or "caps," on how much the interest rate can increase. The net amount of equity in the home spent during the term of a reverse mortgage eventually will be determined by the fluctuation of the interest rate, length of the loan term, appreciation gained, and the spending habits of the borrower. A change in interest rate does not affect the amount of, or the number of, loan advances a borrower receives, but it does cause the loan balance to grow at a faster rate or slower rate. Homes in extremely popular markets could see a majority of the reverse mortgage funds spent replaced by appreciation, whereas homes in flat or depreciating markets would have little, if any, equity remaining after the reverse mortgage is settled. Under no circumstances would the borrower, or the estate, owe more than the value of the home when the borrower moves out of the home. This is what is known as a "nonrecourse loan."

TAX RAMIFICATIONS

The interest that has accrued on the reverse mortgage is not deductible until paid. Remember, the homeowner makes no payments during the term of the reverse mortgage. Therefore, the homeowner usually deducts the accrued interest in the tax year that the homeowner moves out, sells, or refinances the home. If the homeowner dies before the reverse mortgage debt is settled, the interest deduction will be a "Deduction in Respect of a Decedent" and will be treated by the estate or someone who receives the house outside of probate in the same manner as it would have in the hands of the decedent. Because the home is part of the estate, it gets a new "stepped-up" basis equal to fair market value at the time of the homeowner's death. Therefore, its sale usually does not produce a taxable gain.

The timing of the sale of the home and subsequent tax deduction from the reverse mortgage can also be important to consumers. For example, if a senior takes a rather large draw from an ordinary individual retirement account (IRA), the home could be sold in the same year to help offset the taxable income from the IRA. The mortgage interest deduction from the reverse mortgage could help reduce or eliminate the possibility of paying income tax on the IRA.

That total equity in the home is often underestimated in its amount, especially for the generations that are now snapping up second homes for recreation, investment, and retirement, and who will soon reach the traditional retirement age. Dr. Sung Won Sohn, executive vice president and chief economic officer for Wells Fargo Bank, said a greater than expected percentage of wealth in the United States could soon be consolidated into one home.

"The equity in the typical second home often is greater than the assets people have in securities, like stocks and bonds," said Sohn, who once worked with former Federal Reserve Chairman Alan Greenspan and was a senior economist on the president's Council of Economic Advisors. "If you consider a typical Boomer-age homeowner has about $120,000 of equity in the primary home, there is often about $60,000 in a second home."

Sohn believes that when a consumer eventually occupies his or her last home, there's a good chance those equity stakes could be combined—giving the senior greater equity in one place. For example, a senior could move into the investment, recreation, or retirement home he's had for years, making it the primary residence. He then could sell the longtime family home, pocketing up to $500,000 tax free of gain

($250,000 for a single person), making a significant sum of cash available to pay off any mortgage debt on the place he now calls home.

In this chapter, we introduced the concept of a reverse mortgage to help finance future years. The money from a reverse mortgage can be used for any reason, but it will be needed most to enable seniors to age in place. In the next chapter, we will expand on the use of equity. Some consumers wish to have it all in one place, whereas others prefer to be leveraged and have small amounts of equity in a great number of places.

13

CONTINUE TO BORROW, PAY IT OFF, OR CASH IT IN?

Different strategies cater to evolving lifestyles

Protecting or enhancing assets produces different ideas for different people. Some folks would prefer to pay off their home as soon as possible, especially if the balance of the loan is tiny compared to the original amount, whereas others choose to take every additional dime and sock it into a slam-dunk investment they see escalating faster than the value of their home. In this chapter, we consider some of the basic fundamentals for protecting your nest egg, while also considering a few others that are home centered yet produce additional income and enjoyment.

REDUCING YOUR HOME LOAN OFFERS GUARANTEED RATE OF RETURN

There are thousands of homeowners who subscribe to a pay-it-off philosophy when it comes to home loans. They believe there are huge benefits—financial and philosophical—to owning the roof over your head. When that roof now covers your office, as it does for millions of small business owners across the country, isn't there an extra incentive to make a bigger dent in the domestic debt load as we get older? Many financial planners will tell you folks simply don't focus on stashing away retirement dollars until the loan on the family home is paid in full. With the cost of living, coupled with monthly mortgage payments, where do you gather extra cash to be used down the road? It's a sound, logical idea that average consumers should never invest money they can't afford to lose. Folks who take the monthly grocery money and plunk it down on a stock tip they overheard at the coffee shop usually are making a huge mistake.

According to Jack Guttentag, professor emeritus of finance at the Wharton School of the University of Pennsylvania, consumers should view the yield of principal prepayments on their mortgage as equal to the interest rate on their loan—as long as there is no prepayment penalty included in the loan. Hence, if you are paying 6 percent on your loan, prepaying your mortgage would make more sense than tossing any extra cash into a savings account paying 2 percent to 3 percent interest. Guttentag also believes that if the yield on mortgage repayment is being compared to the yield on other taxable investments, it doesn't matter whether yield is measured before tax or after tax (tax-exempt bonds could be an exception).

My pay-it-off philosophy is now consistently laden with potholes. My four children have needed school-related cash—even in public education—so the reality of funding anything more than our annual contribution to an individual retirement account (IRA) is out of the question for the near future. However, down the road there might be a time when discipline and peace of mind begin to play larger roles. For example, would I sleep better at night knowing that I am taking a bigger chunk out of the home loan mountain rather than making a few more percentage points in other markets? Or is the guaranteed return from prepaying the mortgage absolutely no longer acceptable given the potential of stocks, bonds, and other investments? The factors that always need to be weighed are risk, comfort, and discipline. Would I have the discipline to actually invest additional cash instead of paying off the mortgage? How would I feel if a sure-bet stock went bust, blowing not only my hard-earned extra dollars but also the chance of reducing the number of years on my home loan?

Remember, you can save a ton of mortgage interest by prepaying your loan. In fact, if you make an extra payment on the principal portion each month, you can reduce the loan term of a 30-year loan by approximately 12 years. Conversely, by prepaying the loan, you also lose a piece of your mortgage interest deduction. Your actual savings is computed with your marginal tax rate and your mortgage interest rate. Are you one to dig in, do the research, and then work the numbers with a broker or handle the transactions yourself? The real challenge for the average consumer is having the discipline to carry out the challenge. Remember that the biggest mistake common investors make is overestimating net returns over the long term. If you already have investments and feel paying off your home loan would help you "diversify," there are several home loan acceleration computer programs that show you the cost-effectiveness of various options in the mortgage market. Guttentag's site (http://www.mtgprofessor.com) offers several excellent calculators, as does Smartmoney.com.

KEEP YOUR CASH AND USE A VA LOAN FOR YOUR NEXT PURCHASE

The tremendous growth of the housing market is being pushed along by the lower than expected long-term interest rates and the idea that real estate is a wise investment. In addition, consumers are more reluctant to plow their hard-earned cash into the inconsistent conventional financial markets and now are buying an additional piece of real estate sooner in their life. Some of these properties will eventually become retirement homes where seniors and aging Baby Boomers will spend most of their time. Why not purchase one with the help of a VA loan that features a no-money-down option and allows you to keep the cash from the sale of your present home in other investments? Although federal regulations require that all loans insured by the U.S. Department of Veterans Affairs (VA) be used only to acquire a "primary residence," it is possible to purchase your next home using your VA loan guarantee even if it was used on a previous purchase. This could be a boon to the GI generation and other former active military and reservists who believe their VA loan guarantee is "once used then gone." If your original VA loan was paid off, you are eligible to use the guarantee again. If you purchased a previous home with a VA loan and the buyer assumed your loan, your eligibility can be restored only when the assumer has paid off the loan. The only other alternative would be if the assumer is an eligible veteran who is willing to swap his or her available eligibility for yours.

"The law was not intended to help people enter the business of real estate to purchase lots of homes," said Chris Michel, a former naval reservist and founder and president of military.com, an Internet site targeting present and former military personnel and their families. "The law was written to help people afford the home that they are going to occupy. A VA loan can most definitely help purchase that next home or retirement home. It's hoped that, in their retirement years, people are spending most of their time in what was their vacation home."

As in many cases involving the use of real estate, the definition of primary residence is the place you live "most of the year." So if you use the home more than six months of the year, it can be defined as your primary residence. For example, let's say you are getting ready to retire (or can work from a home anywhere) and want to buy a home in Arizona to escape the wetter months of the year in the Portland, Oregon area. However, you also wish to dodge the sizzling desert summers, so the plan is to use the Arizona home October through April. That seven-month period would constitute the largest block of time you live in any one place. Therefore, your new home in Arizona would qualify as your primary residence. The VA requires that you move into the home in a reasonable amount of time and that you keep it as your primary residence. If those are your intentions at the time you apply for the loan, then there is nothing to keep you from using your VA guarantee to purchase a second home or retirement property.

On January 1, 2005, the VA loan guarantee increased to $89,913, and the maximum loan amount was raised to $359,650. The critical requirements for eligibility are an honorable discharge, an eligibility certificate, and the ability to make the loan payments. All VA loans have a funding fee; a borrower's first VA loan fee is 2 percent of the loan. That 2 percent is reduced to 1.2 percent if the borrower puts down more than a 10 percent down payment.

Some seniors and aging Boomers still don't know that reservists are eligible for VA programs. After 50 years of offering loans only to vets who served active duty, the VA changed its ways in 1992. Men and women who have completed six years in the Army, Navy, Air Force, Marine Corps, or Coast Guard Reserves, or the Army National Guard or Air National Guard, are eligible for VA home loans, including no-down-payment programs. In addition, reservists who were called up to active duty after August 1990 and served 90 days continuously on active recall are eligible for VA loans and other benefits. This provision was inserted to help the thousands of men and women who were pressed into service during Operation Enduring Freedom and Operation Iraqi Freedom.

SUBPRIME LOANS DO HAVE THEIR PLACE

Young, first-time homebuyers with little or no funds for a down payment are not the only consumers chasing or protecting the dream of home ownership. Older folks have dreams, too, and some of them include starting over in new areas, with new partners, and perhaps with a new part-time job. These people understand the huge upside of home appreciation and have adopted the mind-set of doing what it takes "to just get in the door" of a home and begin accruing equity. Their backgrounds do not fit seamlessly into the conventional lending bracket, known as "conforming" mortgages, and they are forced to pay high rates and fees brought by the subprime market. If savings is not the challenge, then there are often issues with monthly income cash flow or poor credit.

For example, an elderly couple on fixed incomes (Fred Bartow was in his early 70s, and Mary Eldred had just turned 68) recently married. They had no significant funds for a down payment yet wanted to buy a home in a rapidly appreciating area of North Carolina before home prices got out of sight. They did not want a long-term loan with a high interest rate, so they found a program with a two-year, fixed-rate loan at approximately 3.5 percentage points greater than the 30-year fixed rate. However, that loan allowed the couple to refinance to a lower rate in 24 months after they had built up equity and their monthly income improved. Two years later, even though they still had some credit issues, they refinanced into a long-term, fixed-rate loan very close to the prevailing market rate.

For many borrowers, there is nothing "sub" about subprime. It is simply their only way to purchase a home. What often gives the subprime loan industry a bad name is the lenders chasing down-and-out consumers with open-ended deals with astronomical rates and fees. Some of these loans include hooks that keep the customer in the mortgage for years. A good example was the $484 million settlement reached between Illinois-based Household International and the attorneys general in all 50 states in 2004 to settle several pending lawsuits involving alleged predatory lending practices.

The mortgage game is all about risk and return. Conforming lenders typically abide by the terms and conditions set by the secondary market. A lender will often give a borrower a certain amount of leeway—such as higher debt to income ratios—especially if the lender is keeping the loan. However, many lenders will not stray far from the norm, allowing the lender the flexibility of selling the loan down the road. Lenders, especially those dealing in the subprime market, have been damaged by unscrupulous players who have taken advantage of borrowers unfamiliar with the mortgage process. These borrowers, usually seniors and immigrants, have qualified for better rates and fees than they actually received but simply did not understand what they were signing. Bait-and-switch stories often surface, and language challenges also have been a problem.

For example, a lender often would offer a credit-poor borrower a higher-than-market "rate reduction loan" to consolidate the first mortgage and outstanding consumer (credit card) debt, stating the borrower could not qualify for a better rate because of a blemished credit history. Later in the process, the lender would surface and inform the borrower that the house did not appraise at an amount large enough to justify the loan. The lender would then grant the borrower a second mortgage—sometimes at an interest rate greater than 20 percent.

When applying for a loan, ask friends and neighbors about which companies they would recommend. Conforming or nonconforming, some places are better to work with than others.

WATCH OUT, RETIREES: BOOMERS HAVE HEADED INTO RV WORLD

Mary Jo and Richard McCord sold their home in Belleville, Illinois, a few miles across the Mississippi River southeast of St. Louis, and bought a large recreational vehicle (RV) that now serves as their primary residence. The original idea was to use the portable home to visit college towns during football weekends in the fall, but it evolved into a year-round unit that they park for several months of the year just outside of Tempe, Arizona, near Arizona State University. The facility has a pool, large recreation and meeting rooms, and is close to a golf course.

"We like to travel and usually spend a few weeks in Hawaii every year," said Mary Jo, 66. "We'd also like to go back to Europe a few more times before my knees get really bad, and we didn't want to have all of our money tied up in our house. If we want to visit our kids for an extended period and don't want to drive the RV, we just rent a furnished apartment near them."

According to the IRS, all homes must have basic sleeping, cooking, and toilet accommodations. Virtually all RV types—motor homes, van campers, travel trailers, truck campers, and even some folding camping trailers—are equipped with these facilities. In a capsule, an RV combines transportation and temporary living quarters for travel, recreation, and weekend games. The two main categories are motor homes (motorized) and towables (towed behind the family car, van, or pickup). Types of towable RVs are folding camping trailers, truck campers, conventional travel trailers, and fifth-wheel travel trailers. And, there's a reason you are now seeing more of them on summer roadways, at autumn football tailgate parties, and at winter ski overnight parking areas. Nearly 1 in 12 U.S. vehicle-owning households (approximately 7.2 million) now own an RV, according to a 2001 University of Michigan study commissioned by the Recreation Vehicle Industry Association (RVIA). And—hold on to your reading glasses—more RVs are now owned by Baby Boomers (35- to 54-year-olds) than any other group, according to the University of Michigan study. RVIA reports today's typical RV owner is 49 years old, married, and has an annual household income of $56,000. Nearly 10 percent of those 55 and over own an RV, slightly exceeding the 8.9 percent ownership rates of 35- to 54-year-olds.

The prices for RVs are all over the board. Some of the larger motor homes easily crack the $100,000 plateau, whereas some used, folding camping trailers can be purchased for less than $5,000. In addition, lenders are viewing RV buyers as reliable borrowers. Less than 2 percent of all RV loans are delinquent, RVIA says, sparking lenders to extend RV loan terms and thus making monthly payments more affordable. Loan terms for new, large RVs typically range from 10 to 12 years, with some lenders willing to extend to 20 years. However, homes are real property and recreational vehicles are personal property, so interest rates typically will be higher on RVs. Even though many dealers offer their own in-house financing, RV loans can be obtained from credit unions, banks, savings and loans, and finance companies. According to RVIA, a majority of RV lenders require less than a 20 percent down payment, and some are willing to accept less than 10 percent down.

And there can be an investment side to an RV purchase. Depending on the time of year and area, dealers and rental outlets generally charge between $70 to $170 a day for motor homes and from $50 to $120 a day for truck campers and travel trailers. Individuals who personally rent out their units typically charge less. RVs can be exchanged much like rental homes in a Section 1031 exchange.

MORE BOATS AS HOMES

Even though RVs have been extremely popular for decades, the boat and yacht component is really on the upswing in coastal marinas and inland bays and rivers. A huge boat boom has occurred in the Southwest because Mexico has found a way to further promote its sunshine and tourism by appealing to watercraft enthusiasts. An example of a boater taking full advantage of a boat as a home is Mark McShane. McShane, born and raised in Missoula, Montana, received one-third of the proceeds of his family's longtime summer home on Flathead Lake when his parents' estate was settled several years ago. McShane, 63 and now divorced, purchased a small cabin cruiser that he moors at the lake in the summer and trailers to Mexico in the winter. It qualifies as a home because it has a small galley, bathroom (also called a 'head'), and handheld shower. He owns no conventional home and relies on his computer and the Internet to edit and index small books outsourced from a large publishing house.

CONSIDER SWAPPING YOUR HOME FOR ANOTHER . . . AND FOR CASH

Mary Deakers, 59, was flush with air miles—but not cash—and desperately needed some sunshine. The San Francisco area–based software engineer had just completed a complex project for a longtime friend and client—one of those jobs that somehow stretched into a 90-day assignment instead of the anticipated 45. The idea of spending some winter days in warm tropical sun already was mending her frayed edges.

The plan? Trading homes with a woman in the Canary Islands who had been accepted to study dance at an exclusive San Francisco academy. Deakers would cash her air miles for a flight to London, then on to Santa Cruz de la Palma on the island La Palma. The lush, tropical island, which many European vacationers believe to be their best-kept getaway secret, is often compared to the Hawaiian Island of Kauai (without the humidity) and often is confused with the city of Las Palmas on Grand Canary Island and the island Palma de Mallorca in the Mediterranean. In addition, Deakers would receive $250 a month as an incentive from the dancer who desperately sought Deakers's location.

Home exchanges historically have involved staying in other people's home while they stay in yours—sometimes using each other's cars and boats. Exchange services have been around for decades, but the appeal of the cost savings has recently been augmented by an aging population's desire for the comforts—and safety—of home during extended travel time. Thanks to the increasing popularity and acceptance of the Internet, home swaps in all areas of the country are easier to organize and execute, especially for last-minute single people who do not have to worry about academic calendars or youth sports tournaments.

Representatives from three of the biggest online home-trading companies—Intervac, HomeLink, and HomeExchange.com—say the swap business has also been pushed along by retirees who seek a comfortable alternative to the same old condo in the sun that they have been visiting every year. Costs for home-swap memberships vary depending on the number of pictures you provide and other services you require. Hermosa Beach, California–based HomeExchange.com charges $49.95 for the first year, yet the second year is free if you don't find a match during your first 12 months.

When you join a home-exchange facilitator, you are asked to provide details about your home, your contact information, and your preferred swap locations and available dates. You then gain the same information from other members, allowing you to initiate deals with potential swap partners. Once you've found a match through e-mails and phone calls, make sure you cover the small details. For example, if a car is involved, it's common to make a written agreement on the terms of its use, such as mileage and responsibility for repairs and damages. Many exchange companies have such agreements on their Web site. Similar detailed agreements are also advised for the use of a house and its contents, covering computer equipment, long-distance calls, utility bills, replacement of cooking staples, and other housekeeping matters. Be clear on smoking (especially with Europeans) and pet issues.

Exchange companies suggest locking one room, or cabinet, as "off limits," and storing certain items away. And it's best to check with your insurance company to see what your coverage is in case of an accident.

HOME SHARING: COMPANIONSHIP ALSO BRINGS INCOME

Sometimes, especially after the loss of a spouse, older folks are forced to sell their longtime home and seek less expensive housing. Others find ways of making ends meet—and satisfy their need for human connection at the same time. It's a far cry from the rigors of running a bed-and-breakfast, yet interesting and reliable boarders often come knocking.

Louise Shumacher, 79, is one of the more active and independent members of a senior services home-sharing program, sponsored by the

United Way in several pilot regions of the country. Like many retirees, she participates primarily for extra help with monthly expenses plus the occasional ride to the store or help in the yard. Home sharing is an intergenerational program. In the pilot programs now being tested, one person in the match must be 55 years old or older. All parties must undergo a background check, and home seekers must provide three long-term references. For example, the Seattle program was started 20 years ago and currently has 65 matches in place with a variety of combinations. The process usually takes several weeks to solidify a compatible match, though sometimes it can be very fast. It also has been a lifesaver for older people who really want to stay in their home—or retain a feel of home in another's residence. In Louise's case, for example, it took only one interview to determine some very clear preferences: She enjoys quiet types, free thinkers, and people who spend little time in her kitchen. Her first tenant lasted six months.

The amount of rent charged is up to the homeowner, but the average renter usually pays about $350 to $375 per month. The tenant can reduce that amount by doing household chores, yard work, or running errands for $10 an hour. Not all of the landlords are seniors; some are first-time homebuyers providing shelter for people 55 and older.

BASIC HOME EQUITY LOAN COULD BE A SHORT-TERM SOLUTION

If a senior is not going to occupy a residence for a long period yet still has the income to repay a debt, a basic home equity line of credit could be the answer. The "low documentation" or "no documentation" loans typically are reserved for consumers with obvious monthly incomes. But lenders are more focused on assets than income, and when the asset being leveraged is a single-family home or condominium, the risk of any lenders losing money quickly becomes remote.

A reverse mortgage can really be viewed as a home equity loan without a payment, but both programs tap the built-up cash present in a primary residence. However, conventional home equity loans usually carry no origination fee, and often the lender pays for the appraisal if one is even required. Similar to a reverse mortgage line of credit, no interest is charged on the home equity loan until it is actually used. Most home equity loans do not grow over time as reverse mortgage lines of credit do; yet the up-front fees on the reverse mortgage are far greater. If you do decide to proceed with a home equity loan line of credit, make sure you have some sort of exit strategy—perhaps selling the home in five years and buying "down." If you don't plan carefully, you could find yourself with no money, no place to go, and a fat mortgage payment.

RESEARCH PROPERTY TAXES BEFORE YOU SELL

If you are selling your home as a way to pay property taxes, first check with the county or local senior center about property tax reductions and deferrals. Most states have done a decent job of providing the individual county assessors the ability to reduce or defer property taxes for senior citizens and disabled persons. The amount reduced or deferred is made up when the senior eventually sells the house. These programs usually exempt eligible taxpayers from all excess levies and may exempt a portion of regular levies on a primary residence. Common excess levies are approved by the voters and typically include school construction bonds and maintenance of operation levies.

Income limits and age minimums vary, but let's consider a typical situation in some states. Typically, for a reduced tax, you must be 61 years of age on December 31 of the year of application or unable to work because of a physical disability. In addition, your household income must be $28,000 or less in the year before application. For a deferral of property taxes, you must be 60 years of age with a gross household income of less than $34,000. All sources of income must be reported for yourself, your spouse, and all cotenants. Hundreds of counties now have their own Internet home page, and most now have a common-form address to ascertain assessed values, maps, ordinances, covenants, and countless consumer tips. In some counties, consumers only need a street address to access a variety of information about the property, including information collected by the county assessor's office, a history of sales, and how-to information about tax deferrals and reductions.

LOCAL LOANS PAID UPON HOME SALE

Many jurisdictions have their version of senior home services, a home repair and remodeling service that allows seniors to use funds only on their primary residence. These funds do not require payment until the senior moves out of the home. Some of these loans have a low fee or no fee at all. The homeowner typically receives the cash in a lump-sum payment, and interest accrues on the amount until it is repaid. Local senior centers, libraries, and housing agencies often are a good place to start a search for these loans, sometimes referred to as "deferred payment loans." There usually are income and age guidelines, and some loans are only available in urban areas. Loans sometimes can be "forgiven" if a homeowner remains in the house for a specific amount of time. If you need extra cash only for a home repair, it's a good idea to ask around for deferred payment loans at the senior center.

INQUIRE ABOUT SUPPLEMENTAL SOCIAL SECURITY

According to the American Association of Retired Persons, many citizens age 65 and older who are eligible for monthly cash benefits from Supplemental Security Income (SSI) are not getting them. Income ceilings change regularly, but let's try an example. To qualify for SSI in 2003, your liquid resources (cash and savings) had be less than $2,000 ($3,000 for a couple). Certain resources, such as a home, a small burial fund, or one car, usually do not count. Income ceilings were capped at a monthly amount of $572 ($849 for a couple). If you have a job, those incomes can vary.

BORROWING AGAINST A STOCK OR OTHER ASSET

Stock brokerages and other financial firms often offer borrowers the chance to "pledge" stock as collateral, thereby "borrowing" up to 100 percent of the current value of the stock without cashing it. Because all securities fluctuate, the securities pledged also must have "cushioned" market value of 130 percent of the pledged amount. This program looks great—as long as the stock holds its value. If, for instance, you "pledge" Costco stock and the warehouse shopping company's share value plummets, you will need to add to the pledge account. If you fail to back up your account with more assets, the securities in the pledge account could be cashed to cure the debt. You could also be liable for capital gains tax ramifications on the sale of the stock.

In this chapter, we took a look at some of the alternatives to buying and borrowing and possible strategies for directing cash to other forms of housing. In the next chapter, we will consider capital gains and other rules that continue to be prime influences on real estate decisions for aging homebuyers.

14

TAX RULES ON PROPERTY FAVOR CONSUMERS

Take time to explore the possibilities and ramifications

Although the mortgage interest deduction on first and second homes is a huge incentive for Americans to buy homes, it should not be the only driving force. Older, conventional homeowners often prefer to pay off their home loans, regardless of the benefits of the mortgage interest deduction or the possibility of investing funds earmarked for the home's principal and interest, taxes, and insurance (also known as PITI). Taxes are critical to all real estate, and most federal laws and guidelines passed down since 1997 have favored the consumer. In this chapter, we consider some of the tax ramifications of your next move and also clarify some of the misunderstood basics that have caused seniors and aging Baby Boomers anxiety and a great deal of confusion.

The entire residential real estate landscape improved for the better with the signing of the Taxpayer Relief Act of 1997 on August 5, 1997. The new law changed not only the $125,000, one-time home sale exclusion for persons over 55 but also the "rollover replacement rule." In essence, the home began to move from the "shelter" column into the "financial portfolio" column. Under the old law, a taxpayer could defer any gain on the sale of a principal residence by buying or building a home of equal or greater value within 24 months of the sale of the first home. Tax on the gain was not eliminated but merely "rolled over" into the new residence. If you sold a primary residence and failed to meet the requirements for deferral, you faced a tax on current and previously deferred gain. The old law also contained a once-in-a-lifetime, $125,000 exclusion ($62,500 if single, or married and filing a separate return) of gain from the sale of the primary residence. The intent of the new tax code, which replaces the "rollover" provision and $125,000 over-55 exclusion, is to allow most homeowners to sell their primary residence without tax. It also dramatically simplifies recordkeeping for many people. Although it's still wise to retain proof of the original cost of the home and significant improvements, tedious collection and retention of invoices and other records to substantiate the cost of home improvements probably won't be necessary.

Although some homes in the heartland of the United States had not appreciated at the rate of coastal areas such as San Francisco, Boston, New York, Miami, and San Diego, the one-time, over-55 $125,000 exclusion was absolutely in need of a makeover. Before 1997, the tax-free amount was last raised—to $125,000 from $100,000—on July 20, 1981, which resulted in 16 years of absolutely constant benefit while some homes had tripled in value during the same time. The exclusion, which had jumped from $20,000 to $35,000 in 1976, then to $100,000 in late 1978, was terribly out of date and had not kept pace with inflation. Homeowners, especially retired folks, needed more incentive to be mortgage free. The one-time, over-55 exemption was becoming more of a one-time problem. "Buying down" had begun to carry the connotation of "losing out."

$500,000 EXCLUSION EVERY TWO YEARS

Many taxpayers, including seniors who had already used the one-time, over-55 $125,000 exclusion, did not initially realize that they were eligible to sell their primary home again—and do it every two years—under the Taxpayer Relief Act of 1997. Now, married couples can exclude $500,000 of gain ($250,000 for single persons) on the sale of a primary residence every two years. Theoretically, a couple could move every two years and live off of their equity if they happen to buy in appreciating markets. Some older buyers, with their children moved away and no critical responsibility tethering them to a particular place, are doing just that.

For example, Mark and Diana Schmitz sold their home near Minneapolis, Minnesota, pocketed $275,000 of gain (of a possible $500,000), and moved to Phoenix. They plan to stay two to three years, wait for their home to appreciate, pocket the gain, and move to Santa Fe, New Mexico. From there, they plan to pocket the gain again and buy a waterfront home on the west side of the Sea of Cortez in Baja, Mexico. The cash they make on their homes will be earmarked for everyday living expenses, including groceries.

Here are the keys to one of the best ways the average homeowner can now accumulate more wealth for retirement and an explanation of why the home has become the largest piece in the average taxpayer's financial puzzle.

In order to qualify for the $500,000 exclusion ($250,000 for single persons), you must have owned and used the property as your principal residence for two out of five years prior to the date of sale. Second, you must not have used this same exclusion in the two-year period prior to the sale. So the only limit on the number of times a taxpayer can claim this exclusion is once in any two-year period. What is often misunderstood is that both the earlier one-time exclusion of up to $125,000 in gain for persons over 55 and the deferral of all or part of a gain by purchasing a qualifying replacement residence are now gone. You no longer can combine parts of either portion, and you absolutely do not have to buy a replacement home. Persons who used the $125,000 can make use of the new exclusion if they meet the two-year residency test. The law enables seniors and all homeowners to "buy down" to less expensive homes without tax penalties.

For gains greater than the exemption amounts, a 15 percent capital gains tax usually will apply.[1] If your profits are less than the exemption amounts, you probably will not have to keep tax records and account for the profits at tax time. Homeowners with potential gains larger than the excludable amounts should keep accurate records in an attempt to reduce their gains by the amount of all eligible improvements.

To qualify for the full exclusion, either married spouse can meet the ownership requirement, but both must meet the use requirement. Although exclusion can be used only once in each two-year period, a partial exclusion may be available if the sale results from a change in place of employment or health, or unforeseen circumstances. If you have owned the house less than two years, you would receive a proportional amount of the maximum exclusion under special situations. For example, if you owned a home for one year and made a $65,000 profit, the entire $65,000 would be tax free because your total exclusion was chopped in half to $125,000 from $250,000 because of the one-year time frame. Consumers can turn vacation homes (plus yachts and recreational vehicles) into principal residences simply by meeting the residency requirements. Divorced or separated spouses are also not out in the cold. If an "ex" lived in the home for two of the five years before the sale, that person is able to use the exclusion. However, nothing changes on the loss side of the primary home sale ledger—losses on the sale of the primary home still are not deductible (discussed later). If a nondeductible loss seems unavoidable, it might be a good idea to convert the house to a rental property (where losses are deductible), but you would have to be able to prove the move was not just to avoid taxes. If depreciation were claimed on a property, the maximum capital gains tax liability would be 25 percent to the extent depreciation was claimed.

For married taxpayers who file a joint return, only one spouse need meet the two-out-of-five-year ownership requirement, but both spouses must meet the two-out-of-five-year use requirement. That is, if the husband has owned and used the house as his principal residence for two of the past five years, but his wife did not use the house as her principal residence for the required two years, then the exclusion is only $250,000.

For those who leave their home because of a disability, a special rule makes it easier to meet the two-year requirement, especially if you were hospitalized or had to spend a significant period in a similar facility. In such cases, if you owned and used the home as a principal residence for at least one of the five years preceding the sale, then you are treated as having used it as your principal residence while you are in a facility that is licensed to care for people in your condition. This rule enables the family to sell the home to raise cash for the expenses without incurring a large tax bite.

DON'T PENCIL IN HOME SALE LOSS

Most homeowners are now clear on the ability to pocket up to $500,000 of tax-free capital gain ($250,000 for single people) on the sale of a primary residence. Although most families do not move every two years, the tax-free possibility does exist for folks who may face a job transfer or for others who simply wish to take advantage of rapidly appreciating markets. However, the tax law that provided the new capital help did nothing for capital losses. There still is no benefit for people who made expensive remodels, then had to sell in a hurry and actually got less for their home than the cash they have invested in it. Long-term capital expenditures usually pay off over time but huge changes for the short term are difficult to recover.

For example, Barbara Bradford made significant home modifications to her residence in Houston, Texas, to enable her mother to age in place. Her mother died shortly after the remodel and then Barbara was transferred to Charlotte, North Carolina. The net sales price was less than the total amount invested in the home, but Barbara could not deduct the loss. If you are hoping for some help, don't count on chalking up a capital loss as a big, fat tax deduction. There still is no deduction for a capital loss on the sale of your primary residence. This often causes confusion and provokes questions from consumers, but Uncle Sam will not let you show a loss if you sell for an amount less than the purchase price.

Why? The principal residence has always been viewed as a personal asset. The gain on the sale of a principal residence has been taxable as a capital gain but losses have never been allowed. Although the capital gain thresholds have been increased, proposals to address capital losses have been defeated. The confusion surfaced again a few years ago when several parts of the "Contract with America" included tax law changes. A proposal to allow tax deductions for losses on the sale of a principal residence was part of that package but did not make the cut. Although home values are rising in most regions of the country, some have been flat. In addition, more than a few potential homebuyers get emotionally carried away when bidding for a home. In some cases—especially where there are multiple offers—the offer can exceed the actual fair market value. In a flat market, it could take years to recover an overbid mistake. Those buyers often must move again before the market catches up.

The original capital loss proposal stemmed from complaints from homeowners in the Sun Belt and New England who said they were left with huge losses and no federal tax help when home values plunged during the 1990s—especially when the declining oil industry in Texas really shook the housing market around Houston.

USE AN INVESTMENT PROPERTY TO BUY YOUR NEXT HOME

One of the more talked about subjects for small real estate investors is the tax-deferred exchange. You hear the term "1031 exchange" or "Starker exchange" from business associates, friends at the ball game, and even parishioners after church.

In an exchange, you must trade an interest in real estate (sole ownership, joint tenancy, tenancy in common) that you have held for trade, business, or investment purposes for another "like-kind" interest in real estate. The like-kind definition is very broad. You can dispose of and acquire any interest in real property other than a home or a second residence. For example, you can trade raw land for income property, a rental house for a multiplex, or a rental house for a retail property. A house that is the owner's primary residence cannot be traded for investment property, but you can trade an investment property for another investment property that eventually becomes your home.

For example, let's assume you have one rental property near your local grocery store. You bought it years ago, fixed it up, and rented it out to the supermarket manager. One day, the supermarket manager is transferred, and you no longer want to deal with rents and renters. You sell the home, buy an investment condo on a golf course in Palm Springs, California, and rent out the condo for two years to golfers from your hometown. Two years later, you tire of your job and move into the Palm Springs rental. You have deferred the gain on the grocery store rental and also paid no tax on the sale of your primary residence.

Stocks, bonds, securities, and similar equity investments do not qualify as "like kind." Likewise, if you own land and build a structure on it with 1031 exhange funds, the IRS will probably not consider your investment an exchange. This original process is called a 1031 Delayed Exchange or Starker Exchange. It is named after T.J. Starker, an Oregon man who made a deal with Crown Zellerbach in 1967 to exchange some of his forested property for some "suitable" future property. That agreement ended up in court. Starker's battle was the basis for congressional approval of delayed exchanges through the IRS.

Section 1031 of the Internal Revenue Code specifically requires that an exchange take place. The transaction will proceed just as a "sale" for you, your real estate professional, and parties associated with the deal. However, provided you closely follow the exchange rules, the IRS will "sanction" the transaction and allow you to characterize it as an exchange rather than as a sale. Thus, you are permitted to defer paying the capital gains tax. However, you need to adhere to a few specific guidelines. Those guidelines permit the title to the "new" property to be held by an independent third party (typically a facilitator or attorney) until the "old" property sale closes. There is a reverse exchange, where the new property is purchased before the old property sells, yet relatively few investors, however, have utilized the "reverse exchange".

To totally defer capital gains tax, you must pass the IRS acid test by

- trading even or up in value.
- trading even or up in equity.
- not pocketing any cash from the first sale (you will be taxed on any amount you take).
- identifying the new (or old) property or properties within 45 days of the sale. (Forms are available through a facilitator.)
- closing the transaction within 180 days.

If the taxpayer actually receives the proceeds from the disposition of the relinquished property, the transaction will be treated as a sale and not as an exchange. Even if the taxpayer does not *actually* receive the proceeds from the disposition of the property, the exchange will be disallowed if the taxpayer is considered to have "constructively" received them.

The code regulations provide that income, even though it is not actually reduced to a taxpayer's possession, is "constructively" received by the taxpayer if it is credited to his or her account, set apart for him or her, or otherwise made available so that he or she may draw upon it at any time.

The day you have to pay your capital gains tax will come eventually—unless you leave the property in an instrument like a charitable remainder trust (discussed in Chapter 15). So if you want to sell your investment property, you should weigh the costs of a like-kind exchange against the amount you would have to pay in capital gains tax if you simply sell the property. Professional facilitators charge about $1,300 to $1,500; private attorneys could cost more. To find a competent exchange facilitator in your area, consult a real estate professional, escrow agent, title company, or attorney for references. One may be able to help you do a like-kind exchange that allows your retirement nest egg to grow even bigger until the day you really need the cash.

NEW TAX TIME LINE FOR EXCHANGE PROPERTY RESIDENTS

Deep in the folds of the recently signed American Jobs Creation Act of 2004—the same law that will allow residents of the seven states that don't levy a state income tax to deduct sales taxes from their federal income tax in 2004 and 2005—is a subtle yet important change for homeowners who have acquired their principal residence via a tax-deferred exchange. The new law, signed by President George W. Bush while flying on Air Force One to a campaign appearance in Pennsylvania on October 22, 2004, includes a stipulation that the exchange property must be held for five years to qualify for the $500,000 ($250,000 for a single person) principal residence tax-free exemption.

To qualify for the $500,000 exclusion ($250,000 for single persons), homeowners must have owned and used the property as a principal residence for two out of five years prior to the date of sale. Second, the owner must not have used this same exclusion in the two-year period prior to the sale. So the only limit on the number of times a taxpayer can claim this exclusion is once in any two-year period.

The committee that drafted the section of the new law did not believe the principal residence exclusion "was appropriate for properties that were recently acquired in like-kind exchanges." Under the exchange rules, commonly known as 1031 exchanges or Starker exchanges, a taxpayer who exchanges property that was held for productive use or investment for like-kind property may acquire the replacement property on a tax-free basis. Because the replacement property generally has a low carryover tax basis, the taxpayer will have taxable gain on the sale of the replacement property.

However, when the homeowner converts the replacement property into a principal residence, the taxpayer may shelter some or all of this gain from income taxation. The committee believed that this proposal "balances the concerns associated with these provisions to reduce this tax shelter concern without unduly limiting the exclusion on sales or exchanges of principal residences."

Although the new "Five-Year Rule" is important—especially to people looking to move into a rental property that they have owned—it is not critical. That's because an investment property typically needs to be rented (used as an investment) after an exchange to show the exchange was clearly an investment-for-investment transaction. Accountants say the exchanged property should be held for at least two years as an investment property before an owner considers converting it to a primary residence. In addition, once the homeowners move into the new primary residence, they must stay at least two years before qualifying for the $500,000 exclusion.

When you add the suggested two years as investment property with the two years required under the residency guideline, that's four years minimum needed for the new mandatory Five-Year Rule.

For those who leave their home because of a disability, a special rule makes it easier to meet the two-year requirement—especially, for example, if you were hospitalized or had to spend a significant period in a similar facility. In such cases, if you owned and used the home as a principal residence for at least one of the five years preceding the sale, then you are treated as having used it as your principal residence while you are in a facility that is licensed to care for people in your condition. This rule, especially helpful for some seniors, enables the family to sell the home to raise cash for the expenses without incurring a large tax bite.

A tax-deferred exchange proceeds just as a "sale" for you, your real estate professional, and parties associated with the deal. In fact, Richard Morse, attorney at Washington Exchange Services, refers to exchanges as "legally sanctioned fiction." Section 1031 of the IRS code specifically requires that an exchange take place. That means that one property must be exchanged for another property rather than sold for cash. The exchange is what distinguishes a Section 1031 tax-deferred transaction from a sale and purchase. The exchange is created by using an intermediary (or exchange facilitator) and completing the required exchange documentation.

If you've traded for a golf course getaway condo and now think you would like to live there, make sure you own it for five years before attempting to pocket a principal residence exemption.

BUYING DOWN AND TAKING MONEY OUT OF YOUR FORMER RESIDENCE

In addition, on February 14, 2005, new guidelines were adopted that would allow investors who kept their home and used it as a rental property (under IRS Code 121) to eventually "buy down" and take cash out of the deal without facing federal income tax liability. This money, known as "boot" in tax circles, previously had come with a tax tag.

The new rule, which enables taxpayers to combine Code 121 with the popular Code 1031 for tax-deferred exchanges, is retroactive to January 27, 2005.

For example, let's say Betty Cooper bought a home in Dallas for $150,000 in 1990, raised her large family there, and then moved to Arizona in 2003 after her last child left home. She kept the large family home as a rental property, allowing members of her church to rent the place while they saved for a down payment for their own home. In 2005, when the church family bought its own home, Betty traded her home, now valued at $400,000 via a 1031 exchange, for an Arizona rental condo valued at $200,000 plus $200,000 in cash.

Betty owed no tax because she was able to receive her $250,000 exclusion of gain on the sale of her primary residence ($400,000 value minus $150,000 basis equals $250,000 gain exclusion) because she lived in the home two of the previous five years. However, before the new guidelines, Betty would have faced a tax liability for the amount of cash she put in her pocket ($200,000).

How does the new rule benefit consumers? For the first time, taxpayers are allowed to take tax-free cash out of a property exchange. It also can be a big help to homeowners who are confident their home is going to rapidly appreciate in the next few years and can afford to use their family home as a rental. The 2005 ruling addresses a combination of the above with the ability to pocket $250,000 of gain for a single person ($500,000 for a married couple) on the sale of a primary residence. To qualify for the exclusion, homeowners must have owned and used the property as a principal residence for two out of five years prior to the date of sale. Second, the owner must not have used this same exclusion in the two-year period prior to the sale. So the only limit on the number of times a taxpayer can claim this exclusion is once in any two-year period.

In this chapter, we examined tax consequences and guidelines on home sales. In our final chapter, we will consider how to handle the family home when it's time to move on. Should it go to the children or be put in a trust for a favorite charity?

15

THE FAMILY HOME, THE KIDS, AND TRUSTS

There are options other than selling and moving on

The kids were gone, but the couple did not want to move. She had her garden, weed free and rich in roses. His golf course was down the street where he drove his electric cart to meet the guys for coffee—even when the legs were simply too stiff to play nine holes. They could use some cash but didn't need a ton. Why not stay put and sell the family home to the kids? It might not be the best financial strategy, but it definitely can work if you stay within the proper guidelines.

In this chapter, we take a look at the possibilities of leaving a longtime home to the children in an estate and also the possibility of selling it to them while still protecting Mom and Dad. We'll also consider the important aspects of popular trusts, especially as an exit strategy for investments that have accrued years of appreciation.

My dad always planned to live in the family home with my mom until they both died. That way, the house would have gone into their estate and its value stepped up to the market value at the time of their death. That didn't happen. My dad had to go into a nursing home and Mom decided to sell. If your estate, including your stepped-home's value after you die, is less than the effective estate tax, your heirs will owe no estate tax. The kids can move in or sell it and keep the cash tax free.

DOMESTIC REVERSE MORTGAGE

Children can rent to their parents after buying the family home. It's an attractive alternative for folks who wish to stay put instead of moving to a small apartment or condominium. It's a sort of domestic reverse mortgage. The payments could be a boon to seniors whose only real asset is tied up in their home. Selling the family home to the kids can bring the same result, but be prepared to be probed, prodded, and picked on if you cut corners. Anytime you transact with a family member, Uncle Sam seems to roll over and take notice. Giving a complete stranger a deal is always acceptable, but attempt to give it to a family member and you're often paying dearly.

For example, Molly and Jack Kane sold their Idaho home to their children for $205,000. The kids had the home appraised, and comparable homes in the area had been selling for $194,000 to $215,000. The two kids, Marsha and Ken, put up $5,000 apiece for the $10,000 down payment, and the parents financed the balance of $195,000 on a deed of trust at 6 percent interest for 30 years. The children, as buyers, would owe $1,170 a month ($585 apiece) to the parents. The parents, as renters, initially paid $500 a month to the children. The children, however, selected a payment schedule that also benefited both sides. They decided to pay $1,500 so that they would pay off the loan faster and the parents would receive more tax-excluded income a month.

"We got audited because we were not charging fair-market rent," Marsha said. "So we had to double my parents' rent."

Still, the parents were taking in $500 more than they were paying out. And because of the $500,000 tax-free exclusion on capital gains for a married couple on the sale of a primary residence, the $10,000 down payment and all money paid toward the principal was tax free. Interest income is not excluded from taxable income. The main drawback now to keeping the home in the family is the astronomical price of homes in many popular areas and the inability of the kids to carry the negative cash flow every month brought by a huge mortgage. Plus a lot of retirees need all the proceeds from the home sale just to survive, leaving the children with more expensive conventional financing instead of having their parents "carrying the paper."

For example, the national median price of homes (half the homes sold for more, half for less) in July 2005 was $218,000, up 14 percent from 2004. In the West, that number jumped to $319,000 and with it narrowed the possibility of children saving for the larger down payment and high monthly payments—especially when the money was not going to the children's primary residence. Asking an adult child to plunk down up to $30,000 to $60,000 and pitch in big bucks every month is not easy, yet some, like the Kanes, view their investment as a terrific long-term play.

"I think I will eventually move there, add on a great space to the garage so the parents can have their own space and stay there for a long time," Marsha said. "Who knows . . . maybe our kids will do the same thing and the home will continue to be owned by family members."

KIDS AND YOUR ESTATE

Many senior and middle-aged homeowners are wondering how to handle the financial ramifications of the family home. Should they stay put, get a reverse mortgage, and let the kids divide up what might be left down the road? And, when the kids eventually get the house, will they have to pay tax on the remaining equity? What about cash from stocks and a life insurance policy? At first glance, estate tax rules may seem to apply only to the wealthy. Until recent tax changes were adopted, that was not necessarily the case. Rising values of homes brought the average homeowner serious estate tax consequences.

The Economic Growth and Tax Relief Reconciliation Act of 2001, signed into law by President George W. Bush on June 8, 2001, significantly changed estate taxes. Under current federal law, any U.S. citizen can pass on up to $2 million (in 2006) worth of property free of estate or gift taxes to anyone who is a U.S. citizen. This "passing" is not reserved only for children or immediate family members—it is available to all.

The $2 million federal figure is for the 2006 to 2008 tax years. The ceilings rise to $3.5 million in 2009 before reaching an unlimited amount in 2010. (For more information, consult the IRS's Publication 448, "Federal Estate and Gift Taxes." You can order the form by telephoning 800-TAX-FORM.) However, not all states have adopted the federal schedule. In some states, a taxable estate amount will be owed under the present system when the first spouse dies with what was a properly drafted will. Check with your tax advisor for details. The Tax-

payer Relief Act of 1997 started the effective transfer-tax exemption rolling at $600,000 for the 1997 tax year. The amount was increased to
$625,000 for 1998, $650,000 for 1999, $675,000 for 2000 to 2001,
$700,000 for 2002 to 2003, and then to $1.5 million for 2004 to 2005.

For married couples, there is no limit on the amount of property
one spouse can leave to another tax free. But a married couple, assuming all property is owned as community property, must have at least $4
million in assets (2006), including life insurance, before there is the possibility of a federal inheritance tax if they both exercise their exclusions.

The $2 million exemption is personal to each spouse. If he or she
dies leaving everything to the survivor outright, one of the $2 million
exemptions is wasted. That's because the survivor has only his or her
own exemption left to shelter assets at the time of his or her death (the
exemption at the first death can be protected by using a living will or
living trust, etc., and should be discussed with a professional planner or
attorney). For example, if a single mother dies this year and her estate is
worth less than $2 million when she dies, it will pass tax free to her chil-
dren. The federal government will "step up" the value of the house to
its market value at the time of her death—not its original purchase price.
If that value, plus any life insurance and other assets, is less than $2 mil-
lion, the kids will not owe any federal gift or estate tax (it's best to determine the value at death through a new appraisal).

"It makes sense now for people with large estates to investigate
trusts for their children," said Phil Egger, estate tax attorney based in
Bellevue, Washington. "We often underestimate how quickly assets can
appreciate. What you have today is probably going to be worth a lot
more tomorrow, yet people often don't take the time to handle it
properly."

Take the time to check with a tax attorney or an accountant before
setting up a trust. Be clear about your goals. Accountants say a transfer
to a trust could be treated as a taxable gift, unless the trust is treated as
wholly owned by the donor or the donor's spouse under the grantor
trust provisions of the Internal Revenue Code. This provision was included in the 2001 law to preclude individuals from attempting to shift
income for income tax purposes to lower income tax bracket individuals, thus avoiding gift taxes.

FAMILY GETAWAY IN A TRUST

Have the recent winters left you feeling "too old" to run up and inspect the family cabin? Is it time you made a decision on the future of the wonderful getaway that everybody loves but only you maintain? Two attractive options for keeping the family cabin in the family are an outright sale to the kids—the parents could even rent back from the kids if they choose—or placing the cabin in a Qualified Personal Residence Trust. Both can be beneficial depending on the parents' need for cash and the children's ability to pay. Unlike the couple's personal residence, the cabin will not escape a capital gains tax. If the place has greatly appreciated in value, a tax is almost certain even though most of it could be offset by capital improvements.

The actual gain is the difference between the adjusted sales price (selling price less selling expenses) and their adjusted basis. The adjusted basis is the original cost plus capital improvements. Capital improvements are the cost of improvements having a useful life of more than one year. Examples include the new roof, dock, deck, remodeled bathroom, and finished basement. Generally, an expense is a capital improvement if it adds value to the property or

extends its useful life. If these criteria are not met and the expenditure is considered necessary to maintain current usefulness, it is a maintenance cost.

Under the Qualified Personal Residence Trust (the cabin can be viewed as a second residence), you place the cabin in a trust for a specific period. You choose the term of the trust, for example 10 or 15 years. During that time, you continue to use it. If you survive the term, the cabin goes to the kids and your estate is reduced by the value of the cabin. If you die during the term of the trust, the cabin reverts back to your estate as if no trust were set up.

"I find a Qualified Personal Residence Trust works best for clients who need to reduce the size of their estate and have an heirloom-type property to pass along to the next generation," said Bob Pittman, attorney and radio talk show host. "The tricky—and sometimes delicate to discuss—part is guessing at a parent's life expectancy. The longer the term of the trust, the more you save in estate taxes. But you get a big zero for your efforts if the parent dies too soon."

The government has statistical tables based on age and life expectancy at the time the trust is made on the value of their right to use the cabin. If the kids acquire the cabin and then convert the family getaway to rental property—even temporarily—the rules change significantly. If the kids switch to a rental status, they should do so for periods of at least one year at a time. They would receive all the tax benefits of rental property, including depreciation. The way the individual families use the cabin could change, too. The IRS will not allow the children to show a taxable loss on the property if they personally use it for more than 14 days or 10 percent of the rental period. Personal use includes a rental to any relative unless you charge a fair-market rent.

Pittman said he often encourages families to write a "mission statement" for the family cabin. If a family works together on a mission statement, the chances of long-term success are much greater. Everyone in the family needs to feel they have contributed to and agreed on the elements of the mission statement. It then becomes something they will defend and pass along to succeeding generations, and the legacy of the parents is preserved.

TAKE TIME TO PONDER PROPERTY EXIT STRATEGY

Many people over 55 are small-time real estate players with one or two rental properties.

Very few, though, have explored the exit options available to them by conducting a little research or scheduling a few conversations with a real estate attorney, financial planner, or accountant. For example, many seniors choose to pay the tax on the sale of investment real estate rather than go through the process of a Section 1031 deferred exchange. While even tax-adverse consumers see the value of rolling all of their investment proceeds into the purchase of another investment property, the prevailing philosophy often is "I'll have to pay the tax sometime, so I might as well do it now." This exchange process, the Starker Exchange discussed previously, has two stringent requirements. To defer the gain, the taxpayer must identify another like-kind property within 45 days of the sale of the first property, then close the transaction within 180 days of the sale of the first property. What if you didn't want to go through the exchange process . . . perhaps for a second or third time? What if you found a vehicle that could produce income for you, eliminate the pressure and responsibilities of management, and the large chunk of cash that you would normally pay the IRS went to charity?

Consider a charitable remainder trust as an exit strategy for a real estate asset that may bring you a huge tax bite if simply sold outright. A gift to a charitable remainder trust, or CRT, can produce significant income and gift tax charitable deductions for the donor plus provide a terrific benefit to the hospital, university, relief fund, or senior shelter of your choice. There are thousands of charitable organizations in dire need of funds. According to Heidi Lantz, attorney and personal financial specialist in the Northwest law firm of Keller Rohrbach, a charitable remainder trust "is like giving away the tree yet keeping all the apples." A CRT can be viewed as an irrevocable trust where a portion of the trust's value is distributed each year to one or more individuals for life or for a specific term. At the end of the term when all the annual payments have been made, the designated charity has exclusive benefit of the property.

"The annual amount paid to the donor is the result of a complicated formula," Lantz said. "It involves actuarial tables similar to those used in life insurance. There are also minimum interest rate guidelines that apply once you determine the term of the trust or one's life expectancy."

CRTs come in a variety of packages. The most popular form is the charitable remainder unitrust, or CRUT, which must each year pay out to a "noncharitable beneficiary" (perhaps you, your wife, family, friend, etc.) a fixed percentage of at least 5 percent of the fair market value of the property. Additions to the trust can be made at any time. Because the value must be determined every year, the annual payments usually vary. There are special exceptions. Another commonly used form is the charitable remainder annuity trust, or CRAT, which provides for an annual payment to a "noncharitable beneficiary" of a fixed amount of at least 5 percent of the original value of the property transferred to the trust. Because the amount of the annual payout is fixed at the time the CRAT is created, no additions can be made to it.

"I believe that a charitable remainder trust is an excellent—and sometimes overlooked—exit from real estate," Pittman said. "When an owner has exchanged over the years and now just wants out of real estate, the CRT can be an excellent tool to convert to a lifetime income stream, saving capital gains tax and receiving a charitable tax deduction."

Pittman said any reluctance to go the CRT route rather than leave valuable property to the estate can be alleviated through an insurance policy.

"The kids can be made whole through a special estate planning life insurance policy held in an irrevocable life insurance trust," Pittman said. "The parents get more income, fewer headaches, and a tax deduction. Their favorite charity gets the remaining asset and the kids get the life insurance. Only Uncle Sam is left out."

OUTRIGHT GIFTS AND GIFT AND ESTATE TAX

If you are getting ready to move out of your longtime home and into the sunshine, you can actually gift your home to a child or friend, but that gift will come with a few strings attached. First and foremost, your child's or friend's basis in the house will be what you paid for the property plus major improvements. Because this cost you paid years ago is probably much lower than today's soaring home value, there's a chance tax will be owed on a subsequent sale. For example, if you purchased your home in 1970 for $60,000 and it is now worth $450,000, your child's basis would be $60,000 if you chose to transfer the home to the child as a gift. If the married child sells the home ten years down the road for $760,000, the tax liability would be on $200,000 ($760,000 minus the $60,000 basis, minus the $500,000 exclusion for married couples). Taxpayers in the 15 percent tax bracket would thus owe the IRS approximately $30,000 in capital gains tax.

The outright gift would also reduce your lifetime gift tax and estate tax exemptions. The limits on both the lifetime gift tax and estate tax used to be the same (there was one overall exemption, and the individual used it up by making gifts during life and at death), but the 2001 leg-

Figure 15.1 *Estate and Gift Tax Rates and Exemptions*

Year	Top Estate Tax Rate	Estate Tax Exemption	Top Gift Tax Rate	Gift Tax Exemption
2002	50%	$1 million	50%	$1 million
2003	49	$1 million	49	$1 million
2004	48	$1.5 million	48	$1 million
2005	47	$1.5 million	47	$1 million
2006	46	$2 million	46	$1 million
2007	45	$2 million	45	$1 million
2008	45	$2 million	45	$1 million
2009	45	$3.5 million	45	$1 million
2010	0	Repealed	35	$1 million
2011*	55	$1 million	35	$1 million

* Estate tax reform of 2001 stops in 2011. The law then reverts back to rules in place in 2001.

islation set the gift tax and estate tax on different roads beginning in 2004 (see Figure 15.1). Both were combined into a "unified" exemption because gifts made during life also counted against the total. The overall, or unified, exemption remains for the entire estate, but a gift exemption limits the amount that can be given during a lifetime.

Once the unified exemption is used up, the tax rates that apply are quite high. The estate tax is being phased out over a ten-year period, but the gift tax will remain in place. The gift tax exemption is $1 million in 2006, but the estate tax leaps to $2 million. In future years, the gift tax exemption will remain at $1 million, whereas the estate tax exemption rises until the estate tax is fully repealed in 2010. At that time, the top gift tax rate again will equal the top income tax rate.

If you are going to gift your home to an individual, it's best to offset the amount by first using your annual gift tax exclusion of $11,000 per gift. You can gift $11,000 (this amount will rise and is tied to inflation) to any one person in any year. Hence, if you and your spouse each make a gift to both your child and her spouse, you can offset $44,000 of the home's value. Then, as long as the home's net figure is less than $1 million, you won't owe any current tax (unless you made substantial gifts earlier that reduced your remaining exemption).

A FINAL WORD

In many countries around the world, once the parents die, the children simply move into the home and take over the master bedroom. Although that progression still occurs in the United States, estate taxes, rising home values, job transfers, and the desire for a separate space and different environment have changed the use of the traditional family home. The bottom line is that the home has evolved from basic shelter to the average person's most valuable possession. It needs to be carefully protected, guarded, and even nursed along—much like the responsibilities that took place within the home itself. And the financial value is usually accompanied by priceless memories and experiences, making the family home beyond doubt the ultimate asset.

The house in which I was raised was truly an amazing place. Not only did my parents own and occupy it for 46 years, but it also supplied countless memories for seven children now married with families of their own in other cities. The home's sale provided my mom a financial cushion for the next phase of her life. The sale also sparked many discussions of what other avenues could have been taken. Although other options may not have worked for my mom, they definitely will be brought out on the table when it comes time to make a decision about our present home and future years.

HELPFUL WEB SITES FOR ELDERS AND ADULT CHILDREN, ELDER LAW ATTORNEYS, REVERSE MORTGAGE LENDERS, CERTIFIED AGING IN PLACE BUILDERS AND REMODELERS

Helpful Web sites for Elders and Adult Children
National Sites

AARP
http://www.aarp.org/
Housing Options for Older People
http://www.aarp.org/confacts/housing/housingoptions.html

American Association of Homes and Services for the Aging
http://www.aahsa.org/
AAHSA
2519 Connecticut Avenue NW
Washington, DC 20008-1520
(202) 783-2242
Fax (202) 783-2255
The association represents 5,600 not-for-profit nursing homes, continuing care retirement communities, assisted living and senior housing facilities, and community service organizations.

The Eldercare Locator
http://www.eldercare.gov
800-677-1116
eldercare_locator@aoa.gov
The Eldercare Locator is a national toll-free (and online) directory assistance public service of the U.S. Administration on Aging that helps people locate aging services in every community throughout the United States.

Administration on Aging
http://www.aoa.gov/
One Massachusetts Ave. Stes
4100 & 5100
Washington, DC 20201
Phone: 202-619-0724
Requests for information about
aging issues and programs
should be directed to
aoainfo@aoa.gov

The American Society on Aging
http://www.asaging.org/cdc
The American Society on Aging
creates strategies and materials
to enhance the capacity of
national, state and local
organizations in serving the
health promotion and disease
prevention needs of older adults.
(800) 537-9728 ext. 613
nancyc@asaging.org

Fannie Mae
3900 Wisconsin Avenue NW
Washington, DC 20016-2892
(800) 7FANNIE
Email:
consumer_resources@fanniem
ae.com
http://www.fanniemae.com

Financial Freedom Senior
Funding
7595 Irvine Center Drive, Suite
250
Irvine, CA 92618
(888) REVERSE
Email:
sales@financialfreedom.com
http://www.financialfreedom.com

FirstGov for Seniors
http://www.seniors.gov/
FirstGov for Seniors website will
empower citizens to obtain
valuable health and security
information and services at one
location via the Internet.
FirstGov for Seniors is
maintained by SSA.

National Center for Home
Equity Conversion
360 N Robert, Suite 403
St. Paul, MN 55101
http://www.reverse.org

National Reverse Mortgage
Lenders Assn.
1625 Massachusetts Avenue
NW
Washington, DC 20036
(202) 939-1760
http://www.reversemortgage.org

Seattle Mortgage
601 108th Avenue NE, Suite 700
Bellevue, WA 98004
(800) 233-4601
http://www.seattlemortgage.com

SeniorNet
http://www.seniornet.org/php
121 Second St., 7th Floor
San Francisco, California 94105
415-495-4990
FAX: 415-495-3999
SeniorNet is a nonprofit
organization of computer-using
adults, age 50 and older using
technology to educate and
contribute to a better life.

Senior Housing, Incorporated
http://
www.seniorhousingdirectory.com/
2021 E. Hennepin Ave
Minneapolis, MN 55413
612-617-1025
Senior Housing, Incorporated
offers comprehensive
information on housing and
related services. Click on the
houses to learn more about
housing and services.
Email: shi@isd.net

Wells Fargo Home Mortgages
600 Northern Shores Lane
Greensboro, NC 27455-3441
(800) 543-5642
http://www.reversemortgages.net

National Academy of Elder Law Attorneys, Inc.
National representatives

Lawrence E. Davidow
Davidow, Davidow, Siegel &
Stern
One Suffolk Sq., Ste. 330
Islandia, NY 11749
(631) 234-3030
(631) 630-8846 (Fax)
ldavidow@davidowlaw.com

Donna R. Bashaw
Elder Law Center
23601 Moulton Pkwy., Ste. 220
Laguna Hills, CA 92653
(949) 454-2205
(949) 454-2670 (Fax)
dbeldrlaw@aol.com

G. Mark Shalloway, CELA
Shalloway & Shalloway, PA
1400 Centrepark Blvd., Ste. 700
West Palm Beach, FL 33401
(561) 686-6200
(561) 686-0303 (Fax)
mark@shalloway.com

Craig C. Reaves
Reaves Law Firm, PC
4400 Madison Ave.
Kansas City, MO 64111
(816) 756-2100
(816) 756-0333 (Fax)
craig@reaveslawfirm.com

Ruth A. Phelps, CELA
Phelps, Schwarz & Phelps
527 S. Lake Ave., Ste. 106
Pasadena, CA 91101
(626) 795-8844
(626) 795-9586 (Fax)
rphelps@elderlawyers.com

Stuart D. Zimring
Attorney at Law
12650 Riverside Dr., Ste 100
North Hollywood, CA 91607
(818) 755-4848
(818) 755-4853 (Fax)
zimzim@ElderlawLA.com

Laury A. Gelardi
National Academy of Elder Law
Attorneys
1604 North Country Club Road
Tucson, AZ 85716
(520) 881-4005
(cell phone 770-595-5566)
(520) 325-7925 (Fax)
In Atlanta: (770) 850-0015
(770) 984-8096 (Fax)
lgelardi@naela.com

Susan B. McMahon
National Academy of Elder Law
Attorneys
1604 North Country Club Road
Tucson, AZ 85716
(520) 881-4005
(520) 325-7925 (Fax)
smcmahon@naela.com

Deborah J. Barnett
National Academy of Elder Law
Attorneys
1604 North Country Club Road
Tucson, AZ 85716
(520) 881-4005
(520) 325-7925 (Fax)
dbarnett@naela.com

Edwin M. Boyer
Of Counsel to McConnaughhay,
Duffy
6010 Cattleridge Dr., Ste. 102
Sarasota, FL 34232
(941) 371-4373
(941) 955-6244 (Fax)
emboyer@mcconnaughhay.com

William J. Brisk
Law Office of William J. Brisk
1340 Centre Street, Ste. 205
Newton Center, MA 02459

(617) 244-4373
(617) 630-1990 (Fax)
billbrisk@briskelderlaw.com

Martha C. Brown
Oelbaum & Brown
12166 Old Big Bend, Ste. 99
Saint Louis, MO 63122
(314) 966-5030
(314) 966-5145 (Fax)
mcbrown@elderlawstlouis.com

Gregory S. French
Attorney at Law
1244 Paddock Hills Ave.
Cincinnati, OH 45229-1218
(513) 641-4692
(513) 242-5542 (Fax)
Gfrenchlaw@aol.com

Bradley J. Frigon
Law Offices of Bradley J. Frigon
6500 S Quebec St., Ste. 300
Englewood, CO 80111
720) 200-4025
(720) 200-4026 (Fax)
frigonlaw@qwest.net

Doris E. Hawks
Law Office of Doris E. Hawks
851 Fremont Ave., Ste. 102
Los Altos, CA 94024
(650) 949-4117
(650) 949-4161 (Fax)
dhawks@elderlawadvocate.com

Andrew H. Hook
Oast & Hook, PC
521 Middle St. Mall
Portsmouth, VA 23704
(757) 399-7506
(757) 397-1267 (Fax)
hook@oasthook.com

Barbara S. Hughes
Hill, Glowacki, et. al.
2010 Eastwood Dr., Ste. 301
Madison, WI 53704
(608) 244-1354
(608) 244-4018 (Fax)
bhughes@hill-law-firm.com

Michael F. Loring
Loring & Robinson
50 Cole Pkwy.
Scituate, MA 02066
(781) 545-2600
(781) 545-2695 (Fax)
loringtwo@aol.com

Kerry R. Peck
Peck, Bloom, Austriaco &
Mitchell, LLC
105 W Adams St., 31st Fl.
Chicago, IL 60603
(312) 201-0900
(312) 201-0803 (Fax)
kpeck@peckbloom.com

Stephen J. Silverberg
Certilman Balin, et. al.
90 Merrick Avenue
East Meadow, NY 11554
(516) 296-7044
(516) 908-9601 (Fax)
ssilverberg@certilmanbalin.com

Timothy L. Takacs
Elder Law Practice of Timothy
L. Takacs
201 Walton Ferry Rd.
Hendersonville, TN 37075
(615) 824-2571
(615) 824-8772 (Fax)
ttakacs@tn-elderlaw.com

Lauchlin T. Waldoch
Of Counsel to McConnaughhay,
Duffy, et. Al.
1709 Hermitage Boulevard,
Suite 200
Tallahassee, FL 32308
(850) 425-8182
(850) 222-9766 (Fax)
lwaldoch@mcconnaughhay.com

Wesley E. Wright
Wright Abshire, Attorneys
4949 Bissonnet
Bellaire, TX 77401
(713) 660-9595
(713) 660-8889 (Fax)
wes@wrightabshire.com

Edward E. Zetlin
Legal Services of Northern VA
6066 Leesburg Pike, Ste. 500
Falls Church, VA 22041
(703) 778-6818
(703) 778-4790 (Fax)
Zetlin@comcast.net

Brian W. Lindberg
Consumer Coalition for Quality
Health Care
1101 Vermont Ave., Ste. 1001
Washington, D.C. 20005
(202) 789-3606
(202) 898-2389 (Fax)
bwlind@erols.com

Hugh K. Webster
Webster, Chamberlin & Bean
1747 Pennsylvania Ave., NW
Washington, D.C. 20006
(202) 785-9500
(202) 835-0243 (Fax)
hwebster@wc-b.com

State representatives

Michael B. Cohen
Michael B. Cohen & Associates
700 N Pearl St., Ste. 1650, LB
314
Dallas, TX 75201
(214) 720-0102
Fax: (214) 754-0936
coeldlaw@flash.net

Wendy A. Craig
Wendy A. Craig, PA
204 E State St.
Black Mountain, NC   28711
(828) 669-0799
Fax: (828) 669-5978
wacraig@wncelderlaw.com

Amy Parise Delaney
DeLaney Law Offices
12416 S Harlem, Ste. 103
Palos Heights, IL 60463
(708) 361-8819
Fax: (708) 361-6103
amy@delaneylawoffices.com

Alice Reiter Feld
Law Office of Alice Reiter Feld
Cinnamon Tree Plaza, Ste. 260
5701 N Pine Island Rd.
Tamarac, FL 33321
(954) 726-6602
Fax: (954) 721-0910
reiterfeld@aol.com

Leigh Flynn
Law Office of Leigh Flynn
PO Box 165
Columbia, SC 29202
(803) 791-1991
leigh.flynn@scbar.org

Morris Klein
Attorney at Law
4550 Montgomery Ave.,
Ste. 601N
Bethesda, MD   20814
(301) 652-4462
Fax: (301) 652-1086
morrisklein@netzero.net

Michael F. Loring
Michael F. Loring & Associates
50 Cole Pkwy.
Scituate, MA 02066
(781) 545-2600
Fax: (781) 545-2695
loringtwo@aol.com

R. Shawn Majette
Thompson & McMullan, PC
100 Shockoe Slip, 3rd Fl.
Richmond, VA 23219
(804) 643-4145
Fax: (804) 644-4491
shawn.majette@verizon.net

Beth A McDaniel
Law Offices of Beth A.
McDaniel
15 S Grady Way, Ste. 249
Renton, WA 98055
(425) 227-8700
Fax: (425) 227-5414
bethmcdaniel@seanet.com

Timothy P. O'Sullivan
Foulston Siefkin, LLP
100 N Broadway, Ste. 700
Wichita, KS   67202-2295
(316) 267-6371
Fax: (316) 267-6345
tosullivan@foulston.com

Trudi S. Riley-Quinn
Law Office of Trudi S. Riley-Quinn
2390 Professional Dr.
Roseville, CA 95661
(916)782-8212
Fax: (916)782-8833
trudi@tsriley.com

Eugene Rosner
Fink Rosner Ershow-Levenberg, LLC
1093 Raritan Rd.
Clark, NJ   07066
(732) 382-6070
Fax: (732) 382-7986
gene@finkrosner.com

Vincent J. Russo
Vincent J. Russo & Associates, PC
1600 Stewart Ave., Ste. 300
Westbury, NY   11590-6615
(516) 683-1717
Fax: (516) 683-9393
vincent@russoelderlaw.com

Brian J. Sheppard
Attorney at Law
18075 Ventura Blvd., Ste. 109
Encino, CA 91316
(818) 342-5799
Fax: (818) 342-2470
bjsheppard@aol.com

R. L. Steenrod, Jr.
R.L. Steenrod, Jr. & Associates
2009 Market St.
Denver, CO   80205-2022
(303) 534-5100
Fax: (303) 534-5186
bsteenrod@steenrodlaw.com

Bridget O`Brien Swartz
Law Office of Bridget O'Brien Swartz, PLLC
706 N 44th St.
Phoenix, AZ   85018
(602) 955-7886
Fax: (602) 955-7784
bridget@azspecialneeds.com

Reginald H. Turnbull, CELA
Turnbull Law Office, PC
200 E High St.
Jefferson City, MO 65101
(573) 634-2910
Fax: (573) 634-7418
Ribull@aol.com

J. Gregory Wallace
Monroe, Wyne & Wallace, PA
3225 Blue Ridge Rd., Ste. 117
Raleigh, NC   27612
(919) 876-1400
Fax: (919) 876-1492
jgwallace@ncelderlaw.com

Reverse Mortgage Lenders—Home Keeper and Home Equity Conversion (HECM)

The following list, provided by the National Association of Reverse Mortgage Lenders, includes most of the U.S. lenders offering the Fannie Mae Home Keeper Mortgage and the FHA Home Equity Conversion Mortgage (HECM). Financial Freedom's "jumbo" products are available through its state representatives and "brokered" through many of the other lenders listed below.

Alabama
Financial Freedom Senior Funding Corp.
1-800-588-8044

Wells Fargo Home Mortgage
1-800-336-7359

Alaska
Financial Freedom Senior Funding Corp.
Regional Manager
1-888-REVERSE/1-888-738-3773

Seattle Mortgage Co.
1-800-233-4601

Wells Fargo Home Mortgage
1-800-336-7359

Arizona
Financial Freedom Senior Funding Corp.
1-888-997-9501

First Mortgage Corp.
1-888-608-5868 or
1-602-893-3600

Sun American Mortgage Co.
1-800-469-7383/1-602-832-4343

Wells Fargo Home Mortgage
1-800-336-7359

Arkansas
Financial Freedom Senior Funding Corp.
1-800-336-3135

Wells Fargo Home Mortgage
1-800-336-7359

California
Financial Freedom Senior Funding Corp.
Northern California: 1-800-423-4222
Southern California: 1-800-500-5150

Seattle Mortgage Co.
Northern California: 1-800-489-0986
Southern California: 1-800-656-4045

Wells Fargo Home Mortgage
1-800-336-7359

Colorado
Financial Freedom Senior Funding Corp.
Regional Manager
1-800-843-0480

Wells Fargo Home Mortgage
1-800-336-7359

Connecticut
Wells Fargo Home Mortgage
1-800-299-3135

Financial Freedom Senior
Funding Corp.
1-800-203-4667

Wells Fargo Home Mortgage
1-800-336-7359

Delaware
Financial Freedom Senior
Funding Corp.
1-800-368-3254

Wells Fargo Home Mortgage
1-800-336-7359

District of Columbia
Financial Freedom Senior
Funding Corp.
1-800-368-3254

Wells Fargo Home Mortgage
1-800-336-7359

Florida
Everhome Mortgage Co.
1-888-740-0221

Circle Mortgage Corp.
1-954-981-6800/1-800-576-1338

Financial Freedom Senior
Funding Corp.
1-800-588-8044

Seattle Mortgage Co. d.b.a.
Reverse Mortgages of Florida
1-888-435-7353

Wells Fargo Home Mortgage
1-800-931-3117

Georgia
Everhome Mortgage Co.
1-888-740-0221

Financial Freedom Senior
Funding Corp.
1-800-588-8044

Wells Fargo Home Mortgage
1-800-336-7359

Hawaii
Financial Freedom Senior
Funding Corp.
Regional Manager
1-888-REVERSE/1-888-738-3773

Seattle Mortgage Co., d.b.a.
Reverse Mortgages of Hawaii
1-877-893-1865

Wells Fargo Home Mortgage
1-800-336-7359

Idaho
Financial Freedom Senior
Funding Corp.
1-800-843-0480

Seattle Mortgage Co.
1-800-233-4601

Wells Fargo Home Mortgage
1-800-336-7359

Illinois
Everhome Mortgage Co.
1-888-350-8718

Comcor Mortgage Corp.
1-847-882-6240

Financial Freedom Senior
Funding Corp.
1-800-880-7740

Wells Fargo Home Mortgage
1-800-336-7359

Indiana
Everhome Mortgage Co.
1-888-350-8718

Financial Freedom Senior
Funding Corp.
1-800-860-6983

Wells Fargo Home Mortgage
1-800-336-7359

Iowa
Financial Freedom Senior
Funding Corp.
1-800-880-7740

Wells Fargo Home Mortgage
1-800-945-1700/1-515-273-5769

Kansas
Financial Freedom Senior
Funding Corp.
1-800-336-3135
1-800-798-3946

Wells Fargo Home Mortgage
1-800-336-7359

Kentucky
Financial Freedom Senior
Funding Corp.
1-800-860-6983

Wells Fargo Home Mortgage
1-800-336-7359

Louisiana
Financial Freedom Senior
Funding Corp.
1-800-336-3135

Hibernia National Bank
1-800-562-9007 ext. 35372

Standard Mortgage
1-800-448-4190 ext. 542

Wells Fargo Home Mortgage
1-800-336-7359

Maine
BNY Mortgage – A Bank of
New York Company
1-800-299-3135

Financial Freedom Senior
Funding Corp.
1-800-203-4667

Wells Fargo Home Mortgage
1-800-336-7359

Maryland
Financial Freedom Senior
Funding Corp.
1-800-368-3254

Wells Fargo Home Mortgage
1-800-336-7359

Massachusetts
BNY Mortgage Co. LLC
1-800-299-3135

Financial Freedom Senior
Funding Corp.
1-800-203-4667

Wells Fargo Home Mortgage
1-800-336-7359

Michigan
Everhome Mortgage Co.
1-888-350-8718

Financial Freedom Senior
Funding Corp.
1-800-860-6983

Seattle Mortgage Co., d.b.a.
Reverse Mortgages of Michigan
1-877-590-9648

Wells Fargo Home Mortgage
1-800-336-7359

Minnesota
Financial Freedom Senior
Funding Corp.
1-800-880-7740

Richfield Bank & Trust
1-612-798-3339

Seattle Mortgage Co. d.b.a.
Reverse Mortgages of
Minnesota
1-877-590-9648

Wells Fargo Home Mortgage
1-800-336-7359

Mississippi
Financial Freedom Senior
Funding Corp.
1-800-588-8044

Standard Mortgage
1-800-448-4190 ext. 542

Wells Fargo Home Mortgage
1-800-336-7359

Missouri
Financial Freedom Senior
Funding Corp.
1-800-336-3135

James B. Nutter & Company
1-800-798-3946

Wells Fargo Home Mortgage
1-800-336-7359

Montana
Financial Freedom Senior
Funding Corp.
1-888-REVERSE (1-888-738-
3773)

Intermountain
Mortgage Co.
1-406-252-2600 or 1-800-669-
5138

Seattle Mortgage Co.
1-800-233-4601

Wells Fargo Home Mortgage
1-800-336-7359

Nebraska
Financial Freedom Senior
Funding Corp.
Regional Manager
1-800-843-0480

Wells Fargo Home Mortgage
1-800-336-7359

Nevada
Financial Freedom Senior
Funding Corp.
Northern Nevada 1-800-423-4222
Southern Nevada 1-888-997-9501

National Pacific Mortgage
Corporation
1-818-787-7723

Seattle Mortgage Co. d.b.a.
Reverse Mortgages of Nevada
1-800-405-4539

Wells Fargo Home Mortgage
1-800-336-7359

New Hampshire
Financial Freedom Senior
Funding Corp.
1-800-203-4667

Wells Fargo Home Mortgage
1-800-336-7359

New Jersey
BNY Mortgage
1-800-269-6797

Cardinal Financial Co.
1-800-327-0969

FFinancial Freedom Senior
Funding Corp.
1-800-368-3254

Wells Fargo Home Mortgage
1-800-336-7359

New Mexico
Financial Freedom Senior
Funding Corp.
1-800-843-0480

Wells Fargo Home Mortgage
1-800-336-7359

New York
BNY MORTGAGE
1-800-269-6797

Concord Mortgage Corp.
1-877-795-1100 ext. 257

Financial Freedom Senior
Funding Corp.
1-800-203-4667

M&T Mortgage Corp.
1-800-461-7109

Southern Star Mortgage Corp.
1-516-712-4400

Wells Fargo Home Mortgage
1-800-336-7359

North Carolina
Everhome Mortgage Co.
1-888-850-5100

Centura Bank
1-800-879-5864

Financial Freedom Senior
Funding Corp.
1-800-588-8044

Wells Fargo Home Mortgage
1-800-336-7359

North Dakota
Financial Freedom Senior
Funding Corp.
1-800-880-7740

Wells Fargo Home Mortgage
1-800-336-7359

Ohio
Broadview Mortgage Co.
1-614-854-7045

Financial Freedom Senior
Funding Corp.
1-800-860-6983

Wells Fargo Home Mortgage
1-800-336-7359

Oklahoma
Financial Freedom Senior
Funding Corp.
1-800-336-3135

Seattle Mortgage Co., d.b.a.
Reverse Mortgages of
Oklahoma
1-866-329-3833

Wells Fargo Home Mortgage
1-800-336-7359

Oregon
Financial Freedom Senior
Funding Corp.
1-800-423-4222

Seattle Mortgage Co. d.b.a.
Reverse Mortgages of Oregon
1-888-271-7840

Wells Fargo Home Mortgage
1-503-585-8082 or 1-888-275-
8082

Pennsylvania
Cardinal Financial Co.
1-800-327-0969

Financial Freedom Senior
Funding Corp.
Patty Wills
1-800-368-3254

Seattle Mortgage Co. d.b.a.
Reverse Mortgages of
Pennsylvania
1-888-748-9300

Wells Fargo Home Mortgage
1-800-336-7359

Rhode Island
Financial Freedom Senior
Funding Corp.
1-800-203-4667

Rhode Island Housing &
Mortgage Finance
Community Lending
Department
1-401-457-1289

Wells Fargo Home Mortgage
1-800-336-7359

South Carolina
Everhome Mortgage Co.
1-888-819-4202

centura bank
1-800-879-5864

Financial Freedom Senior
Funding Corp.
1-800-588-8044

First Citizens Bank
1-803-733-2778

First Federal of Spartanburg
1-803-582-2391 or 1-843-596-
8352

Wells Fargo Home Mortgage
1-800-336-7359

South Dakota
Financial Freedom Senior
Funding Corp.
Danielle Fox
1-800-880-7740

Wells Fargo Home Mortgage
1-800-336-7359

Tennessee
Financial Freedom Senior
Funding Corp.
1-800-588-8044

Wells Fargo Home Mortgage
1-800-336-7359

Texas
Financial Freedom Senior
Funding Corp.
1-800-336-3135

Seattle Mortgage Co., d.b.a.
Reverse Mortgages of Texas
1-866-329-3833

Wells Fargo Home Mortgage
1-877-386-5344

Utah
Financial Freedom Senior
Funding Corp.
1-800-843-0480

Sun American Mortgage Co.
1-800-469-7383/1-801-256-0802

Wells Fargo Home Mortgage
1-800-336-7359

Vermont
Financial Freedom Senior
Funding Corp.
1-800-203-4667

Wells Fargo Home Mortgage
1-800-336-7359

Virginia
Everhome Mortgage Co.
1-888-850-5100

Financial Freedom Senior
Funding Corp.
1-800-368-3254

Virginia Housing Development
Authority
1-804-782-1986

Wells Fargo Home Mortgage
1-800-336-7359

Washington
Financial Freedom Senior

Funding Corp.
1-800-423-4222

Seattle Mortgage Co.
1-800-233-4601

Wells Fargo Home Mortgage
1-800-336-7359

West Virginia
Financial Freedom Senior
Funding Corp.
1-800-368-3254

Wells Fargo Home Mortgage
1-800-336-7359

Wisconsin
Everhome Mortgage Co.
1-888-350-8718

Comcor Mortgage Corp.
1-800-775-1666

Financial Freedom Senior
Funding Corp.
1-800-880-7740

Wells Fargo Home Mortgage
1-800-336-7359

Wyoming
Financial Freedom Senior
Funding Corp.
1-800-843-0480

Intermountain Mortgage Co. |
1-800-669-5138

Wells Fargo Home Mortgage
1-800-336-7359

+ = offers only the FHA Home Equity Conversion Mortgage (HECM)

Certified Aging-in-Place Builders and Remodelers
(Arranged by State and City)

Homan Incorporated
P.O. Box 770089
Eagle River, AK 99577
(907) 696-3494

Kitchens & Baths By Design
PO Box 74121
Fairbanks, AK 99707
(907) 479-4056

Lifespan Home Modifications
P.O. Box 65
Sitka, AK 99835
(800) 993-1798

Grandpre' Custom Homes Inc
HC 33 Box 3035
Wasilla, AK 99654-9721
(907) 376-2103

Southern Const. & Design, Inc
5302 Bay Shore Drive
Athens, AL 35611
(256)-797-5426

McKay Building Co. Inc.
7059 Meadowlark Dr
Birmingham, AL 35242-5342
(205) 980-1718

Precision Homecrafters Inc
1215 Lake Forest Circle
Birmingham, AL 35244
(205) 733-9583

Shelton Construction, Inc.
247 East Moulton St., Suite A
Decatur, AL 35601-2350

(256) 351-1112
Norton Construction Company
3412 Frank Ave
Hoover, AL 35226
(205) 978-8206

Medallion Builders
110 Lily Flags Rd
Huntsville, AL 35802
(256) 885-2520

John B Dollison
2214 Shades Crest SE
Huntsville, AL 35801
(256) 534-9647

Baugher Design & Remodel
2106-B Cahaba Rd.
Mountain Brook, AL 35223
(205) 870-8572

J.A.H Design Costruction
3065 Holland Rd.
Newton, AL 36352
(334) 692-3103

Eren Design & Construction Inc
55 N Avenida de la Vista
Tucson, AZ 85710
(520) 885-2500

Dakota Builders Inc
4861 E 29th Street
Tucson, AZ 85711
(520) 792-0438

Southern Construction & Design
Inc
101 Broken Bow Lane
Madison, Al 35758
(256) 652-6857

We Build Corporation
310 N. Palm Street, Suite D
Brea, CA 92821
(562) 694-8766

Cuschieri Horton Architects
927 Sheila Court
Campbell, CA 95008
(408) 772-3623

Home-Prep
3017 Sandi Dr.
Chico, CA 95973
(530) 897-0274

Synergy Design Group
581 Pinto Mesa Drive
Diamond Bar, CA 91765
(909) 861-3071

Bishop Construction Services
PO Box 1527
Highland, CA 923461527
(951) 830-4918

National Resource Center on
Supportive Housing
USC Andrus Gerontology Center
Los Angeles, CA 900890191
(213) 740-1364

Custom Design & Construction
11111 W. Olympic Blvd., #404
Los Angeles, CA 90064
(310) 815-4815

Custom Design & Construction
11111 W. Olympic Blvd.,
Fourth Fl.
Los Angeles, CA 90064
(310) 815-4815

Home for Easy Living Univ. Des
25060 Hancock Ave. #103-186
Murrieta, CA 92562
(760) 409-7565

Complete Design &
Remodeling
P.O. Box 1898
San Marcos, CA 920791898
(760) 801-8900

Churchill Construction
1173 S Sable Blvd #B
Aurora, CO 80012
(303) 898-6215

Churchill Construction
1363 Eagle Street
Aurora, CO 80011
(303) 210-7950

Full Circle Design Group, Inc.
10 Farmer's Lane, Suite 1
Breckenridge, CO 80424
(970) 453-7100

The Remodeler
3205 N Hancock Ave
Colorado Springs, CO 80907
(719) 636-2444

H & H Builders LLC
PO Box 29070
Denver, CO 80229
(303) 450-7006

In Site Design Group Inc.
1280 S. Clayton Street
Denver, CO 80210
(303) 691-9000

Home and Energy Services, Inc.
1030 W. Ellsworth
Denver, CO 80223
(303) 715-0777

Doug Walter Architects
280 Columbine St. Suite 205
Denver, CO 80206-4718
(303) 320-6916

Woodring Construction, Inc.
PO Box 2907
Dillon, CO 80435
(970) 333-4927

Associates in Building & Design
4803 Innovation Dr. #1
Fort Collins, CO 80525
(970) 225-2323

Top Quality Remodeling Inc
29602 Rainbow Hill Rd
Golden, CO 80401
(303) 526-5440

Interior Settings LLC
12655 W Bayaud Ave, Unit 40
Lake Wood, CO 802282025
(303) 985-1980

Hawk Construction Inc
10143 W Chatfield Ave #14
Littleton, CO 80127
(303) 972-0317

GRC Builders
7931 S. Broadway #312
Littleton, CO 80122
(303) 795-8568

Basements by Brooks
1822 Skyway Drive, Suite O
Longmont, CO 80504
(303) 772-1040

Kessler Construction Co, Inc.
5809 Wright Drive
Loveland, CO 80538
(970) 663-4428

Poehlmann Construction/
Basements 4 You
579 W. 66th Street
Loveland, CO 80538
(970) 278-1930

Majestic Development Co LLC
13661 N Travois Trail
Parker, CO 80138
(720) 851-7060

H & H Builders LLC
12061 Pennsylvania St #B102
Thornton, CO 802413146
(303) 450-7006

Scalzo Construction Group
6 Stony Hill Road
Bethel, CT 06801
(203) 790-3250

Mary Jo Peterson, Inc.
3 Sunset Cove
Brookfield, CT 06804
(203) 775-4763

Neighborhood Builders Inc
303 Church St
Guilford, CT 06437
(203) 453-3624

Litchfield Builders, Inc.
2199 State Street
Hamden, CT 06517
(203) 288-8677

John S Cusick Construction
LLC
186 Canner Street
New Haven, CT 06511
(203) 624-2463

House of Hanbury Builders Inc
109 Stamm Road
Newington, CT 06111
(860) 666-1537

CFR Construction
26 Pleasant Hill Road
Newtown, CT 06740-1721
(203) 426-1566

Construction Concepts Corp
87 Brookhollow Lane
Stamford, CT 06902-1039
(203) 325-8102

Sunwood Development
273 North Colony St.
Wallingford, CT 06492
(203) 269-0325

Liljedahl Brothers Inc
17 Oakwood Ave
West Hartford, CT 06119-2128
(860) 232-2229

Sasportas Co Inc
Bx 340/148 Deerfield Rd.
Windsor, CT 060950340
((860)688-1586

Woodstock Building Associates
LLC
78 Prospect Street
Woodstock, CT 06281
(860) 928-0897

Robert Leonard
6117 Deer Run
Fort Myers, FL 33908
(239) 481-7798

Graetz Remodeling and Custom
Homes, Inc
1901 NW 67th Place, Suite B
Gainesville, FL 32653
(352) 371-7730

Smith & Sons Builders
P.O. Box 841
Gulf Breeze, FL 32563
(850) 932-4591

Adaptive Living Concepts
2473 Egrets Glade Dr
Jacksonville, FL 32224
(904) 992-8070

Paul Davis Restoration
12874 Fernbank Lane
Jacksonville, FL 32223
(904) 737-2779

Lawrence Murr Inc
3000-1 Hartley Road
Jacksonville, FL 32257
(904) 262-1434

J&L Homes, Inc
PMB 467, State Road 13 N #26
Jacksonville, FL 32259
(904) 838-9820

Zimmermann Associates, Inc.
PO Box 2036 / 203
Kerneywood Drive
Lakeland, FL 338032036
(863) 682-8874

Davis Construction &
Contracting
P.O. Box 5186
Lakeland, FL 33807
(863) 644-4604

Green Construction Services
Inc
2525 Dranefield Road #13
Lakeland, FL 33811
(863) 665-2767

Home Modifications
Evaluation & Design
4617 Bougainvilla Dr., Apt. 3
Lauderdale by the Sea, FL
33308
(954) 229-6099

JLM Services Inc.
P.O. Box 915292
Longwood, FL 32779
(407) 682-5225

Housing & Assistive Technology
2000 Powerside Terrace, Ste.
505
Miami, FL 33138
(305) 608-0692

Homeworks of Collier County,
Inc.
7424 Bershire Pines Dr.
Naples, FL 34104
(239) 304-5336

The Lykos Group, Inc.
4306 Enterprise Ave # 8
Naples, FL 34104
(239) 263-9660

John R Ranck Inc
601 97th Avenue N
Naples, FL 34108
(941) 597-3867

Abbie Joan Enterprises LLC
4535 Domestic Avenue, Suite A
Naples, FL 34104
(239) 435-0677

Wm. J. Varian Construction Co.
210 31st Street NW
Naples, FL 34120
(239) 775-1178

A.K. Construction, Inc.
555 Bowline Dr
Naples, FL 341034130
(239) 263-6776

Henry Westforth Contracting
Inc
5180 Palmetto Woods Dr
Naples, FL 34119
(239) 455-0272

Kish Builders Inc
1008 Delridge Avenue
Orlando, FL 32804
(407) 297-9392

James M. Krantz Constr. Corp.
1400 Appleton Ave.
Orlando, FL 32856
(407) 857-8869

Adventure in Building, Inc.
927 W Harvard Street
Orlando, FL 32804
(407) 843-4696

Design Solutions!
633 Norwood ST. NW
Port Charlotte, FL 33952
(941) 629-4100

Five Star General Contracting
Inc.
1203 W. Marion Avenue
Punta Gorda, FL 339505393
(941) 637-7848

Access of Sarasota, Inc.
15 Paradise Plaza # 368
Sarasota, FL 342396905
(941) 924-6160

Sawgrass Plantation Ent Inc
2360 Colfax Dr
South Daytona, FL 321193343
(386) 258-7960

Shoreline Building &
Construction Inc
6419 Jack Wright Island Rd
St Augustine, FL 32092
(904) 284-1144

A Carpenters Constructrion Co.,
Inc.
PO Box 14194/ 11013
Pennewaw Trace

Tallahassee, FL 32317
(850) 878-0010

Terry Ward Consulting, LLC
1617 Seminole Drive
Tallahassee, FL 32301
(850) 386-2511

Miramar Palm Realty & D.B.
Property Mgt. Svc., Inc
7300 W. Mcnab Road #218
Tamarac, FL 33321
(954) 328-8001

Emerald Contractors Inc
1118 E Court St
Tarpon Springs, FL 34689
(727) 943-9046

PSG Construction
839 S. Orlando Ave.
Winter Park, FL 32789
(407) 628-9660

Wager Construction Corp.
4555 Mansell Rd. Ste. 300
Alpharetta, GA 30022
(770) 393-8600

LifeSpring Environs Inc
12600 Deerfield Parkway, Suite
100-1053
Atlanta, GA 30004
(678) 762-3330

Integrity Remodeling & Custom
Homes
PO Box 2839
Blairsville, GA 30514
(706) 745-8233

Andrea Hubbard
406 McPherson St.
Bremen, GA 30110
(777) 537-4136

Hobart Builders, Inc.
6113 Seaton Dr
Columbus, GA 31909-3621
(706) 327-3550

Krech CAD Services, Inc.
1316 Milstead Ave
Conyers, GA 30012
(770) 760-8900

The Mike Company
341 Amicalola Forest Dr.
Dawsonville, GA 30534
(770) 294-7867

K Scott Anderson
3138 Robin Lane
Duluth, GA 30096
(678) 584-1213

Georgia Property Assistance
LLC
PO Box 451
Kennesaw, GA 30156
(678) 469-3070

The Home Service Store
1701 Barrett Lakes Blvd., 220
Kennesaw, GA 30144
(770) 261-7145

Stewart Shope & Company
7734 Hampton Place
Loganville, GA 300526770
(770) 987-2609

All in One Accessibility, Inc.
1310 Kennestone Circle
Marietta, GA 30066
(678) 766-1066

Custom Concepts
10800 Alpharetta Highway,
Suite 208-533
Rosewell, GA 30076
(404) 281-6552

Concept Creators
5262 Poplar Springs Rd
Stone Mountain, GA 30083-2905
(770) 469-7299

Summers & Sons
Development Co
1700 Montreal Circle
Tucker, GA 30084
(770) 934-2700

J. Robert Adams & Co., Inc.
115 Lloyd Avenue
Tyrone, GA 30269
(770) 487-4663

Christian Remodeling
1030 Summit Grove Dr.
Watkinsville, GA 30677
(706) 310-0505

Arganbright's Inc.
2366 Sportsman Club Lane
Adel, IA 50111
(515) 993-1166

Magee Construction Co
1705 Waterloo
Cedar Falls, IA 50613
(319) 277-0100

Novak Construction Co
280 50th Ave SW
Cedar Rapids, IA 52404-4913
(319) 363-8890

E C Construction
4489 NW 2nd Street, Suite 7
Des Moines, IA 50313
(515) 280-7633

Tegeler Design Center, Inc.
750 N. Center Point Rd.
Hiawatha, IA 52233
(319) 393-1366

Bea Day Plumbers, Inc.
4954 Dingleberry Rd. NE.
Iowa City, IA 52240
(319) 354-2814

Lammers Construction
Service Inc
35 Imperial Ct
Iowa City, IA 52246
(319) 354-5905

Home Repair Team Inc.
2698 Reservoir Drive NW #3
North Liberty, IA 52317
(319) 626-4663

Able Home Builders
205 West 45th Street
Sioux City, IA 51104
(712) 203-4663

Firstcall Construction
7195 NW 54th Avenue
Urbandale, IA 50322
(515) 202-4976

First Call Construction
7195 NW 54th Ave
Urbandale, IA 50322-6915
(515) 253-2610

Beal Development Corporation
7166 Dakota Drive
West Des Moines, IA 50266
(515) 222-1204

McDermott Remodeling
7301 W Main St
Belleville, IL 62223-3001
(618) 397-8701

Roehm Renovations
2905 Carlene Dr
Bloomington, IL 61704-0000
(309) 663-1909

J J Swartz Company
1605 G E Rd
Bloomington, IL 61704
(309) 662-2611

McCann Construction Co
200 W Buchanan St
Carlinville, IL 62626-1028
(217) 854-6576

Blackberry Builders Inc.
44W 767 Main Street Road
Elburn, IL 60119
(630) 557-2526

Arch Construction Management,
Inc.
15 Spinning Wheel Road # 404
Hinsdale, IL 60521
(630) 654-0537

Design Construction Concepts
Ltd
425 Huehl Rd #15B
Northbrook, IL 60062
(847) 498-1676

Sevvonco Inc
201 E Dundee Rd Suite A
Palatine, IL 60067
(847) 359-3591

Wysong Construction
2338 East 800 North Rd
Pana, IL 62557-6351
(217) 226-4274

KLS Construction, Inc
840 Red Bud
Petersburg, IL 62707
(217) 899-8144

Kraftwerks Remodeling, Inc.
25551 W. 119th St.
Plainfield, IL 605449722
(815) 436-2791

Day & Company Const. Inc
201 So. Walnut Ste. F
Rochester, IL 625630075
(217) 498-7873

Buraski Builders Inc.
3757 South Sixth Street
Springfield, IL 62703
(217) 529-5172

Sutton Siding & Remodeling
Inc
1926 Peoria Rd
Springfield, IL 62702
(217) 528-3911

Fulford Home Remodeling
3318 N. Illinois Street
Swansea, IL 62226
(618) 235-4300

Kraftwerks Remodeling Inc
6441 W 174th St
Tinley Park, IL 604773510
(708) 532-7018

JDC Construction
428 Park Ave
Aurora, IN 47001-1533
(812) 637-2684

Pritchett Bros. Inc.
108 Brairwood Lane
Bedford, IN 47421
(812) 275-3185

Weiss RCMI
PO Box 1066
Carmel, IN 460821066
(317) 873-5991

Heidorn Construction Inc
1455 Stevenson Station Rd
Chandler, IN 47610
(812) 925-7815

Gray Matter, Inc.
3385 W. Lakeshore Dr.
Crown Point, IN 46307
(219) 661-9212

Dalin Remodeling, Inc.
3024 S Main
Elkhart, IN 46517
(574) 296-1056

Oddjob/Creative Interiors Inc
1280 E Morgan Ave
Evansville, IN 47714
(812) 424-2069

Stash Construction Inc.
2701 W 45th Avenue
Gary, IN 46408
(219) 924-0266

Bail Home Services &
Construction, Inc.
1912 Elkhart Rd.
Goshen, IN 46526-2414
(574) 533-4821

The Lifestyle Group, Inc.
6230 Southeastern Ave.
Indianapolis, IN 46203
(317) 352-9022

Dukate Fine Remodeling
110 West Edgewood Ave.
Indianapolis, IN 46217
(317) 736-9961

Jud Construction
5105 West Bradburn Drive
Muncie, IN 47304
(765) 288-1111

Elite Master Builder, Inc.
PO Box 3112
Munster, IN 46321
(219) 712-1329

R E Construction &
Maintenance Services Inc
170 N County Road 400 W
New Castle, IN 47362-9196
(765) 533-6413

Eisenhour Home Improvements,
Inc.
14680 Lincoln Hwy.
Plymouth, IN 46563
(574) 936-8564

Newman Company Inc
PO Box 1006
Riley, IN 47871-1006
(812) 894-2732

Wilbur's Carpentry Service
4139 W 1300 N
Wheatfield, IN 46392
(219) 987-3083

Maxson Remodeling
PO Box 5039
Zionsville, IN 46077
(317) 769-6696

Judy K. Morris
1138 Armstrong Ct.
Derby, KS 67037
(316) 518-1186

McKittrick Construction Inc.
Post Office Box 26445
Shawnee Mission, KS 66225
(913) 402-1961

Jim Goentzel Construction
216 No. Waco, Suite C
Wichita, KS 67202
(316) 264-6333

Guthridge/Nighswonger Corp.
1702 S. Laura
Wichita, KS 67211
(316) 264-7900

John M Considine Contracting
Lexington, KY 45506
(859) 299-1130

Bowersox Remodeling &
Building Co Inc
229 Salem Dr
Owensboro, KY 423037723
(270) 926-6800

EXPAND Inc.
22344 Achord Rd.
Denham Springs, LA 70726
(225) 791-8050

Jay M. Brooks - Wendy Elliott
Foundation
3201 Landfair
Lake Charles, LA 70601
(337) 480-4228

FBN Construction Inc
17 Wolcott Ct
Boston, MA 02136
(617) 333-6821

Sirignano Construction
516 E. 2nd St. Unit #39
Boston, MA 02127
(617) 721-6606

Dale R. Nikula Co.
103 Main St.
Dennisport, MA 02639
(508) 760-6900

The Sullivan Company, Inc.
50 Winchester St Suite 13
Newton Highlands, MA 02461
(617) 527-9989

Twin Peaks Construction, LLC
P.O. Box 337
Norwood, MA 02062
(781) 742-0278

JTC & Company
192 Worcester Rd.
Wellesley, MA 02481
(781) 235-9488

N.R. Bergeron Drywall
Contractor, Inc.
1106 East Mountain Rd.
Westfield, MA 01085
(413) 568-0962

CMHA, Inc. / Elder Home
Repair Program
7-11 Bellevue Street
Worcester, MA 01609
(508) 755-1105

Zwingelberg Enterprises
215 Medwick Garth W
Baltimore, MD 21228-1943
(410) 455-6466

Elegant Builders Inc
1335 Locust Avenue
Bel Air, MD 21014
(410) 836-9433

Van Deusen Construction
P.O. Box 1208
Bel Air, MD 21014
(410) 836-2445

Creative Custom Builders, Inc.
116 Goldsborough Street
Easton, MD 21601
(410) 822-3588

Meyer Sons Builders, Inc.
3 Steuart Lane
Edgewater, MD 21037
(410) 956-4565

Owings Brothers Contracting,
Inc.
1912 Liberty Rd
Eldersburg, MD 21784
(410) 781-7022

Point Enterprises
8409 Old Frederick Road
Ellicott City, MD 21043
(410) 418-9123

Bozzuto Homes
7850 Walker Drive
Greenbelt, MD 20770
(301) 220-0100

Brooks Run Builders
24707 Farmkey Lane
Hollywood, MD 20636
(301) 373-8424

Rebuilding Together
3925 Plyers Mill Rd
Kensington, MD 20895
(301) 933-2700

Dertzbaugh Contruction Inc
PO Box 476
Mt Airy, MD 21771
(301) 865-3658

J & J Builders General
Contractors
3400 Gough Drive
Waldorf, MD 20602
(301) 843-8113

Rollenhagen Builders Inc
6749 Three Mile Rd NE
Ada, MI 49301
(616) 676-1187

Cardea Construction Co
210 Little Lake Dr #12
Ann Arbor, MI 48103
(734) 665-0234

LaRoe Remodeling
2390 Winewood
Ann Arbor, MI 48103
(734) 665-3055

M Rhoades Construction Co
503 E Columbia Avenue
Battle Creek, MI 49015-4498
(616) 962-6011

Shea Company Construction
725 South Adams, Suite 12
Birmingham, MI 48009
(248) 851-7432

Berry Nice Kitchens
01690 Old State Rd
Boyne City, MI 49712-9188
(616) 582-5807

M G M Construction
7090 Matz Rd
Boyne Falls, MI 49713
(231) 549-2596

Tri Square Construction LLC
121 W North Street, Ste. 2
Brighton, MI 48116
(810) 229-8444

Berry Construction, Inc
9711 Reed Rd
Carp Lake, MI 49718-9736
(231) 537-2210

DHI Construction
11862 Gable Street
Detroit, MI 48212
(313) 891-6090

O'Toole Design &
Contruction Inc
836 Plymouth Ave SE
East Grand Rapids, MI 49506
(616) 893-7267

Quality Craftsman
Remodeling LLC
1632 Coolidge Road
East Lansing, MI 48823
(517) 333-2940

Weir Building Company, LLC
11215 Tyrone Trail
Fenton, MI 48430
(810) 629-8400

Woodland House of
Kitchens Inc
6619 S Division SW
Grand Rapids, MI 49548-7805
(616) 281-1300

Bernard Gismondi
Construction
28576 Swan Island
Grosse Ile, MI 48138
(734) 674-1035

Rowen Design
1492 Osborn Drive
Hillsdale, MI 49242
(517) 439-2416

Paulson's Construction Inc
PO Box 2287
Howell, MI 48844
(517) 545-8651

Remodeling Specialist Inc
3140 West F Ave
Kalamazoo, MI 49009
(269) 343-3757

Senior Services Inc.
918 Jasper Street
Kalamazoo, MI 49001
(269) 382-0515

Hall of Fame Homes
6299 Medford Way
Kalamazoo, MI 440099071
(269) 978-2783

Wayne Pavlika Builders, inc.
4172 Clegg Road
Lambertville, MI 48144
(734) 856-7133

R.l. Rider Design/Construction
1121 May Street
Lansing, MI 48906-5508
(517) 487-3713

Q X 2 Contracting, Inc.
2547 W. Main St. Suite 100
Lansing, MI 48917
(517) 204-4406

J & L Johnson
Restoration & Cleaning
7636 Northport Drive
Lansing, MI 48917
(517) 322-3006

All Phase Remodeling Inc
2720 Alpha Access St
Lansing, MI 48910-3608
(517) 482-6433

Johnson Building Co
33550 N Hampshire St
Livonia, MI 48154-2705
(734) 522-0224

Accessible Homes
Remodeling, Inc.
26675 Dequindre
Madison Heights, MI 48071
(248) 321-8951

Grand Bay Builders
2551 Surrey Ln
Pinckney, MI 48169
(231) 995-9057

Brennan/Phelan Construction
4817 Fernlee
Royal Oak, MI 48073
(248) 288-9191

Homeowner Services Of
America
199 W Michgan Ave
Saline, MI 48176
(734) 944-3337

Burkholder Construction Co.,
Inc.
2206 Cass Road
Traverse City, MI 49684-8840
(231) 941-7180

New Dimension Building
2850 Mullins Court
Walker, MI 49544
(616) 453-3470

Borchert Building Co LLC
58459 Van Dyke Avenue
Washington, MI 48094
(586) 992-8400

Plekkenpol Builders Inc.
401 E 78th Street
Bloomington, MN 55420
(952) 888-2225

New Spaces
2105 W 143rd St
Burnsville, MN 55306
(952) 898-5300

Bell's Remodeling
3012 E 2nd St
Duluth, MN 55812-1925
(218) 728-2797

C N Ostrom & Son Inc
PO Box 758
Excelsior, MN 55331-0758
(952) 448-9893

Jeff Nelson Construction
4172 Thunderchief Lane, #204
Hermantown, MN 55811
(218) 727-2197

Sylvestre Construction, Inc.
7708 5th Avenue South
Minneapolis, MN 55423
(612) 861-0188

Built By Design, Inc.
5509 Mayview Rd.
Minnetonka, MN 55345-5938
(952) 939-4133

Jacqueline J Hanson
Hanson Builders & Remodelers
1610 14th Street NW #301
Rochester, MN 55901
(507) 252-5566

Damont, Incorporated
8332 Highway 65 NE
Spring Lake Park, MN 55432
(763) 785-4274

Greg E. Theis Construction
PO Box 7294
St Cloud, MN 563027294
(320) 253-2312

Bisciglia Construction Co
127 E County Road C Ste. 3
St Paul, MN 55117-1383
(651) 766-2511

Patterns of Wellness
686 Arlington Ave W
St Paul, MN 55117
(651) 226-7127

Hamlyne Group LLC
312 N. Meramec, #202
Clayton, MO 631053770
(314) 249-3332

Kliethermes Homes &
Remodeling Inc
1905 Cherry Hill Dr #102
Columbia, MO 65203
(573) 446-2222

Bueler Inc.
13314 Manchester Rd
Des Peres, MO 63131-1709
(314) 966-3191

Riggs Construction Company
212 North Clay
Kirkwood, MO 63122
(314) 821-7646

Mosby Building Arts, LTD
255 E Monroe Ave
St Louis, MO 63122-6126
(314) 909-1800

Miller Building & Remodeling
LLC
550 Beauchamp Rd
Advance, NC 27006-7409
(336) 998-2140

El Grigg Designs
601 S. Cedar Street, Suite 112
Charlotte, NC 28202
(704) 372-0090

Duke University Med. Ctr.
Biological Anthro., Box 3170
Durham, NC 27710
(919) 668-3348

Reynolds House Inc.
1301 Carolina St., Ste. 110
Greensboro, NC 27401
(336) 272-9810

Design/Build Services
2820 Lawndale Dr #309
Greensboro, NC 27408-4127
(336) 282-7800

Bostian Builders Inc
PO Box 19312
Greensboro, NC 274199312
(336) 292-4145

Harkness Builders, Inc.
242 Templeton Road
Morrisville, NC 28117
(704) 799-7744

Corbett Construction Co., Inc.
183 Wind Chime Ct., Suite 202
Raleigh, NC 27615
(919) 845-7670

Hilliard Contracting Inc
5509 Wood Pond Ct
Raleigh, NC 276104533
(919) 231-8314

Quality Design & Construction
3823 Junction Blvd
Raleigh, NC 27603
(919) 779-3964

Hands-On Contracting
5548 Old Still Rd
Wake Forest, NC 27587
(919) 528-8858

Anderson-Moore Builders Inc
8030 North Point Blvd.
Winston-Salem, NC 27104
(336) 759-7343

Rick Duval Construction Inc
2710 5th Ave S #A
Fargo, ND 58103-2338
(701) 293-7688

Fuelling Contracting
5405 Roose St
Lincoln, NE 68502
(402) 432-2700

Foxwood Homes, LLC
10 Commerce Park North,
Suite 13B
Bedford, NH 03110
(603) 644-8100

Gavin Construction Inc
50 Rocky Pond Rd.
Brookline, NH 03033
(603) 672-3200

Gulf Brook Renovations Corp.
52 Hall St
Concord, NH 03301
(603) 226-0212

It Takes Two
P.O. Box 1574
Grantham, NH 03753
(603) 863-1597

Cormack Builders Inc.
46 East Madison Road.
(P.O. Box 180)
Madison, NH 038490180
(603) 367-9938

Maplehurst Construction LLC
26 McKenna Dr
Nashua, NH 03062
(603) 888-8455

Foremost Builders, LLC
179 Main St
New London, NH 03257
(603) 526-6300

A.B.A. Home Remodelers Co.
193 Christie Ave
Clifton, NJ 07011-1857
(973) 478-9277

Accessibility Design Assoc.
28 Harrison Avenue, Suite 234
Englishtown, NJ 07726
(732) 786-9244

Willow Design & Build LLC
1448 York Street
Mahwah, NJ 07430
(201) 934-8636

Fichter Construction
21 Brunswick Road
Montclair, NJ 07042
(973) 509-5200

Creative Design Construction,
Inc.
204 Livingston St
Northvale, NJ 07647
(201) 768-5813

Design Alternatives Inc
147 Oak Ridge Parkway
Tom's River, NJ 08755
(732) 244-7778

Creative Construction Co.
442 Gavilan Pl NW
Albuquerque, NM 87107
(505) 256-7311

Diemer Building &
Remodeling, Inc.
1060 S. Main St.
Las Cruces, NM 88005
(505) 524-5800

Schrader & Co Inc
850 Saratoga Rd
Burnt Hills, NY 12027
(518) 399-1881

Mary Lu Ghezzi
74 Midlake Circle
East Syracuse, NY 13057
(315) 637-1839

Legacy Builders and
Remodelors Corp.
791 Canal Road
Mount Sinai, NY 11766
(631) 331-5305

B D McFarland & Co
59 Hempstead Rd
Spring Valley, NY 10977-2815
(914) 425-9300

Steve Khanzadian
Construction, Inc.
5085 Bradbury Dr.
Syracuse, NY 13215
(315) 469-3258

Sam Pitzulo Homes
400 E. Main St.
Canfield, OH 44406
(330) 533-2137

Universal Concepts &
Design Inc
8454 Blue Ash Rd
Cincinnati, OH 45236
(513) 794-1501

Dave Fox Remodeling Co.
1161 Bethel Rd. Ste. 204
Columbus, OH 43220
(614) 459-7133

Renovations Unlimited Inc.
1933 Harrisburg Pike
Grove City, OH 43123-1453
(614) 594-0004

HC Design Group
6235 Fay Ct., Ste. 1
Loveland, OH 451408119
(513) 931-6300

AVID Construction, Inc.
8353 Mentor Ave.
Mentor, OH 44060
(440) 255-9692

E. H. Duncan
108 S. Main St.
Poland, OH 44514
(330) 757-3764

Owens Construction
9890 Olentangy River Rd
Powell, OH 43065
(614) 846-1149

Riviera Construction, Inc.
34055 Country View Ln
Solon, OH 44139
(440) 349-9744

Al Blyth Construction
12685 Monkey Hollow Rd
Sunbury, OH 43074
(740) 965-4403

Terry Bennett Builders &
Remodelers Inc
26404 Center Ridge Rd
Westlake, OH 44145
(216) 835-4663

R. J. Landis Design &
Construction, Inc.
640 J Lakeview Plaza Blvd
Worthington, OH 43085
(614) 844-6400

Hankins Construction Inc
826 SE 63rd Dr
Hillsboro, OR 97123
(503) 642-3780

Breeding Construction
Company
PO Box 549
Newbury, OR 97132
(503) 538-7380

JB Construction Services, Inc.
10211 SW Barbur Blvd #207-A
Portland, OR 97219
(503) 245-3525

Irving Development Company
10211 SW Barbur Blvd
Portland, OR 97219
(503) 245-2778

In The Works Construction &
Design
15203 NW Burlington Court
Portland, OR 97231
(503) 621-3094

Master Plan Remodeling
8665 SW Canyon Rd
Portland, OR 97225
(503) 297-1281

Steven Heiteen Construction,
Inc.
6049 SW Pendelton Ct.
Portland, OR 97221-1031
(503) 244-3525

NW Renovations & Design Co
13185 NW Westlawn Terrace
Portland, OR 97229
(503) 641-1512

Troy Farnsworth Building
Design and Planning
P.O. Box 3206/
7012 S.W. Nyberg Rd.
Tuaiatin, OR 97062
(503) 692-0777

Personal Mobility
5966 Key Stone Dr
Bath, PA 18014
(610) 837-3000

Quality Building & Remodeling
2424 Toll Road
Effort, PA 183302205
(570) 629-9303

Penn Contractors
419 Dalton Street
Suite 457
Emmans, PA 18049
(610) 965-4204

Siegfried Construction, Inc.
129 Pinchalong Raod
Grove City, PA 16127
(724) 458-4135

Excel Interior Concepts &
Construction
570 S 3rd Street
Lemoyne, PA 17043-2006
(717) 774-4990

North Starr Design &
Construction Services LLC.
42 N Starr Ave
Pittsburgh, PA 15202
(412) 761-6574

Jensco Construction
4690 List Rd
Red Lion, PA 17356-8164
(717) 246-1873

Residential Builders, LLC
1738 Broad Street
Cranston, RI 02905
(401) 941-3388

R.I. Kitchen & Bath
95 Manchester Street
W. Warwick, RI 02895
(401) 826-1550

B&W Construction
4675 Pamlico Circle
Columbia, SC 29205
(803) 738-8027

Remodeling Services
Unlimited Inc
1813 Hampton St
Columbia, SC 29201
(803) 765-9363

A-Therm Remodelors Inc
PO Box 6412
Columbia, SC 29206
(803) 787-8897

Rome Construction Group
PO Box 356
Greenville, SC 29602
(864) 232-3177

Ashmore-Rice Builders, Inc.
364 Crepe Myrtle Drive
Greer, SC 29651
(864) 630-1396

Clark's Construction Co Inc
PO Box 465
Irmo, SC 29063-0465
(803) 781-4884

Citadel Enterprises Inc.
523 Wando Lane
Mt. Pleasant, SC 29464-8211
(843) 884-4303

Ardis-Soules Inc.
872 Oak St
Chattanooga, TN 37403-2408
(423) 756-1600

Prendergast Construction
4033 Fort Henry Dr.
Kingsport, TN 37663
(423) 239-3117

Sr Living Solutions
4029 Wallace Lane
Nashville, TN 37215
(615) 385-7040

Comfort Concepts
4407 West 2nd Ave.
Amarillo, TX 79106
(806) 355-5648

Progressive Insights
5840 W. Interstate 20 Suite 110
Arlington, TX 76017
(817) 919-3587

Steve Gillen Builder Inc
9700 Queensland Dr
Austin, TX 78729
(512) 250-1850

Katz Builders Inc
11107 Aldenburgh Ct
Austin, TX 78737
(512) 301-6000

Liland, Inc. dba Wayland
Construction
5555 W Loops, Suite 315
Bellaire, TX 77401
(713) 528-5898

Donn M. Long
1813 Bluebell Dr
Cedar Park, TX 78613
(512) 336-5664

Quantum Custom Homes, Inc.
820 S. MacArthur Blvd. #105-231
Coppell, TX 75019
(972) 401-1333

Independence at Home, Inc.
1028 Muscadine Vine
Crowley, TX 76036
(817) 447-1330

George Lewis Custom Homes
3100 Monticello
Suite #150
Dallas, TX 75205
(214) 361-8688

Vanguard Construction
Company
12217 Ridgesair Place
Dallas, TX 75234
(972) 243-7198

Tapestry Custom Homes LLC
PO Box 797184
Dallas, TX 753797184
(972) 931-1972

McCollum & Associates Inc
14919 Woodbriar Dr
Dallas, TX 75248
(469) 774-0703

Watermark Design Solutions,
Inc.
703 McKinney Ave. Ste. 402
Dallas, TX 75202
(214) 880-1700

Randall Hall Design/Build &
Remodeling
11837 Judd Court, Suite 122
Dallas, TX 75243
(214) 341-3365

George Lewis Custom Homes
3100 Monticello, #150
Dallas, TX 75205
(214) 361-8688

RSL Company
10675 E Northwest Hwy.,
Ste. 1655-805
Dallas, TX 75238
(214) 340-9936

George Lewis Custom Homes
6517 Hillcrest Ave #211
Dallas, TX 75205
(214) 361-8688

USI Remodeling
2100 N Highway 360 Suite 1603
Grand Prairie, TX 75050
(972) 206-0750

Houston Habitat For Humanity
3607 Fern River Dr.
Houston, TX 77345
(713) 539-6825

2828 Bammel Lane, #900
Houston, TX 77098
(832) 731-9530

Brothers Strong, Inc.
12315 Ann Lane
Houston, TX 77064
(281) 469-6057

Stow's Home Repair &
Remodeling, LLC
7125 W Tidwell, Suite L-108
Houston, TX 77092
(713) 460-2100

LBJ Construction LP
1218 Webster St
Houston, TX 77002
(713) 781-0169

Creative Property Restoration
604 Jackson Hill
Houston, TX 77007
(713) 528-6404

Lone Star Building &
Construction Services Inc
2410 Quenby #200
Houston, TX 77005
(713) 522-7111

Heritage Construction Services
17806 W. Copper Lakes Dr.
Suite 100
Houston, TX 77095
(281) 345-6525

Premier Remodeling &
Construction, L.P
PMB 314; 5773 Woodway Dr.
Houston, TX 77057
(713) 410-2983

Houston Structural Inc
7632 Hammerly
Houston, TX 77055
(713) 686-5900

Relocate & Renovate Inc.
11931 Wickchester Suite 201
Houston, TX 77043
(281) 497-3017

Legal Eagle Construction Co
5530 Yarwell Dr
Houston, TX 77096-4012
(713) 723-8850

Greymark Construction Co
701 N Post Oak Rd # 340
Houston, TX 77279-9628
(713) 722-7226

William Shaw & Associates, Inc.
4206 Law St
Houston, TX 77005-1036
(713) 666-1931

Enviro Custom Homes
4829 Cortina Dr.
Irving, TX 75038
(972) 679-8133

QHS-Quality Home Solutions
1914 River Falls Dr
Kingwood, TX 77339
(281) 312-4411

Ashworth Construction Inc
3218 Holly Green Drive
Kingwood, TX 77339
(281) 360-6117

Michael Land Design/Build
5309 Village Creek Dr.
Plano, TX 75093
(972) 250-2005

Mackenzie Roofing &
Remodeling
240 Sherwood Drive
San Antonio, TX 78201
(210) 732-7319

Beaver Builders
2970 FM 455 W #1
Sanger, TX 76266
(940) 458-7354

Construction Services Grp Inc
26308 Aldine Westfield Rd
Spring, TX 77373-2609
(281) 350-1222

Construction Services Group
26308 Aldine Westfield Rd
Spring, TX 77373
(281) 350-1222

DreamMaker Bath & Kitchen
1020 N. University Parks Dr.
Waco, TX 76712
(254) 745-2432

McDowell Custom Homes Inc.
1007 Woodridge Drive
Waxahachie, TX 75165
(972) 935-0655

Don Schmerse Custom Homes
PO Box 691
Waxahachie, TX 75165
(972) 938-0224

Homes By Hanes, Inc.
711 Ferris Avenue Suite 102
Waxahachie, TX 75165
(972) 938-2311

Blue Ridge Home Improvement
PO Box 903
Blacksburg, VA 24063-0903
(540) 951-3505

Richmond American Homes
5336 Blue Aster Circle
Centerville, VA 20120
(703) 396-1311

Rinehart Homes Ltd.
1110 Rose Hill Drive, #100
Charlottesville, VA 22903
(434) 977-7000

Case Handyman Services
1327 Poindexter St.
Chesapeake, VA 23324
(757) 545-7100

Bateman Custom Construction
5217 Concordia St
Fairfax, VA 22032-3409
(703) 323-1454

Augustine Homes
100 Riverside Parkway,
Suite 229
Fredricksburg, VA 22406
(540) 372-7770

Laura Stemper
231 Dixie Ave.
Harrisonburg, VA 22801
(540) 433-7905

Butler Brothers Corp
5750 White Funt Ct.
Manassas, VA 20112
(703) 878-3300

Design for Spaces
8047 Counselor Rd.
Manassas, VA 20112
(703) 928-5028

Regent, Inc.
105 Baker St
Manassas Park, VA 20111
(571) 437-1073

Access 1st Inc.
224 Brunswich Place
Newport News, VA 23601
(757) 592-5355

Realty Inc.
566 Denbigh Blvd.
Newport News, VA 23608
(804) 874-7484

Realty Builders, Inc.
566 Denbigh Blvd.
Newport News, VA 23608
(757) 874-7484

Richmond American Homes
7 Steed Place
Potomac Falls, VA 20165
(703) 898-3929

Lauten Construction Co.
133 East Main St.
Purcellville, VA 20132
(540) 338-5341

FLF Services
3413 Paxford Rd
Richmond, VA 23234
(804) 641-8433

Osborne Company Inc
7420 Alban Station Ct
Suite B210
Springfield, VA 22150
(703) 455-6688

Benson Builders Inc.
1728 Virginia Beach Blvd.,
Suite 118
Virginia Beach, VA 23454
(757) 496-9613

Criner Construction Co Inc
300 Criner Ln
Yorktown, VA 23693-2430
(757) 868-6200

Prime Construction Company
PO Box 1236
Burlington, VT 05402
(802) 865-9276

Posey & Associates
PO Box 542
Milton, VT 05468
(802) 893-7932

HCS Construction Services Co.
15227 NE 20th
Bellevue, WA 98007
(425) 747-9347

Cornice Construction Co.
16035 SE 45th Pl
Bellevue, WA 98006-6800
(425) 643-8292

Sweatman-Young, Inc.
PO Box 7105
Bonney Lake, WA 98390
(253) 863-3786

J M Bogan Company Inc
4519 196th St SE
Bothell, WA 98012
(425) 788-2272

Fourth Dimension Housing Inc
190 N Livingston Bay Rd
Camano Island, WA 98282
(360) 387-1438

Shirey Contracting Inc
230 NE Juniper St
Issaquah, WA 98027
(425) 427-1300

Craig Smith Construction, Inc.
24850 SE Mirrormont Dr
Issaquah, WA 98027-6946
(425) 392-4751

Butler Construction
118 SW 2nd Avenue
Kelso, WA 98626
(360) 423-6176

Kitchen ReStylers Inc
516-A W Deschutes Ave
Kennewick, WA 99336
(509) 582-1893

Sound Builders Inc.
23528 110th Place SE
Kent, WA 98031
(253) 859-7978

Hudson Remodeling
912 Loomis Trail Rd
Lynden, WA 98264-9112
(360) 354-7006

Britson Construction
22006 Sweeney Rd SE
Maple Valley, WA 98038-6415
(425) 432-3013

Booth Construction, Inc.
5622 90th Ave SE
Mercer Island, WA 98040
(206) 232-0868

Booth Construction, Inc.
5622 90th Avenue SE
Mercer Island, WA 98040
(206) 232-0868

Parks & Associates
324 S Main
Montesano, WA 98563
(360) 249-5054

The Artisans Group
2316 4th Ave E #B
Olympia, WA 98506
(360) 280-9444

John Erwin Remodeling
310 South Bay Road, Suite C
Olympia, WA 98506
(360) 705-2938

Doyle Custom Homes, Inc.
PO Box 13049
Olympia, WA 98508
(360) 789-8030

Accurate Builders
7621 NE Harborview Dr
Poulsbo, WA 98370
(360) 697-3593

Shattuck & Associates Inc
11905 74th Ave E
Puyallup, WA 98373
(253) 845-6245

Tenhulzen Remodeling
PO Box 987
Redmond, WA 98052
(425) 885-9871

Marymoor Construction Inc
15328 NE 96th Place, #A-11
Redmond, WA 98052
(425) 556-9475

Tenhulzen Remodeling
8550 164th Ave. NE
Redmond, WA 98052
(425) 885-9871

J W Bratton Design/Build LLC
15209 SE Fairwood Blvd
Renton, WA 980588645
(425) 271-2057

Northwest Homecrafters Inc
6910 Roosevelt Way NE #332
Seattle, WA 981156635
(206) 601-9725

Cascade Construction Design
Build Inc
4902 Aurora Ave N Suite A
Seattle, WA 981036520
(206) 632-4300

Conner Remodeling & Design
Inc
3929 Stone Way North
Seattle, WA 98103
(206) 782-6959

L. Susan Penning
317 N. 137th
Seattle, WA 98133
(206) 418-0644

Adaptive Installations
9740 43rd Place SW
Seattle, WA 98136
(206) 762-6130

Hines Construction
PO Box 3336
Sequim, WA 983825022
(360) 681-6698

Irons Brothers Construction,
Inc.
15304 Ashworth Ave. N
Shoreline, WA 98133
(206) 306-7767

JAFA Enterprises Inc
PO Box 1568
Silverdale, WA 98383-1568
(360) 698-9233

First Team Construction
5124 N Vista Ct
Spokane, WA 99212
(509) 924-8224

Wright Brothers Sunrooms, LLC
320 S. Sullivan Road
Spokane Valley, WA 99037
(509) 927-1190

Rainier Construction &
Remodeling
720 Galloway Street
Steilacoom, WA 983883922
(253) 581-4050

Frank & Sons Construction
8204 Portland Ave.
Tacoma, WA 98404
(235) 476-8042

Reier Construction
6124 Alameda Ave W
University Place, WA 98467
(253) 305-0753

T Square Remodeling
10600 NE 94th Avenue
Vancouver, WA 98662
(360) 256-3946

Skill Construction Services Inc
11282 Washougal River Rd
Washougal, WA 98671
(360) 256-2790

Westhill Inc.
PO Box 306
Woodinville, WA 98072
(425) 483-0999

Peter Dell Custom
Remodeling Inc
3201 W Nob Hill Blvd
Yakima, WA 98902-4960
(509) 453-2234

Stebnitz Builders, Inc.
1102 Ann St.
Delavan, WI 53115
(262) 728-8027

Knutson Brothers, II, LLC
West 792 Potters Cir
East Troy, WI 53120-0092
(262) 642-5211

JDJ Builders Inc
12340 W Layton Ave
Greenfield, WI 53228
(414) 425-2100

Doneff Building Systems, Inc.
115 E. Waldo Blvd. Suite 300
Manitowoc, WI 54220
(414) 682-0066

Baeten Building & Remodeling
1112 Merritt Ave
Oshkosh, WI 54901
(920) 235-8372

Luther Home Improvement
LLC
PO Box 220
Portage, WI 53901
(608) 745-0771

A-A Exteriors
6897 Clow Rd
Winneconne, WI 54986
(920) 836-2423

Introduction

1. John Burns Real Estate Consulting, Retirement Housing Forecast, 2003.

2. William Strauss and Neil Howe, *Generations: The History of America's Future 1584–2069.*

3. Barbara Butrica and Cori Uccello, *How Will Boomers Fare at Retirement?*, AARP, March 2004.

4. William Strauss and Neil Howe, *Generations: The History of America's Future 1584–2069.*

5. Strauss and Howe, *Generations.*

Chapter 1

1. "The State of the Nation's Housing 2005," The Joint Center for Housing Studies, Harvard University.

Chapter 2

1. 2003 Senior-Boomer Survey, National Association of Homebuilders, Countrywide Home Loans.

2. John Burns Real Estate Consulting, 2005.

3. Zoomerang Research, January 2005, for Coldwell Banker Previews International.

Chapter 4

1. Lee Fisher, "The Art of Retirement: An Economic Development Program for Rural Towns and Counties", Seattle, WA March 1992.

2. National Association of Realtors.

3. National Association of Realtors.

4. Partly, these statistics are skewed by the fact that the South is the largest of the census regions, stretching from Delaware to New Mexico. In a later section, we look at the more finely divided nine census regions.

5. Warren R. Bland, *Retire in Style: 60 Outstanding Places Across the USA and Canada.*

Chapter 7

1. Belden Russonello and Stewart for AARP; "In the Middle: A Report on Multicultural Boomers Coping with Family and Aging Issues," July 2001.

2. U.S. Census, *Geographical Mobility: 2002 to 2003.*

3. John Burns Real Estate Consulting.

Chapter 9

1. Belden Russonello and Stewart for AARP; "In the Middle: A Report on Multicultural Boomers Coping with Family and Aging Issues," July 2001.

2. Belden Russonello and Stewart for AARP; "Caregiving in the U.S.," funded by The National Alliance for Caregiving, MetLife Foundation, April 2004.

Chapter 10

1. Matthew Greenwald & Associates, Inc. for AARP, *These Four Walls . . . Americans 45+ Talk About Home and Community*, May 2003.

2. Andrew Kochera and Audrey Straight, AARP Public Policy Institute; and Thomas Gutterbock, University of Virginia for AARP, "Beyond 50.05—Livable Communities: Creating Environments for Successful Aging," May 2005.

3. Andrew Kochera and Audrey Straight, AARP Public Policy Institute; and Thomas Gutterbock, University of Virginia for AARP, "Beyond 50.05—Livable Communities: Creating Environments for Successful Aging," May 2005.

Chapter 11

1. Barbara Basler, *Suing to Get Out in the World*, AARP Bulletin, June 2004.

Chapter 14

1. Reduced from 20 percent to 25 percent in 2003. The base rate for long-term capital gains tax stood at 15 percent in 2006. Depreciation recapture could add to tax liability.

Tom Kelly is a nationally syndicated newspaper feature writer and radio talk show host. He served the *Seattle Times* readers for 20 years—several of them as real estate editor—and his work now appears in the *Los Angeles Times,* the *Houston Chronicle, St. Louis Post Dispatch,* the *Oakland Tribune, Kansas City Star,* the *Sacramento Bee, San Jose Mercury News,* the *Tacoma News Tribune,* the *Reno Gazette-Journal,* the *Louisville Courier-Journal,* and the *Des Moines Register,* plus more than two dozen other newspapers.

In 2006, Tom's award-winning radio show "Real Estate Today" began its 13th year on *710 KIRO-AM,* the CBS affiliate in Seattle and the state's largest station. The show is syndicated by Business Talk Radio to approximately 40 domestic markets and airs on 450 stations in 160 foreign countries via American Forces Radio.

Tom is the author of *The New Reverse Mortgage Formula* and coauthor of *How a Second Home Can Be Your Best Investment* and *Cashing In on a Second Home in Mexico.*

Tom was president of the Santa Clara University class of 1972. He and his wife, Dr. Jodi Kelly, an associate dean and professor at Seattle University, have four children and live on Bainbridge Island, Washington.